More

MAKE YOUR OWN GROCERIES

More

MAKE YOUR OWN GROCERIES

by Daphne Metaxas Hartwig

The Bobbs-Merrill Company, Inc.
Indianapolis/New York

PREVIOUS BOOKS BY AUTHOR:

- *Make Your Own Groceries*
- *Classic Greek Cooking*

Published by The Bobbs-Merrill Co., Inc.
Indianapolis/New York
Manufactured in the United States of America
First Printing
Illustrations by Maggie Marinaro
Designed by A. Christopher Simon

Library of Congress Cataloging in Publication Data

Hartwig, Daphne Metaxas.
   More make your own groceries.

   Includes index.
   1. Cookery. I. Title.
TX652.H3724   1983   641.5   83-3806
ISBN 0-672-52671-9
ISBN 0-672-52774-X (pbk.)

To Glenn and Theone
with thanks for their support

INTRODUCTION

More Make Your Own Groceries is a further collection of recipes for all the processed foods that you would normally buy at your supermarket. I included recipes in this book only if they met the following criteria: (1) The recipe must cost less to make at home than the cost of its commercial counterpart; (2) The recipe must not require any special processing techniques or equipment. If a recipe for a food is equal in price to its store-bought cousin but is a superior product because it is considerably higher in quality and nutrition, then it is included here. When a store-bought grocery item is of the same quality as its homemade version and it costs the same or less to buy, a homemade recipe is not included.

All the homemade food products in this book either save you money or give you added quality. No knowledge of techniques like canning, freezing, or food processing is needed to make the recipes in this book; neither do you need any special equipment, hard-to-find ingredients, or a lot of time. Pickles and relishes cure and store in your refrigerator or freezer; candy recipes are formulated so that there is no need for a thermometer; ice creams are made without an ice cream machine; jams, jellies, and preserves are made to be stored in your freezer; and

cold cuts are made without a meat grinder or casings. When recipe directions tell you to use a machine such as a blender, directions for an alternative method are given wherever possible. The recipes also give directions for a food processor whenever one can be used, and there is always an alternative method to the food processor.

The result of all these homemade grocery recipes is a book that, like a supermarket, has something for everyone's tastes and everyone's inflation-burdened pocketbook. There are freezer-to-oven convenience foods, instant breakfasts, and package-your-own dinnertime and baking mixes for the working woman. There are staples like cream cheese and cottage cheese, frozen no-thaw soup concentrates, lunchmeats, and homemade dog and cat food for those who wish to save money on these necessities. Then there are reduced-calorie salad dressings, diet ice creams and candy, and egg and sausage substitutes for dieters. Nutritious snacks and frozen vegetarian dinners made with strictly wholesome ingredients will appeal to those who care about what they put into their own and their children's bodies. For those who are concerned about value and nutrition in their foods, there are freezer-to-oven dinners that contain well over twice as much meat as the commercial variety, minus the chemical preservatives.

I hope you will enjoy this book and turn to it often. Besides the savings and quality you will gain from these recipes, I know you'll enjoy the simple, self-reliant pleasure of creating your own basic foods to share with your family and friends.

CONCISE TABLE OF CONTENTS

METRIC CONVERSION CHART
These charts are rounded off to the nearest equivalent.

LIQUID MEASURES

** To convert quarts into liters, multiply the quarts by 0.94635.

** To convert liters into quarts, multiply the liters by 1.056688.

** To convert liquid ounces into milliliters, multiply the ounces by 29.573.

** To convert milliliters into liquid ounces, multiply the milliliters by 0.0338.

U.S. SPOONS, LIQUID OUNCES CUPS AND QUARTS	METRIC EQUIVALENT	U.S. SPOONS, LIQUID OUNCES CUPS AND QUARTS	METRIC EQUIVALENT
1 TEASPOON	5 MILLILITERS	¾ CUP or 6 liquid ounces	180 milliliters
1 TABLESPOON or 3 teaspoons or ½ liquid ounce	15 MILLILITERS	⅞ cup or 7 liquid ounces	200 MILLILITERS
2 TABLESPOONS or 1 liquid ounce or ⅛ cup	30 milliliters	1 CUP or 8 liquid ounces	240 milliliters
3⅓ tablespoons or 3 tablespoons *plus* 1 teaspoon	50 MILLILITERS	1 cup *plus* 1 tablespoon and ¾ teaspoon	250 MILLILITERS or ¼ liter
¼ CUP or 4 tablespoons or 2 liquid ounces	60 milliliters	2 CUPS or 16 liquid ounces or 1 pint	480 milliliters *minus* 1½ tablespoons
⅓ CUP or 5 tablespoons *plus* 1 teaspoon	80 milliliters	2 cups *plus* 2½ tablespoons	500 MILLILITERS or ½ liter
⅓ cup *plus* 1 tablespoon or 3½ liquid ounces	100 MILLILITERS	4 CUPS or 32 fluid ounces or 1 quart	1 liter *minus* ⅓ cup and 1 tablespoon (or 6 tablespoons and 1 teaspoon or 900 milliliters)
½ CUP or 8 tablespoons or 4 liquid ounces	120 milliliters		
⅔ CUP or 10 tablespoons *plus* 2 teaspoons	160 milliliters	4⅓ cups *plus* 1 tablespoon	1 LITER or 1,000 milliliters

WEIGHT MEASURES

** To convert weight ounces into grams, multiply the ounces by 28.3495.
** To convert grams into weight ounces, multiply the grams by 0.35274.

U.S. WEIGHT OUNCES AND POUNDS	METRIC EQUIVALENT	U.S. WEIGHT OUNCES AND POUNDS	METRIC EQUIVALENT
⅛ ounce	5 GRAMS	scant 4½ ounces	125 GRAMS
⅓ ounce	10 GRAMS	8 OUNCES or ½ pound	227 grams
½ OUNCE	15 GRAMS	9 ounces	250 GRAMS
scant 1 ounce	25 GRAMS	1 POUND or 16 ounces	464 grams
1 OUNCE	28⅓ grams	1 pound *plus* 1⅓ ounces	500 GRAMS
1 ounce *plus about* 1/12 ounce	30 GRAMS	2 POUNDS or 32 ounces	928 grams
1¾ ounces	50 GRAMS	2 pounds *plus* 3⅓ ounces	1 KILOGRAM or 1,000 GRAMS
2⅔ ounces	75 GRAMS		
3½ ounces	100 GRAMS		
4 OUNCES or ¼ pound	114 grams		

DETAILED LIST OF RECIPES

Chapter 1:

INSTANT MEALS AND SIDE DISHES

Sections:

☐Cereals and Instant Breakfasts
☐Freezer-to-Oven Dinners
☐Freezer-to-Oven Vegetables

NANCY'S GRANOLA

Makes 8 cups

5 cups regular rolled oats
1 cup *each:*   sesame seeds
                 sunflower kernels
                 shredded coconut
                 regular wheat germ
                 chopped almonds
                 nonfat dry milk
                 soy flour (sometimes called soya
                     flour) available at health food
                     stores
                 honey
                 oil

Grease a 14-by-9-by-2-inch or similar large baking pan with vegetable shortening; set it aside. Combine all the dry ingredients; mix well. In a small saucepan, blend the honey and oil; heat gently to dissolve the honey. Pour the honey-oil mixture into the dry ingredients; stir well to coat thoroughly. Spread the mixture in the baking pan and bake at 250° for 45 to 50 minutes, or until toasted to your liking; stir every 15 minutes. Cool thoroughly. You can also add raisins or chopped dried fruits if desired. Store at room temperature in an airtight container.

OVERNIGHT INSTANT CEREAL

Makes 2 cups

Set this up the night before for a hot, nutritious breakfast in an instant.

½ cup cracked bulgur wheat
1 tablespoon sugar
½ teaspoon cinnamon
Dash of salt
1 ⅓ cups boiling water

Stir all the ingredients together in the top part of a double boiler. Cover; place the top part into the bottom part of the double boiler; let stand at room temperature overnight.

In the morning, the bulgur will have absorbed all the water. Uncover and heat to serving temperature over boiling water. Serve topped with your choice of butter, milk, sugar, or maple syrup.

WITH RAISINS

Add ¼ cup raisins to the raw bulgur wheat and increase the boiling water by 1 tablespoon. Chopped dried apricots or apples or shredded coconut can be used instead of the raisins.

HOMEMADE CREAMED CEREALS

*Makes 2 cups powdered cereal
or ten ¾-cup servings*

Process your own creamed cereals for a fresher taste, more nutrition, and greater savings, and to make varieties not sold in supermarkets.

CREAM OF RICE

Measure out 2 cups of uncooked rice. Pour ⅛ cup of the rice into a blender container. Cover and blend at medium speed for 1 minute. Change to highest speed and blend for 2 to 3 minutes, or until the rice turns into a powder. The rice will not harm your blender, but it's a good idea to stop and let your blender rest and cool from time to time as you continue. If you have a food processor, the job will be easier. Empty the rice powder into a large clean frying pan. Continue the process until all 2 cups of rice are powdered and in the frying pan.

Put the frying pan over medium heat and stir to remove the moisture from the cereal. Do this only briefly for storage purposes and do not allow the cereal to toast or brown. Let cool. Store at room temperature in an airtight container.

Cooking Directions: Allow 3 tablespoons cereal, 1 cut water or milk, and a good dash of salt for each ¾-cup serving. Bring salted liquid to a rapid boil over medium heat. Sprinkle the cereal atop and stir continuously for 45 seconds. Turn off the heat, cover, and let stand for 3 minutes. Serve topped with your choice of sugar, syrup, honey, fresh fruit slices, jam, raisins, or butter.

CREAM OF WHEAT

Blend cracked bulgur wheat into a powder as described on previous page. Allow 3 tablespoons powdered cereal, 1⅓ cups water or milk, and a good dash of salt per serving. Bring salted liquid to a rapid boil. Slowly sprinkle and stir in the cereal. Continue stirring as you return cereal to a boil. Reduce heat; simmer for about 8 minutes, stirring often.

CREAM OF BROWN RICE

Make powdered cereal from raw brown rice. Allow 3 tablespoons cereal, 1½ cups liquid, and a good dash of salt per serving. Prepare as for Cream of Wheat, cooking for about 12 minutes.

CREAM OF BARLEY

Make powdered cereal from pearl barley. Allow 3 tablespoons cereal, 2¼ cups liquid, and a good dash of salt per serving. Bring salted liquid to a rapid boil, reduce heat to a steady simmer, and slowly sprinkle and stir in the cereal. Cook, stirring constantly, for about 10 minutes.

CREAM OF CORN

Use yellow cornmeal straight from the box. Allow 3 tablespoons cornmeal, 1½ cups liquid, and a good dash of salt per serving. Prepare as for Cream of Wheat, cooking about 6 minutes.

EXTRA-CREAMY CEREALS

Combine the cereal, salt, and *cold* liquid in a saucepan, bring to a boil, and cook as directed.

Note: To make cleaning the cereal pan easier, fill it with *cold* water immediately after serving.

CORNFLAKES AND APPLES BREAKFAST BARS

Makes ten 3-by-5-inch bars

1 cup crushed cornflakes or wheat flakes
⅓ cup packed brown sugar
2 tablespoons butter, melted
½ cup packed brown sugar
½ cup granulated sugar
½ cup vegetable shortening
1 cup applesauce
2 cups flour
1 teaspoon baking soda
½ teaspoon salt
1½ teaspoons cinnamon
1 teaspoon nutmeg
1 cup raisins or chopped dried apples

Combine the crushed cornflakes, ⅓ cup brown sugar, and melted butter in a small bowl; use your fingers to blend the mixture, then set aside. In a large mixing bowl, cream together the two sugars and the shortening until fluffy. Mix in the applesauce and set aside. In a smaller bowl, combine the flour, baking soda, salt, cinnamon, and nutmeg. Stir these dry ingredients into the applesauce mixture and fold in the raisins.

Spread the mixture in a greased 10-by-15-by-1-inch or similar size pan. Sprinkle the batter evenly with the cornflake mixture. Bake at 350° for about 20 to 30 minutes, or until a knife inserted in the center comes out clean. Cool in the pan, then cut into bars.

To Serve: These hearty bars will store well in their covered pan for a full week, or you can package them individually in sandwich bags and freeze them; they can thaw overnight in time for breakfast, or they will thaw in 1 hour at room temperature.

WHEAT AND OATS BREAKFAST BARS

Makes 8 bars

The wheat, oats, and nuts provide the vitamins and protein while the dried fruit filling adds plenty of iron. One bar should see you through the morning.

6 ounces dried mixed-fruit bits
1 cup water
3 tablespoons sugar
1 teaspoon strained fresh lemon juice
7 tablespoons butter, softened
½ cup honey
1¼ cups whole wheat flour
1¼ cups regular rolled oats
½ cup chopped almonds
2 tablespoons wheat germ
½ teaspoon baking soda
½ teaspoon salt

Combine the dried fruits and water in a saucepan. Cover and slowly simmer for about 10 to 15 minutes, or until the fruits are tender, then stir continually over low heat until the mixture thickens. Mix in the sugar and lemon juice. Set aside to cool.

In a large mixing bowl, beat the butter and honey together until smooth. In another bowl, combine the remaining ingredients. Gradually stir the dry ingredients into the butter-honey mixture; mix with a wooden spoon until blended. Press half of this oat mixture into a greased 8-inch square pan. Spread the fruit filling evenly atop. Crumble the remaining oat mixture as a topping over the fruit filling. Bake at 350° for 25 to 35 minutes, or until the topping is golden. Let cool in the pan before cutting into bars.

To Serve: The bars store well in their covered pan for a week, or you can package them individually in sandwich bags and freeze them; they will thaw overnight in time for breakfast.

CHOCOLATE-STRAWBERRY GRANOLA BARS

Makes 6 to 9 bars

½ cup semisweet chocolate morsels
¾ cup strawberry jam
2 cups any granola cereal
1 cup quick-cooking oats
½ cup chopped walnuts

Butter an 8-by-8-by-2-inch pan; set it aside. Over very low heat, melt the chocolate in a quart-size saucepan, stirring constantly. Stir in the jam until blended, then remove the pan from the heat. Add the remaining ingredients; mix until they are coated; spread the mixture evenly in the pan. Refrigerate until firm, then cut into bars. You can double this recipe by using a 9-by-14-by-2-inch pan.

OTHER-FLAVORED GRANOLA BARS

Use butterscotch-flavored morsels with grape jelly. Experiment with different flavored jams or jellies and different kinds of nuts.

INSTANT BREAKFAST DRINKS

*Each recipe makes about
one 14-ounce serving*

Directions: Combine all ingredients in a blender. Whirl until smooth and frothy. You can also use an eggbeater, electric mixer or, when possible, a shaker-jar to blend. Use a food processor only when the recipe does not call for an egg.

CHOOSE-A-FRUIT SHAKE

¾ cup milk
1 egg white
1½ teaspoons sugar
½ cup any fresh fruit, peeled and diced

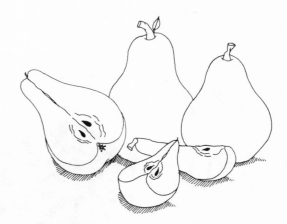

TROPICAL FRUIT DRINK

1 cup orange or pineapple juice
½ ripe banana, peeled and sliced
1½ teaspoons sugar

GRAPE NOG

½ of a 6-ounce can frozen grape juice
    concentrate, thawed
½ cup milk
1 egg
Dash of nutmeg

STRAWBERRY HEALTH DRINK

1 cup fresh strawberries (or a 5-ounce frozen
    package, thawed)
½ cup milk
½ cup plain or vanilla yogurt
2 tablespoons wheat germ
1 or 2 tablespoons honey or sugar

CRANBERRY-BANANA DRINK

¾ cup cranberry juice cocktail
1 egg white
1½ teaspoons sugar
½ ripe banana, peeled and sliced

WINTER SHAKE, MELBA

1 cup low-sugar canned peaches or pears with
    some liquid from the can
½ cup raspberry yogurt
Dash of allspice

POP-UP TOASTER TARTS

Makes 8 to 10

½ cup sugar
½ cup vegetable shortening
2 eggs
2½ cups flour
2 teaspoons baking powder
Choice of Filling: any flavor jam, marmalade,
    preserves, or fruit butter
1 egg white, optional
Milk, optional
Sugar, optional

Cream together sugar and shortening, beating until light. Beat in the eggs until creamy, then stir in the flour and baking powder to make a soft dough. Divide the dough evenly into 16 parts. Roll each part into a flattened ball; set the balls on a plate. Wrap the plate in plastic wrap and refrigerate for 2 hours.

Grease a cookie sheet and set it aside. Roll 1 dough ball into a vaguely rectangular shape, about ¹⁄₁₆-inch thick. Spread 1 heaping teaspoon of filling evenly over the dough, as pictured on the following page, leaving a generous margin. Roll out another dough ball into a similar shape and

POP-UP TOASTER TARTS

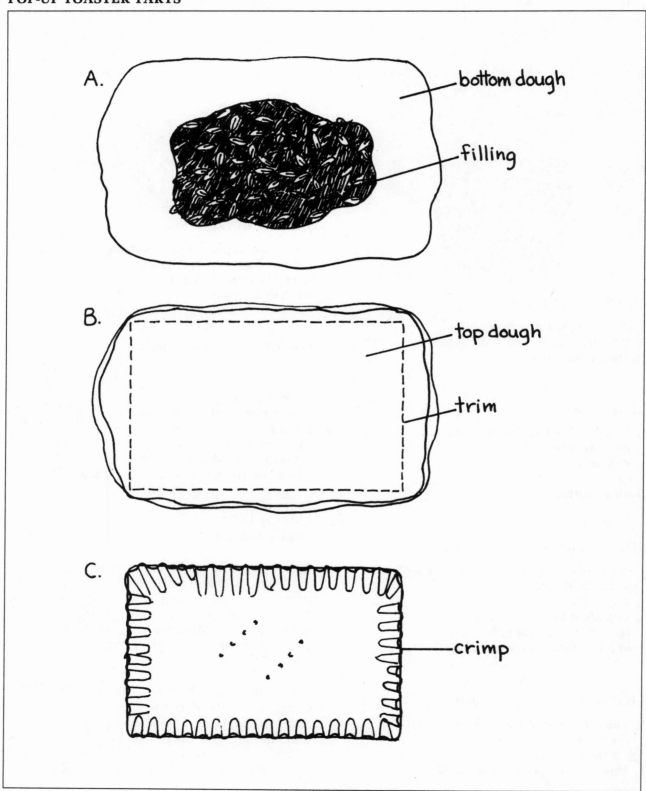

A. bottom dough

filling

B. top dough

trim

C. crimp

lay it neatly over the first. Use a knife to trim the filled Pop-Up Tart to 3½ by 5 inches, then crimp the edges together with your fingertips or the tines of a fork. Place the tart on the cookie sheet, then prick the top crust with a fork. Repeat this procedure with the remaining dough balls and any trimmed-off dough. Optional: Lightly beat an egg white with 1 tablespoon milk; brush the tops with this mixture for a golden crust; sprinkle with sugar.

Bake the tarts at 350° for about 25 minutes, or until the edges become browned. Prick the Pop-Up Tarts again during the first 10 minutes of baking to keep them flat. When cool, wrap and store at room temperature or in the refrigerator.

To Serve: Place a Pop-Up Tart in the toaster and toast once. Let cool slightly before removing as it will get very hot.

FROZEN PEANUT TOASTER SLICES

Makes 1 dozen slices

1¾ cups flour
½ cup sugar
3 tablespoons baking powder
½ teaspoon salt
¾ cup peanut butter
¾ cup milk
2 eggs, beaten

Grease a 9-by-5-by-3-inch loaf pan and set it aside. In a mixing bowl, sift together flour, sugar, baking powder, and salt. Use your fingers to cut in the peanut butter, much as you would make a pie crust, until the mixture is crumbly. Add the milk and eggs; stir just until the mixture is well combined, but do not overbeat. Turn the batter into the loaf pan and bake at 350° for 40 to 45 minutes, or until a knife inserted in the center comes out clean. Remove the loaf from the pan and cool on a rack. When completely cool, use your sharpest knife to slice the loaf into ¾-inch slices. Stack with a small sheet of wax paper between each slice, wrap the stack of slices in a plastic bag, label with this page number or the following directions, and freeze.

To Serve: Put frozen slices in a toaster and toast once or twice or heat briefly on both sides under a broiler or toaster oven. Like toast, these slices are good buttered.

FROZEN PEACH-LOAF TOASTER SLICES

Makes 1 dozen slices

3 or 4 ripe peaches or nectarines, peeled and pitted
1 teaspoon fresh lemon juice
1 teaspoon orange extract
2 cups flour
2½ teaspoons baking powder
½ teaspoon salt
4 tablespoons butter, softened
4 tablespoons vegetable shortening
¾ cup sugar
2 eggs

Whirl enough of the fruit in a blender or food processor to make 1 cup of purée; blend in the lemon juice and orange extract; set aside. In a medium-size bowl, stir together the flour, baking powder, and salt; set aside. In a large mixing bowl, use an electric mixer to cream together the butter, shortening, and sugar. Beat in the eggs until well blended, then the peach purée. Don't worry if your batter appears curdled. Add the flour mixture by hand, stirring only until the flour becomes moistened.

Turn the batter into a greased 9-by-5-by-3-inch loaf pan. Bake below the center rack at 350° for 50 to 60 minutes, or until a clean knife inserted in the center comes out clean. Let stand 10 minutes before turning out onto a rack to cool. When the loaf is completely cool, wrap it and let it ripen for 24 hours so that it will slice without crumbling.

With your sharpest knife, cut the ripened loaf into ¾-inch slices. Stack with a sheet of wax paper between each slice; wrap the stack of slices in a plastic bag; label and freeze.

To Serve: Put frozen slices in a toaster and toast once or twice, or heat briefly on both sides under a broiler or in a toaster oven. Like toast, these slices are good buttered.

HIGH ENERGY BREAKFAST CUPCAKES

Makes 1 dozen

4 tablespoons butter, softened
½ cup honey
1 egg
1 teaspoon vanilla extract
¾ cup all-purpose flour
½ cup whole wheat flour
½ teaspoon baking soda
½ teaspoon cinnamon
¼ teaspoon nutmeg
¼ teaspoon salt
Several dashes of ground cloves
½ cup applesauce
½ cup raisins
½ cup chopped dried apricots
¾ cup chopped walnuts

Put the butter in a medium-size mixing bowl and beat, briefly, with an electric mixer at medium speed. Gradually beat in the honey followed by the egg and vanilla. In a small bowl, stir together both flours, baking soda, cinnamon, nutmeg, salt, and cloves. At slow speed, mix these dry ingredients into the batter alternately with the applesauce until just blended. By hand, stir in the raisins, apricots, and ½ cup of the chopped walnuts.

Spoon the batter into well-greased or paper-lined cupcake pans, filling each ¾ full. Sprinkle the tops with the remaining ¼ cup of nuts. Bake 350° for about 30 minutes, or until the tops spring back when touched. Remove the hot cupcakes from their pans and cool on racks.

To Serve: These nourishing cupcakes will store well in a plastic bag for a full week and take only 1 hour to thaw if frozen. Serve cupcakes at room temperature or re-warm by placing them back in the muffin tin in which they were baked; cover loosely with foil; heat at 450° for 5 minutes.

MAKE-AHEAD MUFFIN BATTER

Makes batter for 2½ dozen
medium-size muffins

4 cups flour
2½ tablespoons baking powder
1½ teaspoons salt
⅓ cup sugar
2 eggs
2 cups milk
½ cup corn oil
Five 16-ounce lidded plastic containers

Sift the flour, baking powder, salt, and sugar into a bowl. In a larger mixing bowl, briefly beat together the remaining liquid ingredients. Quickly pour the dry ingredients into the liquid mixture and, with a few swift strokes, mix just to moisten the flour; the mixing should only take 15 seconds and should produce a coarse and lumpy batter; if you beat the batter to near-smoothness, the gluten in the flour will quickly develop and result in tough, rubbery muffins.

Pour the muffin batter equally into the 5 containers; cover, label, and freeze immediately.

To Serve: Each container will yield 6 muffins. Let the batter thaw in the refrigerator for 12 hours or more. Very briefly, stir the muffin batter; at this point you can gently fold in your choice of the following variations. Fill greased or paper-lined muffin tins ⅔ full with batter and bake at 400° for 20 to 25 minutes, or until the tops spring back when touched. Let the muffins remain in their tins for several minutes before serving.

BLUEBERRY OR STRAWBERRY

Fold in 1 cup of fresh berries; if using frozen or canned, drain well and pat dry with paper towels.

CRANBERRY

Chop ¾ cup fresh cranberries, sprinkle with 4 tablespoons sugar, and fold in.

CANDIED FRUIT

Fold in ½ cup finely chopped candied orange peel or mixed citron.

NUT

Fold in ¾ cup coarsely chopped walnuts or pecans.

RAISIN AND DRIED FRUIT

Fold in ½ cup dried mixed fruit bits, or raisins, or chopped dried apricots.

CHEESE

Fold in ⅔ cup grated Cheddar or Muenster cheese.

BACON

Fold in ½ cup cooked, drained, and crumbled bacon. For Cheese and Bacon Muffins, use ⅓ cup cheese with ¼ cup bacon.

Section: FREEZER-TO-OVEN DINNERS

SOME THINGS TO KNOW ABOUT FREEZER-TO-OVEN FOODS

• The aluminum foil pans used in many of the following recipes are doubly convenient since you can freeze and bake your finished meal in just one pan—and sometimes pre-cook in it as well. These foil pans are re-usable and are readily available in the baking aisle of most supermarkets or wherever aluminum foil broiler pans are sold.

• When making Freezer-to-Oven foods, never use a pan that is drastically different in size from what the recipe calls for. The cooking times and temperatures are given only for the pan size specified. Changing the pan size could result in a ruined recipe.

• Foil pans tend to wobble when filled. Whenever you are removing one from the oven or placing one in the freezer, either hold it by opposite corners or, better yet, slip it from the rack onto a cutting board.

• There are many ways to wrap foil pans. Choose from: (1) fitting a doubled piece of aluminum foil over the pan and tucking the edges underneath the pan's rim; (2) slipping the pan into a plastic food storage bag (not for long-term freezing); or (3) wrapping the entire pan in the Drugstore Wrap as described in the following recipe.

• Many of the following recipes will tell you to cool a pot or pan-full of food by immersing the pot in a sinkful of cold water while stirring the contents. One reason for this is to stop the cooking that continues in a pot even after it is removed from the heat. The extra cooking will make for a mushy, overcooked product when the frozen food is heated through. The other reason for rapid cooling is to prevent a film from forming atop gravies and sauces and to prevent them from separating out upon freezing.

• Beef comsommé is used in many of the gravies and sauces rather than beef broth. The reason is that the gelatin in the consommé prevents the gravy or sauce from separating out or curdling upon reheating from the frozen state. If you can't find consommé, add ⅛ teaspoon of unflavored gelatin to every 2 cups of beef broth you substitute. Be sure to dissolve the gelatin in a bit of cold water before adding it to the broth. Gelatin is used in other recipes for the same reason and should not be omitted.

• Most recipes are for one or two dinners and are meant to be doubled, tripled, or quadrupled by you—all according to your own particular serving needs.

• The uncooked meat called for in these recipes can either be fresh, or frozen and defrosted because it is cooked before refreezing it. (There is only one exception—Michigan Pasties—where raw meat is assembled in a recipe and frozen raw.)

• All cooking directions will tell you to preheat your oven before putting in the frozen food to be cooked. If you preheat your oven for a full 10 minutes before adding the food, the specified cooking times will be exact.

• When cooking directions tell you to keep a pan loosely or tightly covered while the frozen food bakes, use doubled or heavy-duty aluminum foil as the cover.

• When cooking directions tell you to heat a frozen meal until it is hot at the center, test for this by inserting a dinner knife into the center of the pan for about 10 seconds; remove the knife and briefly feel it with your fingertips. If it's hot, then so is the meal; if it's cool to lukewarm, let the meal bake 10 more minutes before retesting.

• Whenever you place a pan or container to be frozen in the freezer, make sure it is level. Cooking directions are calculated only for even depths.

DRUGSTORE WRAP

Wrap all your foods to be frozen in the Drugstore Wrap for freezer-to-oven convenience without any baking pans to clean up. Foods wrapped in this manner maintain freshness, do not get freezer burn, and stay moist and flavorful even under high oven heat. (See illustrated instructions on following page.)

Step One: Measure off a length of aluminum foil long enough to completely envelop the food to be wrapped, plus about 3 more inches. Use heavy-duty or doubled aluminum foil if you plan to keep the food frozen longer than one month.

Step Two: Bring the two long ends of the foil up to meet each other over the center of the food.

Step Three: Fold the foil edges together once, folding in ½ to 1 inch. Then continue folding down until the folds are snug against the food.

Step Four: With the newly folded line horizontal to you, press the two open side edges of foil together. Take the upper right-hand corner and fold it down over itself as illustrated. Fold the lower right-hand corner in the same way. Repeat this folding-in with the upper and lower left corners.

Step Five: Fold in the right-hand edge, much as you folded in Step Three. Then fold in the left edge. Both folded-in, right and left edges should be snug against the food.

Step Six: Use a permanent ink marker to label the wrapped package. You can also use masking tape, but be sure to leave it on the package even as you bake it—the tape will scorch from the heat when you bake it, but it won't affect the food in any way. Pulling the tape off a frozen package will only rip the foil and cause the food to dry out upon baking.

Step Seven: After labeling, set the frozen Drugstore-Wrapped package on a level surface in your freezer. When solidly frozen, stack as you wish.

CHICKEN À LA KING

Makes 6 servings

5 tablespoons butter (not margarine)
1 cup sliced fresh mushrooms
½ cup green pepper sliced in thin strips
4 tablespoons flour

1 cup chicken broth
1 cup milk
½ cup light cream, milk, or broth
¼ to ½ cup canned pimiento sliced in thin strips
⅛ teaspoon unflavored gelatin, dissolved in 1 tablespoon cold water
2½ cups diced cooked chicken
Six 16-ounce lidded plastic containers

Melt the butter in a heavy saucepan; add mushrooms and pepper; cook over low heat for 5 minutes, or until soft. Remove the pan from the heat and stir in the flour until blended. Return the pan to very low heat and slowly stir in chicken broth and milk; stir until thick and smooth. Stir in cream, pimiento, and gelatin; heat to scalding then remove from heat. Place saucepan in a sink filled with cold water and stir the sauce continuously until it is well cooled.

Distribute the diced chicken equally among the plastic containers. Ladle the cooled sauce equally into the containers, covering the chicken. Briefly stir the containers—they will barely be halfway filled. Cover each container and place in the freezer overnight or until solid. Remove the frozen Chicken à La King discs and either package them in plastic freezer bags or wrap them individually in aluminum foil. Label with this page number or the following cooking directions and return to freezer.

Cooking Directions: Each frozen disc makes 1 serving. Put 1 tablespoon water in the top part of a double boiler; place 1 unwrapped frozen disc in the water. Place the pot over simmering water, cover tightly, and cook about 5 to 10 minutes, or until thawed; turn the disc over once during this cooking time. When thawed, stir the sauce vigorously to smooth out the lumps, then add the next disc to the pot. Cover and heat until thawed; repeat for as many servings as you want. Stir the mixture well as it warms to smooth out the sauce; you may add a few tablespoons of water or milk should the sauce thicken too quickly. When both sauce and chicken are heated through, add salt and pepper to taste and 1 or 2 teaspoons dry sherry per serving. Serve immediately over toast points or patty shells.

DRUGSTORE WRAP

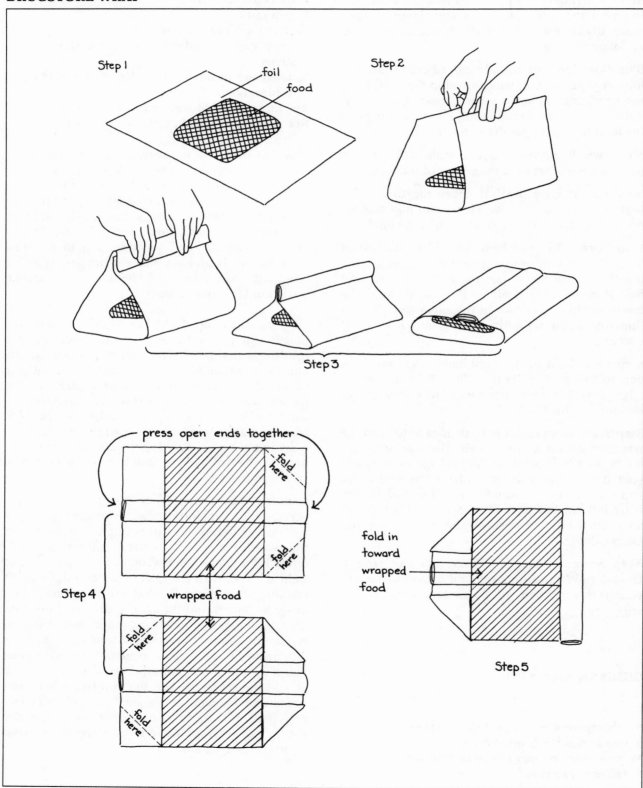

Step 1
foil
food

Step 2

Step 3

press open ends together
fold here
fold here

Step 4
wrapped food

fold here
fold here

fold in toward wrapped food

Step 5

TURKEY À LA KING

Use cooked diced turkey meat in place of chicken.

CHICKEN À LA KING, SOUTHERN STYLE

Use 1½ cups diced chicken along with 1 cup diced cooked ham.

CREAMED CHICKEN OR TURKEY WITH MUSHROOMS

Omit peppers and pimientos. Replace chicken broth with milk.

CHICKEN OR TURKEY FRICASSEE

Omit mushrooms, peppers, pimientos, and sherry. Replace milk and cream with broth.

CURRIED CHICKEN FRICASSEE

When heating discs of frozen Chicken or Turkey Fricassee, stir in a paste of ¼ teaspoon curry powder and 1 teaspoon water per serving.

CHICKEN CORDON BLEU

Makes 2 pans each serving 4 to 6

ROLL-UPS:

12 chicken breast halves, skinned and boned
12 thin slices cooked ham
12 slices Swiss cheese
24 eight-inch lengths of clean cotton string
⅓ cup flour
½ teaspoon salt
⅛ teaspoon pepper
2 eggs
2 tablespoons milk
1 cup fine dry breadcrumbs
4 tablespoons butter
2 foil pans, 8 by 8 by 2 inches

WINE SAUCE:

8 tablespoons butter
¾ cup flour
1 teaspoon salt
2 cups whole milk
2 cups chicken broth
1½ cups dry white wine
1 teaspoon strained fresh lemon juice
¼ teaspoon unflavored gelatin, dissolved in 1 tablespoon cold water
1 can (1 pound) sliced mushrooms, drained (or four 4-ounce cans)

Roll-Ups: Sandwich each chicken breast between two 12-inch square layers of plastic wrap. Place one of the sandwiched chicken breasts on the kitchen floor and pound it vigorously with a heavy iron skillet or a wooden mallet until the chicken breast spreads evenly to about double its original size; stop pounding before the meat becomes so thin that it begins to fray. Repeat this procedure to flatten all 12 chicken breasts.

Peel the top layer of plastic wrap off 1 breast; place a slice of ham atop, followed by a slice of cheese. Roll as you would a jelly roll, removing the bottom layer of plastic as you roll. Tie the roll with a length of string near each end, much as you would tie up a sleeping bag; snip the string ends to 1 inch. Repeat this procedure to make 12 roll-ups.

Combine flour, salt, and pepper in a shallow bowl; beat the eggs and milk together in another bowl; place the breadcrumbs in a third bowl. Dredge each roll-up in flour; dip it in the egg mixture; roll it in breadcrumbs. Melt the butter in a skillet and sauté the roll-ups on all sides for about 10 minutes, or until browned. Place 6 roll-ups in a single layer in each foil pan. Preheat oven to 375°. Set the pans aside while you make the wine sauce.

Wine Sauce: Melt butter in a saucepan over medium-high heat; use a wire whisk to blend in the flour and salt; stir and cook for 1 minute, but do not let the flour brown. Add milk and broth; cook over low heat, stirring constantly, until thickened; this will take about 10 to 15 minutes. Add the remaining ingredients and cook over low

13

heat another 5 minutes. Cover the roll-ups in each pan with half of the sauce and bake for 30 minutes.

Cool the pans for 30 minutes at room temperature, then wrap, label with either this page number or the following cooking directions, and freeze.

Cooking Directions: Preheat oven to 375°. Bake, uncovered, for 2 hours and 15 minutes, or until hot at the center.

CHICKEN PARMIGIANA CASSEROLE

Makes 2 casseroles, each serving 4

6 eggs, lightly beaten
4 cups finely chopped cooked chicken or turkey
1¾ cups grated Parmesan cheese
⅔ cup fine dry breadcrumbs
3 tablespoons olive oil
3½ cups spaghetti sauce
⅔ cup water or dry red wine
12 ounces mozzarella cheese, shredded
2 foil pans, 8 by 8 by 2 inches each

Combine the eggs, chicken, Parmesan, and breadcrumbs. Use your hands to shape the mixture into 16 oval patties ½- to 1-inch thick. Heat the oil in a skillet and sauté the patties on both sides until browned; set aside to drain and cool on paper towels.

When the patties are cool, arrange them equally between the 2 foil pans. Combine the spaghetti sauce (cooled if it is homemade) and water or wine; pour equal amounts over the patties in each pan. Sprinkle each pan with equal amounts of mozzarella. Wrap each pan by fitting a doubled piece of aluminum foil over the pan and crimping the edges underneath the rim. Label pans with this page number or the following cooking directions and freeze.

Cooking Directions: Preheat oven to 400°. Place the covered pan in the oven and bake for 50 minutes; uncover and bake 25 more minutes, or until hot at the center.

INDIVIDUAL TURKEY TETRAZZINI CASSEROLES

Makes 8 or 9 individual servings

Here's a hearty, gourmet meal to enjoy on even your busiest days. Serve with a salad and a glass of white wine.

1 box (8 ounces) linguine spaghetti, regular or thick
3 cups cooked, diced turkey
1 can (10¾ ounces) condensed cream of mushroom soup
1 can (4 ounces) sliced mushrooms, liquid drained and reserved
⅔ cup chicken broth
⅔ cup dry white wine
½ teaspoon salt
White pepper to taste
8 or 9 round foil pot-pie or tart pans, 5 inches across and 1¼ inches deep
6 tablespoons butter
1 cup dry breadcrumbs
⅓ cup grated Parmesan cheese

Cook the linguine only ¾ of the time specified by the manufacturer: If the instructions are to cook the linguine 10 to 12 minutes, cook it 8 to 9 minutes. Rinse the linguine in a colander under cold running water until completely cool; let it drain. Use the empty linguine pot to combine the turkey, soup, mushrooms, broth, wine, salt, and pepper. Stir in the drained linguine: *Pour* this mixture equally among the 8 or 9 foil pans and freeze, uncovered, while you make the buttered crumbs.

Melt the butter; stir in and heat the breadcrumbs until light amber in color. Spread the hot crumbs on a plate and refrigerate for 30 minutes, or until cool to the touch. Blend the Parmesan into the cooled crumbs. Spread the crumbs evenly and equally over the filled pans; wrap; label with this page number or the following cooking directions and return the pans to the freezer.

Cooking Directions: Preheat oven to 400°. Uncover the desired amount of frozen casseroles and bake 55 to 60 minutes, or until hot at the center.

FAMILY CASSEROLES

To serve 3 or 4, pour the casserole mixture equally between two 8-by-8-by-2 inch foil pans. Cover with the same amount of prepared crumbs; wrap, label, and freeze. Bake the frozen casserole, uncovered, in a preheated 400° oven for 1 hour, or until hot at center.

COMPANY CASSEROLE

To serve 6 or 7, pour the casserole mixture into an 8-by-12-by-1 inch foil, ready-mix cake pan. Cover with the same amount of prepared crumbs; wrap, label, and freeze. Bake the frozen casserole, uncovered, in a preheated 400° oven for 1 hour and 15 minutes, or until quite bubbly at the edges and a teaspoon inserted at the center comes out hot. Always slide this size pan onto a large cutting board before handling.

MICHIGAN PASTIES

Makes twelve 8-inch pasties, serves 12

These meaty, hand-held turnovers are easy to assemble in advance because they are frozen without any cooking.

7⅓ cups flour
3¾ teaspoons salt
2½ cups vegetable shortening or lard, chilled
6 tablespoons butter, chilled
About 1¼ cups ice water
2½ pounds boneless chuck steak, never frozen
1½ cups finely chopped onions
About 4½ medium potatoes (1⅓ pounds)
About 3 medium turnips (½ pound)
2 or 3 teaspoons prepared horseradish
1½ tablespoons salt
½ teaspoon plus a few shakes pepper

Combine flour and salt in a mixing bowl. Pinch off shortening and butter into ¼-inch pieces and add to flour. Working quickly, use your fingertips to rub the shortening and butter pieces into the flour so that you get coarse flakes. Sprinkle the ice water over this mixture, just 3 tablespoons at a time, mixing well with a fork after each addition. Continue working in as much water as you can, but do not let the dough become sticky. Still working fast, divide the dough into 12 equal balls. Wrap the balls in wax paper and refrigerate them either 3 hours or overnight.

MICHIGAN PASTIES

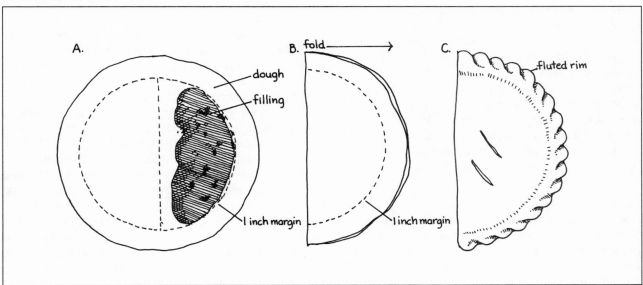

Prepare the filling only when you're ready to assemble the pasties; otherwise the potatoes and turnips will turn brown. Trim and cut the steak into ¼-inch cubes and place them in a large mixing bowl along with the chopped onions. Peel and dice the potatoes into ¼-inch cubes measuring 3½ cups; add to the bowl. Scrape, then dice the turnips into ¼-inch cubes measuring 1½ cups; add to the bowl. Add horseradish, salt, and pepper, then mix the filling with your hands to blend well.

On a lightly floured surface, roll out 1 ball at a time (keep the rest refrigerated) into a circle about ¼-inch thick and roughly 8 inches in diameter. In your mind, imagine a center line dividing the circle. Place between ¾ and 1 cup of the filling 1 inch to the right of that center line, making sure that you also leave a 1-inch margin along the circle's edge; see Illustration A. Fold the left half of the circle over the filling-covered right half. You should get a semicircle whose curved upper and lower edges will meet each other perfectly; see Illustration B. Trim off the extra, ragged dough edges but be sure to leave a 1-inch, unfilled edge of dough. Fold this curved edge of dough on top of itself by ½ inch so as to form a snug and fluted rim—much as you would flute a pie. Do this at ½-inch intervals around the curved edge of the pasty; see Illustration C.

Make two 1-inch slashes in the top of the pasty with a sharp knife, then use a spatula to transfer the finished pasty to a cookie sheet. Repeat this procedure to complete the remaining pasties. When the first cookie sheet is filled, cover it loosely with wax paper and place it in the freezer; repeat for the second cookie sheet. Freeze pasties overnight or until solid. Remove the pasties from the cookie sheets, then package them in empty cereal or cracker boxes or in foil or in plastic freezer bags. Label with this page number or the following cooking directions and return to freezer.

Cooking Directions: Preheat oven to 425°. Place desired amount of pasties on an ungreased cookie sheet and bake for 35 minutes, or until edges become golden. For an extra-golden crust, brush frozen pasties with 1 beaten egg yolk mixed with 2 teaspoons milk.

For tonight's dinner: You can bake some of the pasties, before freezing them, at 400° for 45 minutes.

MEXICAN BURRITOS AND CHIMICHANGOS
Makes 25 to 28, about 9 to 12 servings

Use this recipe for two different dinners—a freshly made Burrito dinner for tonight and a frozen Chimichango dinner for later use. For a Burrito dinner, follow the recipe directions but do not fry the rolled-up Burritos in oil; instead, serve them as a hand-held entrée. Burritos are surprisingly filling and you can count on two or three per serving. Burritos become Chimichangos when you fry them. Use the remaining ingredients from your Burrito dinner to make fresh and/or frozen Chimichangos. Both Burritos and Chimichangos are eaten with your hands and are best accompanied by a crisp, tossed salad.

2 cans (1 pound each) pinto beans
2 medium onions, chopped
½ cup bacon fat or ¼ cup oil
2 pounds ground beef
1 cup shredded Cheddar cheese
1 teaspoon Tabasco sauce (or to taste)
1 teaspoon garlic salt
½ teaspoon chili powder
Salt to taste
28 eight-inch flour tortillas, sold in supermarket dairy case or in frozen foods section
Vegetable oil for frying

Check the amount of liquid in the cans of beans; if minimal, pour beans, undrained, into a mixing bowl and use a potato masher or your hands to squish them into a mushy paste; set aside. If bean cans contain a lot of liquid, reserve the liquid and add as needed. Sauté onions in bacon fat; when soft, add meat and sauté until no longer pink. Add beans and sauté until they are blended and have absorbed all excess grease. Add cheese, Tabasco, garlic salt, and chili powder. Heat through to melt the cheese and adjust salt to taste. Remove from heat and set aside.

To Make Burritos for Tonight's Dinner: Steam the flour tortillas, 1 at a time, on a cake rack placed above a pan of boiling water; turn once on each side so that the tortilla becomes soft and pliable. Spoon about 2 heaping tablespoons of filling onto the warm tortilla and fold as shown in the illustration. Serve Burritos immediately.

To Make Chimichangos for Tonight's Dinner: Fill and fold tortillas as described above, using a little less filling (which you can cool) to make the folding neater. Fasten the filled tortillas with wooden toothpicks. Pour vegetable oil into a heavy skillet to a depth of about 1 inch. Heat over medium-high heat until hot but not smoking. Fry several rolled-up Chimichangos at a time, turning when necessary, for about 2 minutes, or until they are brown and crisp on all sides. Lower the heat as necessary. Drain on paper towels. Remove toothpicks. Serve hot.

To Make Freezer-to-Oven Chimichangos: Make and fry Chimichangos as described above. Drain and cool thoroughly on paper towels. Wrap in aluminum foil, label with this page number or the following cooking directions, and freeze.

To heat the frozen Chimichangos, preheat oven to 350°. Unwrap the frozen Chimichangos and place them in a single layer on a shallow pan or cookie sheet. Bake, uncovered, about 15 minutes on one side then another 10 minutes on the other, or until crisp and hot.

BEEF BOURGUIGNON

Makes 8 servings

2 **pounds stewing beef, cut into 1-inch cubes**
1 **cup Burgundy wine**
2 **cans (10½ ounces each) condensed beef consommé**
1 **teaspoon salt**
½ **teaspoon pepper**

BURRITOS

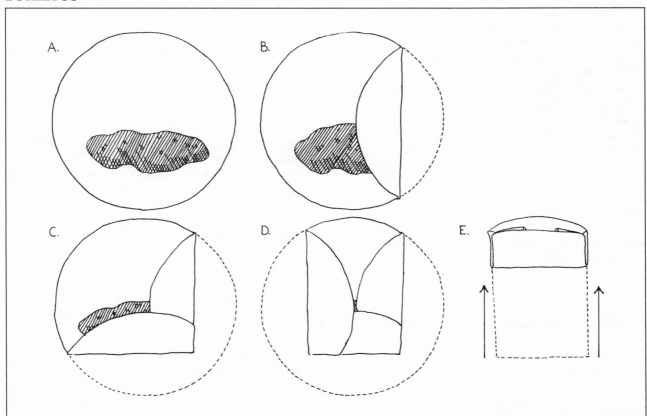

½ cup fine dry breadcrumbs
½ cup flour
2 medium onions
Eight 16-ounce lidded plastic containers

Combine the beef, wine, consommé, salt, and pepper in a large, heavy, non-ceramic casserole with a tight-fitting lid. Mix the crumbs with the flour; stir into the casserole mixture. Slice the onions into rounds; separate the rounds into rings and use your hands to mix the rings into the casserole mixture. Cover and bake at 300° for 2½ hours; stir occasionally. Let the hot casserole stand, covered, at room temperature for 1 hour, then immerse it in a sink filled with cold water, uncover and stir to somewhat cool the stew.

Ladle the stew equally among the 8 containers—they will barely be halfway filled. Cover each container and place in the freezer overnight, or until solid. Remove the frozen Beef Bourguignon discs and either package them in plastic freezer bags or wrap them individually in aluminum foil. Label with this page number or the following cooking directions and return to the freezer.

Cooking Directions: Each frozen disc makes 1 serving. Put 2 tablespoons of water in the top part of a double boiler; place the unwrapped frozen disc in the water. Place the pot over simmering water; cover tightly and cook about 10 to 15 minutes, or until thawed; turn the disc over once during this cooking time. When thawed, stir the sauce vigorously to smooth any lumps, then add the next disc to the pot. Cover and heat until thawed; repeat for as many servings as you want. Stir the mixture as it warms; you may add a few tablespoons of water or wine should the sauce become too thick. When both sauce and beef cubes are heated through, add salt and pepper to taste. Serve this flavorful stew over wide egg noodles or rice pilaf.

SPICY CARIBBEAN BEEF TURNOVERS

Makes 12

1½ pounds ground beef
1 large garlic clove, smashed and minced
¾ cup thinly sliced scallions

½ cup tomato sauce
¼ to ¾ teaspoon crushed red pepper, or to taste
Salt to taste
1 tablespoon cornstarch
¾ cup beef broth
2 cups flour
1 tablespoon curry powder
1 teaspoon salt
⅔ cup vegetable shortening
About ⅓ cup ice water

Sauté the ground beef in a skillet until no longer pink; drain off all excess fat. Add garlic and scallions; sauté briefly. Add tomato sauce, red pepper, and salt; simmer and stir until most of the liquid has evaporated. Combine the cornstarch and beef broth in a jar; shake well and pour into the beef mixture. Cook and stir until the mixture boils and thickens. Set aside, stirring occasionally, to completely cool.

Make the pastry by sifting together the flour, curry powder, and salt. Using a pastry blender, cut in the shortening until the mixture looks like coarse meal. Sprinkle ¼ cup of the ice water into the flour and toss with a fork to mix. Working quickly, use your hands to press the dampened dough into a ball and set it aside. If any flour mixture remains in the bowl, drizzle in enough water to dampen it, too. Press all the dough together. On a floured surface, roll the dough about ⅛-inch thick, then cut it into twelve 6-inch rounds.

Spoon about 2 heaping tablespoons of the filling onto half of each of the rounds. Brush the margin of each round with a little warm water. Fold the empty half of each round over the filling to make a half-circle turnover. Use fork tines to seal the edges and to prick each top in several places. Use a spatula to transfer the finished turnovers to the cookie sheets; cover loosely with wax paper and freeze overnight, or until solid. Remove the frozen turnovers from the cookie sheets, then package them in foil or plastic freezer bags. Label with this page number or the following cooking directions and return to the freezer.

Cooking Directions: Preheat oven to 425°. Place desired number of turnovers on an ungreased cookie sheet and bake for 50 to 60 minutes, or until the edges become golden. Serve along with a tossed, green salad. One turnover a person is ample for lunch; 2 turnovers per person make a hearty dinner.

AMERICAN TURKEY TURNOVERS

Sauté ½ cup finely chopped onion and ½ cup finely chopped celery in 4 tablespoons of butter. Stir in 1 can (10½ ounces) condensed cream of chicken soup, ½ teaspoon salt, ¼ teaspoon pepper, several dashes of poultry seasoning, and 3 cups cooked and very finely chopped turkey or chicken. Make the same pastry as directed above, with or without the curry powder, depending on your taste; roll and cut into twelve 6-inch rounds. Assemble, freeze, and cook turkey turnovers as directed on the page opposite.

FISHSTICKS

Makes 5½ to 6 dozen

When you make this quickly done recipe, you'll save half the cost of the same amount of commercial fishsticks. The convenience will be the same, but your own homemade product will taste better and will contain twice the fish.

3 pounds perch fillets, thawed if frozen
¾ cup flour for dusting
3 eggs
1 tablespoon milk or water
3 cups fine dry breadcrumbs
½ cup plus 1 tablespoon flour
1½ teaspoons salt
Scant ½ teaspoon pepper
Scant ½ teaspoon paprika
Oil for frying

If the fish has a skin, remove it, but only if it comes off easily. Slice the fish into strips about ¾-inch wide and about 3½ inches long. Set up a bowl containing the dusting flour. Set up a second bowl containing the eggs and milk; beat slightly. Set up a third bowl containing blended breadcrumbs, flour, and the 3 seasonings. Dust all the fish strips in the first bowl of flour; shake off excess.

Heat oil in a frying pan over medium heat to a depth of ½ inch. When the oil is hot, dip a floured fish strip into the egg, then coat it well in the crumb mixture. Put the strip in the hot oil and repeat with the next 6 strips. Fry the fish strips, turning once, until golden and crisp. They will be done in a matter of minutes, so do not let them overcook. Drain on a section of newspaper lined with a paper towel, then repeat with all the fish strips. Let the cooked fishsticks cool to room temperature, then freeze, uncovered and still atop the newspaper, overnight or until solid. Transfer the fishsticks to a plastic bag, label with this page number or the following cooking directions and return to the freezer.

Cooking Directions: Preheat oven to 400°. Place frozen sticks on an ungreased baking sheet. Bake for 12 to 15 minutes, or until the largest fishstick is heated through.

CRUNCHY FISHSTICKS

Add ⅓ cup cornmeal to the breadcrumb mixture.

FRIED FISH FILLETS

Do not cut the fish into strips; instead, cut the fillets into chunks about 2½ by 4 inches. Coat, fry, and freeze as directed. Cook frozen, fried fish fillets on an ungreased baking sheet in a preheated 350° oven for 30 minutes, or until the largest one is hot at the center.

SHRIMP CREOLE

Makes 6 servings

3 tablespoons butter (not margarine)
¾ cup chopped onion
¾ cup chopped celery
1 can (16 ounces) tomatoes
½ of a 6-ounce can tomato paste
Water
1½ tablespoons Worcestershire sauce
2 teaspoons chili powder
1 teaspoon salt
1 teaspoon sugar
Tabasco sauce to taste

⅛ teaspoon unflavored gelatin, dissolved in 1 tablespoon cold water
12 ounces frozen, precooked shrimp, not thawed
Six 16-ounce lidded plastic containers

Melt the butter in a saucepan; sauté the onion and celery until tender, but not brown. Pour the entire contents of the can of tomatoes into a bowl; use your hands to squish the tomatoes into small pieces; add the contents of the bowl to the saucepan. Put tomato paste in a measuring cup; add enough warm water to make 1 cup; stir until smooth and add to the saucepan. Stir Worcestershire, chili powder, salt, sugar, and Tabasco into the saucepan. Simmer, uncovered, for 40 minutes. Stir in the gelatin, then place the saucepan in a sink filled with very cold water and stir the sauce until it is well cooled.

Set up the plastic containers. Distribute the shrimp, still frozen, equally among the containers. Ladle the cool sauce equally among the containers, covering the shrimp; the containers will barely be halfway filled. Stir briefly, cover each container, and place in the freezer overnight or until solid. Remove the frozen discs and either package them in freezer bags or wrap them individually in aluminum foil. Label with this page number or the following cooking directions and return to the freezer.

Cooking Directions: Each frozen disc makes 1 serving. Put 1 tablespoon of water in the top part of a double boiler; place 1 unwrapped frozen disc in the water along with a dash of garlic powder. Place the pot over simmering water; cover tightly and cook about 15 minutes, or until both the sauce and shrimp are heated through; turn the disc over once during this time; stir the sauce until smooth. For additional servings, add the next disc to the pot along with another dash of garlic powder; cover and heat; repeat for as many servings as you want. Serve Shrimp Creole over a bed of pilaf.

CHICKEN CREOLE

Replace the shrimp with 2½ cups of diced cooked chicken.

HAM AND VEGETABLE CASSEROLE

Makes 4 to 6 servings

You may want to double or triple this quickly assembled casserole since no prebaking is necesaary.

6 tablespoons butter
4 tablespoons flour
¾ teaspoon salt
Pepper to taste
2 cups milk
1 small package (3 ounces) cream cheese, in small cubes
1 large onion, chopped
2 to 2½ cups cooked ham cut into ½-inch cubes
2 packages (10 ounces each) frozen mixed vegetables, partially thawed
One 8-by-8-by-2-inch foil pan

Melt 4 tablespoons of the butter in a 2-quart pot over low heat. Remove pot from heat and stir in flour, salt, and pepper until smooth. Return pot to heat and gradually stir in milk. Cook, stirring constantly, until the sauce is well thickened and beginning to bubble. Remove pot from heat and stir in cream cheese cubes until they dissolve into the white sauce. Quickly cool the mixture by placing the pot in a sinkful of cold water, stirring frequently to prevent a film from forming.

While white sauce cools, melt the remaining 2 tablespoons of butter in a skillet. Add onion and sauté until limp and slightly browned. Scrape both onion and butter into the cooled white sauce. Use a rubber spatula to uniformly fold in the cubed ham and the mixed vegetables. Spread this mixture into the foil pan; cover with doubled aluminum foil; label with this page number or the following cooking directions and freeze.

Cooking Directions: Preheat oven to 350°. Remove foil cover from the frozen casserole and bake, uncovered, for 1 hour and 30 minutes, or until bubbly at the edges. For a more attractive casserole, melt 5 tablespoons of butter or bacon drippings in a skillet; add 1 cup dry breadcrumbs; sauté briefly until lightly golden. Sprinkle these buttered crumbs over the casserole after 1 hour of baking.

INDIVIDUAL CASSEROLES

Instead of turning the prepared casserole mixture into an 8-by-8-inch pan, divide it among 4 foil baby-loaf pans (5¾ by 3¼ by 2 inches each) allowing about 1½ cups mixture per pan. Cover each pan with doubled foil, label with this page number and freeze. Each pan will generously serve 1 person. For smaller servings, divide mixture among 5 or 6 pans.

To cook individual casseroles, preheat oven to 350°. Remove foil covering and bake for 1 hour and 15 minutes, or until bubbly at the edges. Pans containing less than 1½ cups should bake for only 1 hour. To make a buttered crumb topping for 1 individual pan: Melt 1 tablespoon butter in a skillet; add 3 tablespoons breadcrumbs; sauté briefly. Sprinkle crumbs over casserole after first 30 minutes of baking.

RAVIOLI

Makes about 30. Serves 4 to 6

This homemade ravioli puts the frozen, supermarket version to shame in both taste and price.

MEAT FILLING:

1 pound lean ground beef
1 small onion, chopped
3 tablespoons water
½ teaspoon salt
¼ teaspoon pepper
1 egg, lightly beaten

PASTA DOUGH:

2 cups flour
2 eggs, at room temperature
2 teaspoons oil
½ teaspoon salt
3 to 6 teaspoons lukewarm water
2 non-terrycloth towels, dampened

Prepare Meat Filling: Lightly sauté the meat in a skillet until the pink is almost gone; add onion and sauté until limp; add water, salt, and pepper and continue to cook and stir until no pink remains. Simmer, uncovered, for 8 to 10 minutes, or until the water evaporates leaving a crumbly filling. Adjust salt and pepper to taste. Set aside and allow filling to cool completely.

Prepare Pasta Dough: If you have a food processor, follow the dough directions at the end of this recipe. If you are making the dough by hand, mound the flour in a large mixing bowl and make a well in the center; put the eggs, oil, and salt into the well. Use your first two fingers to break the yolks and to swirl the eggs in a clockwise direction around the walls of the well. Keep swirling so that the flour combines with the egg, first into a paste, then into a crumbly, crude-looking, dough-like mixture. When the mixture cannot absorb any more flour, resist the temptation to squeeze it into a dough. Instead, sprinkle 1 teaspoon of water over it and swirl again, using all your fingers. If the mixture gets a little sticky and looks as if it wants to adhere, squeeze it into a ball of dough; if not, continue adding more teaspoons or drops of water until you get a crude-looking ball of dough.

Knead the dough on a lightly floured surface for about 15 minutes, or until smooth and elastic. If the dough becomes too sticky, knead with floured hands; if the dough is too stiff or crumbly, knead it with water-moistened palms; if your dough is too elastic from overworking, wrap it and let it rest 10 minutes before continuing. When kneaded, wrap the dough snugly in plastic wrap and let it rest at room temperature for 30 minutes.

Assemble Ravioli: Go back to the cooled filling and stir in the egg; set the filling aside. Divide the dough in half; rewrap one half and set it aside. On a lightly floured surface, roll the unwrapped dough-half into a rough rectangle as large and paper thin as you can get it. Trim the top edge straight with a ravioli cutter, a pizza or pastry wheel, or a very sharp knife. Cover the dough with the damp, non-terrycloth towel leaving a 5-inch-wide strip uncovered along the top, trimmed edge; see Illustration A on page 22. The towel should be damp, but not wet; if it dries out as you work, redampen it to prevent your dough from drying out.

Place teaspoonfuls of the meat filling 1½ inches apart down the center of the exposed 5-inch dough strip. Use a small brush or your fingertip dipped in cold water to draw straight vertical lines between the mounds of filling and long, horizontal lines across the top and bottom borders of the dough; see Illustration B. Use just enough water to dampen the dough into stickiness.

Bring the trimmed, top edge of the dough up and over the mounds of filling so that the trimmed dough edge almost meets with the towel as shown in Illustration C. To seal the two layers together, gently press the length of your finger between and around the mounds of filling on all the places you previously dampened with water. Use a ravioli wheel or a sharp knife to cut along the line the

RAVIOLI

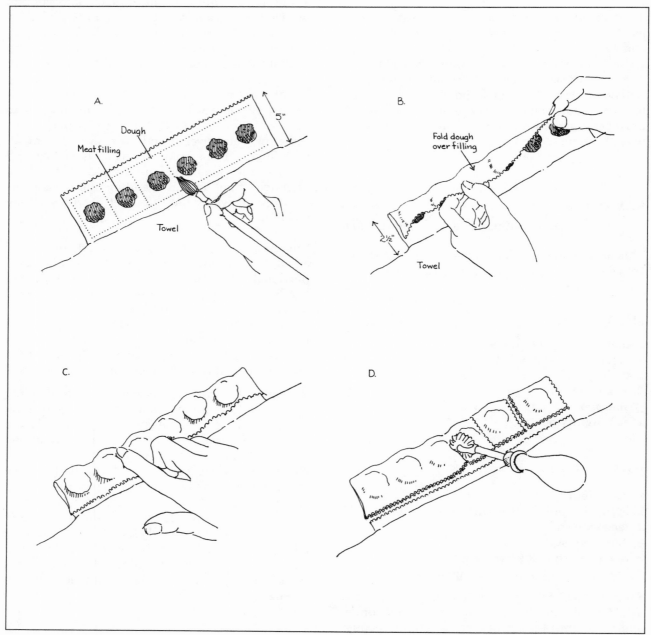

towel makes and between each mound. If any of the seals between the two dough layers look as though they might burst open, use fork tines to reseal them. Place the finished ravioli on a lightly floured cookie sheet and cover with the other dampened towel.

To make more ravioli, simply move the towel down the dough another 5 inches and repeat what you have just done. When the cookie sheet is full, remove the towel and place the cookie sheet, uncovered, in the freezer overnight, or until solid. Transfer the ravioli to plastic bags, label with this page number, and return to the freezer.

Cooking Directions for Fresh Ravioli: Ravioli are awfully good when freshly made, so if you want some for tonight's dinner, cook them right away for best results (or they can wait for up to 2 hours under the dampened towel). For a wait longer than 2 to 3 hours, cover with plastic wrap and refrigerate. For a wait longer than 3 hours, it is best to freeze them.

To cook fresh ravioli, drop them one by one into a very large pot of rapidly boiling salted water. Reduce the heat slightly to prevent too much churning and boil, uncovered, for about 8 to 10 minutes, or until cooked to desired tenderness. Drain well and serve with your favorite spaghetti sauce or with melted butter and freshly grated Parmesan cheese.

Cooking directions for Frozen Ravioli: Bring a very large pot of salted water to a rapid boil. Drop frozen ravioli in, one by one, waiting between additions. Bring the pot to a second boil and boil gently for 15 to 20 minutes, or until cooked to desired tenderness. Drain well and serve as described for Fresh Ravioli, above.

RICOTTA CHEESE FILLING

Replace the meat filling with a gently stirred-together mixture of: 1½ cups ricotta cheese, ¾ cup freshly grated Parmesan cheese, 3 egg yolks at room temperature, 1 tablespoon grated onion, and 1 teaspoon salt.

SPINACH FILLING

Replace the meat filling with a lightly blended mixture of: 1 package (10 ounces) frozen chopped spinach, cooked and absolutely, thoroughly, drained until almost dry, ½ cup ricotta cheese, ½ cup freshly grated Parmesan cheese, 1 egg yolk at room temperature, 1 tablespoon grated onion, and ⅛ teaspoon nutmeg.

To Prepare Pasta Dough with a Food Processor: If you have a food processor that will handle a small quantity of dough, use it to make a dough that will knead more easily. Do not use an ordinary blender.

Use the Pasta Dough ingredients; combine the flour and salt in the food processor container. Turn the machine quickly on and off to blend the ingredients. Turn the machine on and add the eggs, one at a time, until they are well mixed into the flour. With the machine still running, pour in enough water in a thin, steady trickle to make a medium-soft dough that is not sticky. Cover and let rest for 30 minutes. If your processor has a kneading attachment, refer to the machine's directions and knead until smooth and elastic (the equivalent of 15 minutes hand kneading). Wrap the dough snugly in plastic wrap and let it rest for 30 minutes. Continue with the recipe at "Assemble Ravioli."

TORTELLINI

Makes about 12 servings

1 **whole chicken breast**
1 **loin pork chop**
1 **cup chicken broth**
¼ **cup grated Parmesan cheese**
1 **egg, lightly beaten**
⅛ **teaspoon grated fresh lemon peel**
⅛ **teaspoon nutmeg**
Salt and pepper to taste
Pasta Dough from previous Ravioli Recipe
1 **non-terrycloth towel, dampened**

In a saucepan, combine chicken, pork chop, and broth; cover and simmer 15 minutes, then remove chicken breast; continue cooking the pork chop

20 more minutes. Let the meats cool slightly, then skin, defat, and bone them; either grind them together in a food processor or dice them as fine as possible with a sharp knife; you should have 1 cup of ground meat or 1⅛ cups finely diced meat. Discard broth or save it for another cooking use. Mix the meats, cheese, egg, lemon peel, and nutmeg in a bowl until well blended; season with salt and pepper; set aside.

Make and knead the same pasta dough that appears in the previous Ravioli recipe (page 23), and let it rest for 30 minutes. If you have a food processor, use the directions that appear at the end of that recipe. Divide the dough in half; rewrap one half and set it aside. On a lightly floured surface, roll the unwrapped dough into a rough rectangle as large and as paper thin as you can get it. Trim the sides into a straight rectangle

TORTELLINI

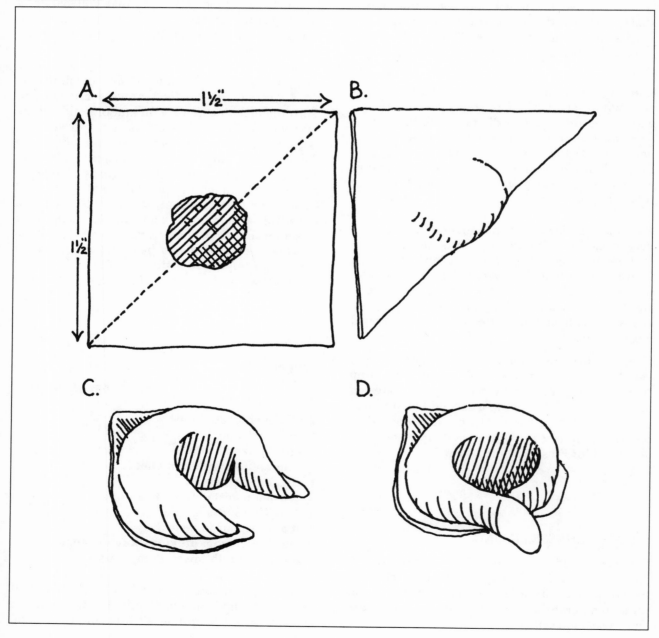

using a ravioli cutter, a pastry or pizza wheel, or a very sharp knife. Cut this rectangle into 1½-inch squares.

Place ¼ teaspoon of the meat mixture on each square. Use your fingertips to moisten the edges of each square; use only enough water to dampen the dough into stickiness. Folding away from yourself, fold each square into a triangle; press the edges to firmly seal them together. Place your index finger against the fold and pull the two corners of the triangle toward you; pinch the corners together to form the Tortellini; see Illustration A for further instruction.

Place each of the Tortellini on a lightly floured cookie sheet. Cover the first set with a damp, non-terrycloth towel while you repeat the procedure with the remaining dough and filling. When all the Tortellini have been made, remove the towel and place the cookie sheet(s), uncovered, in the freezer overnight, or until solid. Transfer the Tortellini to plastic bags, label with this page number, and return to freezer.

Cooking Directions for Fresh Tortellini: Tortellini are best when cooked at once, but they may be covered in plastic wrap and refrigerated for up to 8 hours; for a wait longer than 8 hours it is best to freeze them.

To cook fresh Tortellini, drop them into a very large pot of rapidly boiling, salted water. Stir carefully with a wooden spoon for the first few moments to prevent them from sticking to each other, then boil, stirring occasionally, for about 10 minutes or until they are tender. Drain well in a sieve or colander. Serve with your favorite spaghetti sauce or in hot chicken or beef broth.

Cooking Directions for Frozen Tortellini: Cook as for fresh Tortellini, increasing the boiling time to 15 minutes.

FROZEN PIZZA CRUSTS

Makes 4 pizza crusts
serving 4 each

Frozen pizzas can never taste freshly made because: (1) frozen toppings and frozen crusts bake at very different rates and this causes the topping to sink down into a soggy crust; and (2) the many seasonings in frozen toppings either disappear or change flavor upon freezing. The answer is in handy Frozen Pizza Crusts: they enable you to assemble a fresh-tasting pizza using your own ready-made, partially-baked, never soggy crust.

6¼ to 6½ cups flour
2 packages active dry yeast
2 teaspoons salt
2 cups lukewarm-to-warm, 110° to 115° water
2 tablespoons olive oil
Four 12-inch pizza pans or ample cookie sheets, lightly greased and sprinkled with cornmeal

Stir together 3 cups of the flour, the yeast, and the salt in a large mixing bowl; add water and oil. Use an electric mixer at low speed to beat for 30 seconds; continuously scrape down the sides of the bowl as you beat. Change to high speed and beat for 3 minutes. Using a wooden spoon, stir in ½-cup measures of the remaining flour to make a stiff dough. If you have a food processor or other appliance for mixing dough, follow the manufacturer's directions. Knead the dough on a lightly floured surface until smooth, elastic, and slightly blistered beneath the surface; this should take from 10 to 15 minutes.

Shape the dough into a ball and place it in a lightly oiled bowl; turn the dough over to grease the top, then cover the bowl loosely with plastic wrap followed by a towel. Let the dough rise in a warm draft-free spot for 1½ to 2 hours, or until it has approximately doubled in volume.

Punch the dough down with your fist; pull the edges to the center; form a ball and knead briefly until smooth. Use a knife or scissors to cut the dough into 4 equal pieces; form the pieces into balls. Cover the dough balls with plastic wrap and a towel; let them rest on a floured board for 10 to 15 minutes. While the dough rests, preheat oven to 425°.

Use the palm of your hand to flatten 1 of the dough balls into a circle about 1 inch thick. With both hands, hold the circle along its rim and stretch the dough by turning the circle and gently pulling your hands apart at the same time. When the circle measures about 8 or 9 inches across, spread it out on a lightly floured surface. Use a rolling pin to roll the dough out from the center to the edges; turn the dough slightly after each roll until you get a circle of dough about 11 or 12 inches across. Place the circle on one of the greased and cornmeal-dusted pans. Use your thumbs to crimp the edge of the circle until it forms a rim.

Bake for 10 minutes; the crust will not be brown and it may be a bit uneven due to baked-in air bubbles, but this will not affect the finished pizza. Remove the crust from the oven and let it cool in its pan. Repeat this stretching, rolling, and baking procedure for all the dough balls. When all the baked crusts are completely cool, freeze them in their pans, covered loosely with wax paper, overnight or until solid; then wrap each crust separately in foil or freezer paper in the Drugstore Wrap (see page 10); label with this page number and return to the freezer.

Cooking Directions: Preheat oven to 450°. Pour ¾ cup of your favorite pizza sauce or spaghetti sauce on the completely unwrapped, frozen crust; swirl it around with the back of a spoon. Sprinkle the sauce with ¾ cup shredded mozzarella and 3 tablespoons of grated Parmesan cheese; add any extra topping you wish; then drizzle the surface with 1 to 2 tablespoons of olive oil.

Set the pizza directly on the lowest oven rack (not in a pan) or on the floor of the oven; bake 15 to 25 minutes, or until the crust is lightly browned and the filling is bubbling hot. Let the pizza set for 5 minutes before scoring and serving.

HOMEMADE PIZZA SAUCE

Sauté a medium, chopped onion in 2 teaspoons of olive oil; add and sauté 1 minced garlic clove. Add: 1 small can (8 ounces) of tomato sauce, ½ teaspoon oregano, ½ teaspoon basil, ½ teaspoon salt, ¼ teaspoon sugar, and pepper to taste. Simmer, uncovered, until thickened, about 20 minutes. Provides sauce for 1 pizza.

TOPPINGS

Add your choice of topping after distributing the mozzarella and Parmesan and before drizzling on the olive oil. Some topping suggestions are: cooked and crumbled Italian sweet sausage with casings removed; canned or sautéed sliced mushrooms; additional shredded mozzarella; pepperoni or hard salami slices; anchovy strips; ham or prosciutto strips; tiny, cooked meatballs; onion rings or green pepper strips, parboiled until softened.

INDIVIDUAL PIZZAS

After you have punched down the risen dough, knead it briefly and divide it into 16 equal balls. Continue with the recipe, rolling each ball into a 5-inch circle; bake on prepared cookie sheets; cool, freeze, and wrap as directed. On each frozen crust, use 3 or 4 tablespoons of sauce, ¼ cup mozzarella, 2 teaspoons Parmesan, and a sprinkling of oil. Bake at 425° for 15 to 25 minutes.

INDIVIDUAL MACARONI AND CHEESE CASSEROLES

Makes 8 individual servings

Quickly made, these double-cheese casseroles make a good freezer staple.

4 **cups (1 pound) uncooked elbow macaroni**
3 **tablespoons butter**
2 **teaspoons grated onion**
4 **tablespoons flour**
1 **teaspoon dry mustard**
¼ **teaspoon pepper**
2½ **cups milk**
2 **teaspoons Worcestershire sauce**
1 **medium package (8 ounces) cream cheese, cut into cubes**
3 **cups shredded sharp Cheddar cheese**
Salt to taste
8 **round foil pot-pie or tart pans, 5 inches across and 1¼ inches deep**

Cook the macaroni only ¾ of the time specified by the manufacturer: If the box tells you to cook the macaroni 8 to 12 minutes, cook it 6 to 9 minutes, or until just barely *al dente*. Rinse the macaroni in a colander under cold running water until completely cool; let it drain.

Melt the butter in a large saucepan over medium heat; do not let it brown. Briefly sauté the grated onion, then stir in the flour, mustard, and pepper until absorbed. Gradually stir in the milk and Worcestershire sauce and continue to cook over low heat, stirring constantly, until thickened and bubbly. Stir in the cream cheese until melted and blended. Cup by cup, stir and blend in the Cheddar cheese; set aside.

Pour the drained macaroni into a large bowl. Pour the cheese sauce atop and mix thoroughly; adjust salt to taste. Pour the macaroni and cheese mixture equally among the 8 foil pans. Cover and secure each with aluminum foil; label with this page number or the following cooking directions.

Cooking Directions: Preheat oven to 425°. Place desired number of frozen, covered pans on a cookie sheet or aluminum foil. Bake 30 minutes; remove foil cover and continue to bake for 10 more minutes, or until hot at center, bubbly at the edges, and lightly browned.

CHEESE STRATA CASSEROLE

Makes 2 casseroles serving 4 each

25 slices of bread, each about 3 inches square and at least ¼-inch thick
2 foil pans, 8-by-8-by-2 inches, greased with butter
4 cups (16 ounces) shredded Cheddar, Swiss, or Muenster cheese
1 cup grated Parmesan cheese
6 eggs
4 cups whole milk
¼ cup finely chopped chives, onions, or parsley
½ teaspoon salt
¼ teaspoon paprika
Several dashes cayenne pepper or Tabasco

Choose a bread that is sturdier than the average soft supermarket bread: 1½ loaves of Pepperidge Farm white or whole wheat bread will fit the rec-

ipe nicely as will any comparable counterpart. Trim the crusts from the bread slices (do not use the heels); cut all the slices vertically in half. Cut 2 of the halves vertically to make 4 narrow strips. Arrange 12½ half-slices of bread in the bottoms of each of the greased pans; do not let the slices overlap. Sprinkle the Cheddar and Parmesan equally atop the bread in the pans. Cover the cheese in each pan with equal amounts (12½ half slices each) of the rest of the bread.

Beat together the remaining ingredients; pour this mixture evenly and equally over both pans. Let the pans stand for 5 minutes, then wrap each in foil, label with this page number or with the following cooking directions and freeze.

Cooking Directions: Preheat oven to 350°. Bake the frozen, wrapped pan for 1 hour and 15 minutes; unwrap and bake 15 minutes more, or until hot at the center and browned.

INDIVIDUAL TUNA-SPINACH CASSEROLES

Makes 8 individual servings

A meal-in-one for busy people; you get protein, carbohydrate, and vegetable in one tasty dish.

2 packages (10 ounces each) frozen chopped spinach, completely thawed
2 cups uncooked narrow or medium noodles
1 cup cream-style cottage cheese
1 cup shredded Monterey Jack cheese
1 can (10¾ ounces) condensed cream of celery soup
1 can (7 ounces) tuna in water, drained and well flaked
1½ tablespoons strained fresh lemon juice
½ teaspoon salt
8 round foil, pot-pie or tart pans, 5 inches across and 1¼ inches deep

Cook the spinach for only half the time the package directions specify; drain in a strainer; press out any excess liquid; set aside to drain further. Cook the noodles according to package directions just to the *al dente* stage; rinse them in a colander under cold running water; set aside and let drain. Place the cottage cheese in a large bowl; use an egg beater to beat out any large lumps. Use a spoon to mix in the shredded cheese, soup, tuna, lemon juice, and salt. Drain the spinach as thoroughly as possible and stir it into the cheese-tuna mixture. Gently mix in the cooked noodles.

Divide the mixture among the 8 foil pans and let cool. Cover with aluminum foil, label with this page number or the following cooking directions, and freeze.

Cooking Directions: Preheat oven to 450°. Bake, loosely covered, for 40 minutes; remove foil and bake 5 more minutes, or until hot at the center and bubbly around the edges.

VEGETARIAN VARIATION

Omit the tuna, increase the noodles to 3 cups; you may wish to use whole wheat or high protein noodles instead of the ordinary variety.

CHEESE SOUFFLÉ

Makes 1 soufflé, serves 6

6½ tablespoons butter
2 tablespoons finely grated Parmesan cheese
6 tablespoons flour
¾ teaspoon salt
½ teaspoon paprika
Dash of cayenne pepper
1½ cups whole milk at room temperature
1½ cups (6 ounces) diced, sharp Cheddar cheese
6 large eggs, separated and at room
  temperature
⅛ teaspoon cream of tartar

Grease a 2-quart, 4-inch-deep, straight-sided soufflé or casserole dish with ½ tablespoon of the butter; make sure the bottom is well coated; dust the Parmesan around to coat the bottom and sides. Set this dish in your freezer to chill.

Melt but don't brown the remaining butter in a saucepan; with a wire whisk, blend in the flour and seasonings; cook slowly, stirring for 1 or 2 minutes without browning. Add the milk; cook and stir vigorously over high heat until smooth and thickened. Add the cheese; stir until melted; remove from heat.

Use an egg beater or an electric mixer to beat the egg yolks until smooth and thick; gradually stir them into the cheese mixture. Clean your beater well, then beat the egg whites in a large mixing bowl until they begin to foam; add the cream of tartar, then beat vigorously until the whites can hold stiff peaks with slightly drooping points. Use a rubber spatula to fold the cheese mixture into the egg whites until well combined. Fold swiftly, turning the bowl as you do, so that the whites do not collapse. Spoon the mixture into the prepared soufflé dish, cover tightly (because the egg whites can pick up many freezer smells), and freeze for up to 3 weeks. Label with this page number or with the following cooking directions.

Cooking Directions: Uncover the frozen soufflé and place it in a cold oven. Set the temperature at 350°; bake for 1½ hours or until the top has browned and the sides show a faint line of shrinkage from the dish. Serve plain or with a creamy mushroom or seafood sauce.

SWISS CHEESE SOUFFLÉ

Replace the Cheddar with Swiss (or Monterey Jack) cheese; omit the paprika and cayenne, replacing them with several dashes of pepper and a pinch of nutmeg.

INDIVIDUAL VEGETARIAN PIES

Makes 6

1 package (10 ounces) frozen chopped spinach,
  completely thawed
5 tablespoons butter
2½ cups (½ pound) sliced fresh mushrooms
4 eggs
2 cups (1 pound) ricotta cheese
1 cup shredded Monterey Jack or Muenster
  cheese
2 teaspoons minced fresh dillweed (or
  ½ teaspoon dried)
½ teaspoon salt
¼ teaspoon pepper

6 round foil, pot-pie or tart pans, 5 inches across and 1¼ inches deep, well greased

Set the thawed spinach in a strainer; press out any excess liquid; set aside to drain further. Melt the butter in a frying pan and sauté the mushrooms until soft and limp; set aside.

In a large bowl, beat the eggs until frothy, about 3 minutes. Stir in the ricotta with a wire whisk; when the mixture is smooth and free of lumps, stir in the shredded cheese. Press out any remaining liquid from the spinach before stirring it into the egg and cheese mixture. Add the dillweed, salt, and pepper, then the sautéed mushrooms. Pour equally among the 6 foil pans.

Bake at 325° for 35 to 40 minutes, or until the centers feel firm when touched; cool completely. Cover each pan with aluminum foil and seal by crimping under the edges. Label with this page number or the following cooking directions and freeze.

Cooking Directions: Place desired number of covered frozen pans in a preheated 350° oven for 1 hour. Remove from oven; uncover and briefly cut around the edges to loosen. Invert a dinner plate and serve with a tossed salad.

WITH SALMON

Add ¾ cup canned salmon, skinned, deboned, and shredded with your fingers, when you add the spinach.

WITH HAM

Sauté 1 cup diced cooked ham along with the mushrooms.

MEATLESS MOUSSAKA

Makes 2 pans serving 4 each

EGGPLANT AND FILLING:

3 pounds eggplant, about 2 or 3 of medium size
Salt

4 tablespoons butter
¾ cup cracked bulgur wheat
1½ teaspoons salt
¼ teaspoon pepper
1⅞ cups water or chicken broth
2 medium onions, chopped
1 small can (6 ounces) tomato paste
¼ cup water
1 teaspoon allspice
½ cup grated Parmesan cheese
Butter
¼ cup fine dry breadcrumbs
2 foil pans, 8 by 8 by 2 inches

MOUSSAKA SAUCE:

4 tablespoons butter
2 tablespoons flour
2 cups whole milk
4 eggs
½ cup grated Parmesan cheese
½ teaspoon salt
Dash of pepper

Many people dislike eggplant because it has a slightly bitter taste. The following salting procedure will draw out all bitterness: Peel the eggplants and slice them into rounds ⅛-inch thick. Sprinkle both sides of each slice generously with salt and place the slices in a large deep bowl. Fill the bowl up to the rim with cold water and cover with a heavy dinner plate to keep the slices submerged. Set aside for 1 hour at room temperature while you make the filling.

Melt 2 tablespoons of the butter in a heavy saucepan over medium heat. Stir in the bulgur, salt, and pepper and sauté, stirring constantly, until the wheat takes on a slightly translucent quality; do not let the particles pop or get brown. Slowly stir in the broth; bring to a full boil; cover and lower the heat to a simmer. Simmer for 25 to 30 minutes, or until nearly all the liquid is absorbed and the bulgur looks just a bit too moist to serve. Turn off the heat and let the saucepan stand, without removing the cover, for 15 more minutes. When done, remove the cover and let the bulgur cool to room temperature while you make the tomato sauce.

Melt the remaining 2 tablespoons of butter in a

frying pan and sauté the onions until limp, but not brown. Mix in the tomato paste, ¼ cup of water, and allspice; stir until smooth, then set aside.

When the eggplant is ready and the bulgur is completely cool, prepare the foil pans by greasing them liberally with butter and sprinkling each of the bottoms with ⅛ cup of breadcrumbs. Thoroughly rinse and drain the eggplant slices in a colander.

Spoon half of the bulgur into a bowl; leave the other half in its saucepan. Pour half of the onion-tomato sauce into the bulgur bowl and the other half into the saucepan containing the bulgur. Pour ¼ cup of the grated Parmesan into the bowl; pour the remaining ¼ cup Parmesan into the saucepan. Mix the ingredients in the bowl; do the same with the saucepan. Adjust the salt and pepper in both bowl and saucepan.

Divide the eggplant slices into 6 equal piles. Arrange eggplant pile #1 over the breadcrumbs in the first foil pan. Cover with half the contents of the bulgur bowl. Arrange eggplant pile #2 over this; cover with the remaining contents of the bulgur bowl. Finally, cover with eggplant pile #3 and set aside. Repeat this same procedure to fill the second foil pan, using the remaining 3 eggplant piles and the bulgur in the saucepan. Set aside while you make the following Moussaka Sauce.

Melt the butter in a large saucepan over low to medium heat. Use a wire whisk to stir in the flour. Slowly pour in milk and stir constantly until smooth and thickened; this will take some time; remove from heat and set aside. In a bowl, beat the eggs to a froth for about 5 minutes. Add a small amount of the cooked white sauce into the bowl of eggs to equalize the temperatures, then, stirring constantly, slowly pour the bowl's entire contents back into the saucepan. Mix in the Parmesan, salt, and pepper. Gradually pour this sauce equally into the 2 foil pans; you will have to jiggle the pans to get the sauce between the layers, or else you can poke your finger to the bottom layer in various places and at the pan edges so that the sauce will sink down.

Bake both pans at a preheated 375° for 1 hour. If you wish to serve one of the casseroles for tonight's dinner, let it set for 5 or 10 minutes before cutting it into 4 squares. Let the pans cool completely on wire racks, then wrap in foil, label with this page number or the following cooking directions, and freeze.

Cooking Directions: Bake, uncovered, in a preheated 425° oven for 1 hour, or until a knife inserted at the center comes out hot. Let the Moussaka set for 5 or 10 minutes before cutting and serving.

VEGETARIAN EMPANADAS

Makes 8 servings

3   medium-size carrots, well scrubbed
4   tablespoons butter
1   large onion, chopped
½   pound fresh mushrooms, coarsely sliced
2   medium-size zucchini cut in ½-inch slices
3   stalks celery, cut in ½-inch slices
1   green pepper, cut in ½-inch squares
2 or 3 garlic cloves, smashed and minced
1   can (1 pound) tomatoes, undrained
1   teaspoon chili powder
½   teaspoon ground cumin
½   teaspoon oregano
¼   teaspoon cayenne pepper
2   tablespoons flour
¼   cup cold water
1   cup shredded Monterey Jack cheese
Salt
3½ cups sifted all-purpose or whole wheat flour
1½ tablespoons baking powder
4   tablespoons butter, chilled
4   tablespoons vegetable shortening, chilled
2   teaspoons soy sauce
1⅛ cups ice cold water
1   egg mixed with 1 tablespoon water

Put the carrots in a pot with enough water to just cover them, bring to a boil, then lower heat and simmer for about 10 minutes, or until just tender; drain, cut into ¾-inch slices, and set aside. Melt the butter in a large frying pan over medium heat. Add the onion, mushrooms, zucchini, celery, green pepper, and garlic. Sauté, stirring continuously, just until the onion is limp; set pan aside. Pour the entire contents of the can of tomatoes into a bowl; use your hands to squish the tomatoes into small pieces; blend the chili powder, cumin, oregano, and cayenne into this.

Put the flour into a small cup; thoroughly blend in the ¼ cup cold water; pour this mixture into the tomato mixture and stir to blend well, then stir it into the frying pan containing the vegetables. Bring to a simmer; cover and simmer for 2 or 3 minutes, then uncover and cook for about 5 minutes over medium-high heat, stirring constantly, until the liquid evaporates and the vegetables are just tender. Stir in the carrots and the shredded cheese; adjust salt to taste. When the cheese has melted, set the frying pan in the refrigerator to quickly cool the vegetables; gently stir them now and then to accomplish this.

When the vegetable filling is cooled, begin the empanada crust. Resift the flour along with the baking powder into a bowl. Working fast, cut the butter and shortening into the flour mixture until it looks like coarse meal. Make a well in the center; add the soy sauce and cold water, all at once, and stir vigorously with a fork just until the dough follows the fork around the bowl; this should only take 30 or 40 seconds. Turn the dough onto a lightly floured surface and knead gently for another 30 seconds (about 10 folds) to remove stickiness.

Divide the dough into 8 equal balls. Roll out 1 ball on a lightly floured surface to make an 8-inch circle. Spoon about ¾ cup of vegetable filling on the circle's center. Lightly moisten the entire circle's edge with water. Bring the edges of the circle together at the top of the filling. Use your fingers to pinch and flute the edges to make a sealed

semicircle. Use a spatula to lift the empanada to an ungreased cookie sheet.

Repeat the above process, using all remaining dough balls and filling. Place the bundles 1 inch apart on 2 or 3 cookie sheets; refrigerate the first filled cookie sheet before going on to the next. Prick the top of each empanada with a fork and brush thoroughly with the egg and water mixture. Freeze the uncovered empanadas overnight, or until solid. Wrap each frozen empanada individually in foil or in a freezer bag, label with this page number and return to your freezer.

Cooking Directions: Preheat oven to 425°. Place desired amount of unwrapped frozen empanadas on an ungreased cookie sheet and bake for about 30 minutes, or until the crust appears firm and golden brown and each empanada is hot at the center. Let cool just slightly on racks before serving.

For Tonight's Dinner: Bake the just-made, not-yet-frozen empanadas, uncovered, on an ungreased cookie sheet in a preheated 400° oven for 25 to 30 minutes, or until firm and golden.

OTHER VEGETARIAN RECIPES

Other vegetarian recipes in this chapter-section are:

RAVIOLI WITH RICOTTA CHEESE FILLING
RAVIOLI WITH SPINACH FILLING
FROZEN PIZZA
INDIVIDUAL MACARONI AND CHEESE
   CASSEROLES
CHEESE STRATA CASSEROLE
CHEESE SOUFFLÉ
INDIVIDUAL TUNA-SPINACH CASSEROLE,
   NOODLE VARIATION

CORN CASSEROLE

*Makes 2 casseroles serving
4 to 6 each*

3 packages (10 ounces each) frozen corn
  kernels (or 4½ cups fresh kernels)
8 tablespoons butter
2 tablespoons flour
1 tablespoon cornstarch
3½ cups milk
1½ teaspoons salt
2 dashes paprika
2 tablespoons snipped chives
8 eggs, at room temperature
2 foil pans, 8 by 8 by 2 inches, well buttered

Pour the frozen corn into a bowl; fill with hot tap water and swish with your hands to thaw the corn; let drain in a colander. Briefly melt the butter, but do not let it brown; let it cool to room temperature. Preheat oven to 325°.

Combine the butter, flour, and cornstarch in a large bowl; gradually blend in the milk, salt, paprika, and chives, then stir in the drained corn. In another bowl, beat the eggs until they are frothy; add them to the milk mixture.

Pour the combined ingredients equally between the 2 well-buttered foil pans and bake for 45 minutes, or until slightly browned on top; stir once during the baking time. When cooked, let the casseroles cool to room temperature; cover with foil; label with this page number or the following cooking directions and freeze.

Cooking Directions: Bake the frozen, uncovered casserole in a preheated 325° oven for 30 minutes, or until a knife inserted at the center comes out hot.

GLAZED CARROTS

Makes 1 pan, serving 4 to 6

1 pound carrots
4 tablespoons brown sugar
2 teaspoons flour
½ teaspoon salt
2 teaspoons freshly grated orange or lemon peel
2 tablespoons fresh lemon juice
½ cup strained orange juice
3 tablespoons butter
1 foil pan, 8 by 8 by 2 inches, buttered

Peel the carrots and slice them on the diagonal into ¼-inch thick ovals. Bring a large pot of water to a rapid boil; add the carrots and when the water returns to a boil, let them boil for 5 minutes. Immediately rinse the carrots in a colander under cold running water and set them aside to drain. Mix the sugar, flour, salt, and peel in a saucepan; stir in the 2 juices and bring to a boil. Add the butter and simmer, uncovered, for 5 minutes. Let cool to room temperature.

Arrange the drained carrots in the foil pan; pour the cooled sauce atop. Cover the pan with foil, label with this page number or the following cooking directions, and freeze.

Cooking Directions: Preheat oven to 350°. Bake covered pan for 30 minutes; remove cover and continue baking another 30 minutes, or until bubbly at edges and hot at the center.

CRISPY PARMESAN-EGGPLANT STICKS

Makes 3 dozen

Save over the commercial sticks while you enjoy a much tastier product. These crispy sticks make a good, ready-in-a-minute appetizer, too.

1 pound eggplant
2 tablespoons salt
About ¾ cup flour for dusting

1 large egg
1 teaspoon milk
¾ cup fine dry breadcrumbs
¼ cup grated Parmesan cheese
2 tablespoons plus 1 teaspoon flour
¼ teaspoon garlic powder
¼ teaspoon pepper
Oil for frying
Vegetable shortening for frying

Peel eggplant; cut into strips ¼-inch thick, 1-inch wide, and 3 or 4 inches long. Arrange some of the sticks on a paper plate and generously sprinkle both sides with some of the salt; place salted strips in a colander. Repeat for all remaining strips and salt. Put a dinner plate atop the strips in the colander, then weight it down with several heavy cans or a brick. Let the bitter juices drain out of the eggplant for 1 hour at room temperature. Rinse the limp sticks well in water and let drain.

Set up a bowl containing the ¾ cup of dusting flour. Set up a second bowl containing the egg and milk; beat slightly. In a third bowl blend the breadcrumbs, cheese, 2 tablespoons plus 1 teaspoon flour, garlic powder, and pepper. Heat half oil and half vegetable shortening in a frying pan over medium heat to a depth of ¾ to 1 inch. When the oil is hot, dust about 6 of the drained strips in the flour. Dip a floured strip into the egg; coat it well in the crumb mixture; place it in the hot oil. Repeat with the next 5 strips. Fry the eggplant sticks, turning once, until they are a deep golden brown. Sticks will fry in a matter of minutes. Drain on paper towels set on a newspaper section, then repeat for all the eggplant strips.

Let the cooked sticks cool to room temperature, then freeze uncovered and still atop the newspaper overnight, or until solid. Transfer the sticks to a plastic bag, label with this page number or the following cooking directions, and return to the freezer.

Cooking Directions: Preheat oven to 400°. Place frozen sticks in a single layer on an ungreased baking sheet. Bake for 10 to 12 minutes, or until the largest stick is heated through. You can also re-fry the frozen sticks in a skillet.

CHINESE GREEN BEAN CASSEROLE

*Makes 2 casseroles
each serving 2 to 4*

1 tablespoon corn oil
½ cup celery peeled and thinly sliced on the diagonal
1½ cups thinly sliced fresh mushrooms
1 can (10¾ ounces) condensed cream of celery or mushroom soup
¾ cup chicken broth
1 tablespoon soy sauce
1 can (8½ ounces) water chestnuts, drained and sliced
2 packages (9 ounces each) frozen cut green beans, unthawed
2 foil roll pans, 8 by 5 by 1 inches

Heat the oil in a skillet and sauté the celery and mushrooms until just tender and limp; set aside. In a mixing bowl, blend the soup, chicken broth, and soy sauce; stir in the celery and mushrooms and the water chestnuts. Separate the frozen green beans with your hands or by slamming any solid blocks of beans against your work surface; stir the frozen beans into the other ingredients. Pour this mixture equally into the 2 foil pans. Cover both pans with foil, label with this page number or the following cooking directions, and freeze.

Cooking Directions: Preheat oven to 400°. Remove the foil cover from the frozen pan and bake for 1 hour, or until hot at the center and bubbly around the edges.

PEA POD CASSEROLE

Replace the 2 packages of green beans with two 6-ounce packages frozen pea pods.

POTATO PANCAKES

Makes about 12

6 cups peeled, diced raw potatoes (about 4 pounds)
4 eggs
¼ cup fine cracker meal (or ½ cup flour)

1 **small onion, coarsely sliced**
2 **teaspoons salt**
½ **teaspoon pepper**
Oil for frying

Blender Method: Peel and dice potatoes into a bowl of cold water; when ready to use, drain them thoroughly and pat dry on paper towels. Put only half of the eggs, cracker meal, onion, salt, and pepper in a blender container; briefly whirl to mix. Gradually add 1 cup of the diced potatoes, blending at low speed. With the blender still going, gradually add handfuls of diced potatoes until a total of 3 cups has been whirled in and coarsely chopped into the batter. Pour the blender container's contents into a bowl, cover, and set aside while you repeat the same procedure with the remaining half of the ingredients.

Pour oil in a skillet to a depth of ½ inch and heat over high heat; do not let the oil smoke. Use several big dollops of potato batter for each 3½-inch pancake, frying them on both sides until crispy, golden brown, and somewhat moist and fluffy inside. Drain on paper towels and let cool thoroughly. Place 1 layer of pancakes on a cookie sheet and set, uncovered, in your freezer until solid. Pack frozen pancakes in a plastic freezer bag along with this page number or the following cooking directions.

Cooking Directions: Heat ½ to 1 inch of oil in a skillet over high heat; do not let it smoke. Fry the desired amount of frozen pancakes on both sides until crisp and heated through. Drain on paper towels and sprinkle with any extra desired salt before serving.

Food Processor Method: This is the same as the Blender Method except that you can process the entire amount of ingredients at once. Do not whirl the potatoes past the coarsely shredded stage. Fry and freeze as directed.

Hand Method: Peel the potatoes and grate them on a cheese or vegetable grater; place them in a bowl of cold water; when ready to use, drain thoroughly and pat dry on paper towels. Beat the eggs in a large bowl; mix in the cracker meal, 3 tablespoons of grated onion, and the salt and pepper; fold the potatoes into this batter. Fry and freeze as directed.

HOME FRIES

Makes about 8 cups

Here's a tasty solution to having too many potatoes and not enough time to use them before they sprout.

8 **medium-size (about ½-pound each) all-purpose potatoes**
Vegetable shortening for frying

Wash and peel the potatoes; cut them uniformly into slices ¼-inch thick; place them in a large bowl of cold water. When ready to use, drain thoroughly and pat them dry on paper towels.

Melt enough shortening in a large skillet to make a depth of ½ inch. Heat the shortening over high heat, but do not let it smoke. Put enough slices into the skillet to cover the bottom in 1 layer and cook until lightly browned; turn all the slices over and brown the other sides as well; the potato slices should be almost completely cooked. Use a slotted spatula to transfer the slices in 1 layer to a shallow baking pan; do not drain off the oil. Repeat this frying and transferring procedure until several baking pans are filled.

Let the slices cool to room temperature, then place them, uncovered, in the freezer overnight or until solidly frozen. Transfer the slices to plastic freezer bags, label with this page number or the following cooking directions, and return them to the freezer.

Cooking Directions: Arrange desired amount of frozen home fries on a shallow baking pan. Let them brown in a preheated 450° oven for 3 to 5 minutes; turn them all over and continue to bake for several more minutes until nicely browned and hot throughout. Drain on paper towels and sprinkle with salt and pepper to taste while still hot.

MUSHROOM-STUFFED POTATOES

Makes 8

4 **baking potatoes of uniform size**
Vegetable shortening or butter

½ **pound fresh mushrooms**
6 **tablespoons butter**
1 **tablespoon very finely chopped onion**
1 **teaspoon minced fresh dillweed (or ¼
     teaspoon dried)**
½ **teaspoon strained fresh lemon juice**
Milk
Salt and pepper to taste

Wash, scrub, and dry the potatoes. Grease the palms of your hands with a bit of the shortening or butter and rub it into the skin of each potato. Prick the potato skins a few times with a pointed knife tip. Bake the potatoes in a 450° oven for about 45 minutes, or until tender throughout. While the potatoes cook, go on to prepare the mushrooms.

Slice the mushrooms thinly, then chop them coarsely into, very roughly, ¼-inch square pieces. Melt the 6 tablespoons of butter in a large skillet over medium heat; add the onion and mushroom pieces and sauté until just tender; let cool to room temperature. When cool, stir in the dill and lemon juice; set aside.

When the potatoes are cool enough to handle, cut each in half lengthwise. Scoop the potato pulp into a large bowl, leaving empty, boat-like shells of skin; set these shells aside. Mash the potatoes in the bowl along with the juices from the skillet until smooth, then gradually beat in enough milk so that the potatoes become fluffy and as moist as medium-dry mashed potatoes. Mix in the mushroom-onion mixture and add salt and pepper to taste.

Pile the mashed potato mixture into the 8 potato-skin shells, place them on a baking pan and freeze, uncovered, until solid. Transfer the frozen, stuffed potatoes to plastic freezer bags, label with this page number or the following cooking directions, and return to the freezer.

Cooking Directions: Preheat oven to 400°. Place desired amount of frozen potatoes on an ungreased baking pan. Bake for 30 to 45 minutes, or until lightly browned and a pointed knife tip inserted in the center of the biggest potato comes out hot to the touch.

GREEN BEAN STUFFED POTATOES

Replace mushrooms with ½ pound fresh green beans; remove the ends; cut the beans into ¼-inch slices. Sauté as for mushrooms but increase the onion to 3 tablespoons and omit the lemon juice; sauté time will be about 5 minutes, or until just tender to the bite.

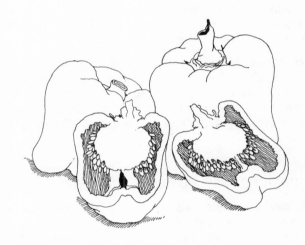

COMBINATION VEGETABLES

*Each package makes about 2 cups
and serves 3 or 4*

Your own home-assembled version of combination vegetables will cost you less than half the amount you'd pay for the commercially-assembled variety. Combine the vegetables in quart-size, plastic food storage bags (the Zip-Loc varieties are very good) and label with this page number for cooking directions.

PEAS AND MUSHROOMS

Sauté ½ to ⅔ cup thinly sliced fresh mushrooms in 2 tablespoons butter; let cool. Measure 2 level cups frozen peas (or one 10-ounce package) into a plastic bag. Pour in mushrooms and their butter; seal, label, and freeze.

To Cook: Put 1 tablespoon water and 1 tablespoon butter in a saucepan. Add frozen peas and mushrooms; heat to a full boil, separating all frozen chunks; cover tightly and simmer for about 6 or 7 minutes, or until the peas are done. If you need more water in the pan, add a few teaspoons.

PEAS AND PEARL ONIONS

Assemble plastic bags, each containing 1⅓ cups frozen peas and 1 cup frozen pearl onions (available in 20-ounce bags). Seal, label, and freeze.

To Cook: Heat to boiling ½ cup lightly salted water. Add one homemade package Peas and Pearl Onions. Bring water to a second boil. Cover pan, reduce heat, and simmer until both vegetables are tender, about 10 minutes. Drain and serve.

GREEN BEANS AND PEARL ONIONS

Assemble plastic bags, each containing 1⅓ cups frozen green beans and ⅔ cup frozen pearl onions. (Buy both green beans and onions in 24- and 20-ounce bags.) Seal, label, and freeze.

To Cook: Heat to boiling ½ cup lightly salted water. Add one package Green Beans and Pearl Onions; return water to a boil. Cover, reduce heat, and simmer until both vegetables are tender, about 10 minutes. Drain and serve.

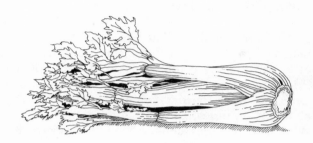

PEAS AND CELERY

Sauté ½ cup thinly sliced celery stalks in 3 tablespoons butter until limp; let cool. Measure 2 level cups frozen peas (or one 10-ounce package) into the plastic bag. Pour in sautéed celery with its butter. Seal, label, and freeze.

To Cook: cook exactly as for Peas and Mushrooms, above.

OTHER FREEZER-TO-OVEN VEGETABLES IN THIS BOOK ARE:

ZUCCHINI PANCAKES, PAGE 159
PUMPKIN TEMPURA, PAGE 163

Chapter 2:

MAKE-AHEAD CONVENIENCE MIXES

Sections:

☐Oven-Top Dinner Mixes
☐Side Dish Mixes
☐Miscellaneous Dinnertime Mixes
☐Baking Mixes
☐Cake and Cookie Mixes

MACARONI AND BEEF SKILLET MIX

Makes 1 pre-packaged mix to serve 3 or 4

Pre-packaged by you, this easy ground beef-helper dinner with several variations lets you make a wholesome meal in 30 minutes or less.

¼ cup dried chopped onion
1 teaspoon salt
¼ teaspoon pepper
¼ teaspoon chili powder
¼ teaspoon sugar
1 large can (1 pound, 12 ounces) tomatoes (or two 15-ounce cans)
1 cup uncooked elbow macaroni
1 sandwich bag
1 brown paper bag, lunchbag size

Combine the onion, salt, pepper, chili powder, and sugar in a small paper envelope or in a small homemade packet of aluminum foil; seal well and tape this seasoning packet to the top of the can of tomatoes. Measure the macaroni into the sandwich bag and seal well. Before unfolding the brown paper bag, label it with this recipe title (or whatever variation you are using) and page number. Place the taped can(s) of tomatoes and the bag of macaroni in this bag; fold down the top edges; staple them shut and store in your cupboard until needed.

To Use: Sauté 1 pound of ground beef in a skillet; when no pink remains, drain off all excess fat; set aside. Pour the can(s) of tomatoes, undrained, into a mixing bowl; use your hands to squeeze all the tomatoes into shreds; pour these tomatoes and their liquid into the skillet. Sprinkle the seasoning packet atop and stir to blend all the ingredients. Bring the skillet ingredients to a steady simmer and let them continue to cook, uncovered, for 10 minutes: the mixture will be thickened slightly but still somewhat soupy.

Stir in the macaroni; cover and simmer, slowly now, for 15 minutes. Uncover and simmer until thickened to your liking. Serve at once.

CHILI-MAC

Increase the chili powder in the seasoning packet to 2 to 3 teaspoons and add to it the following: ⅛ to ¼ teaspoon ground cumin; ¼ teaspoon garlic powder; several dashes of cayenne pepper. Use a larger brown paper bag and include in it one 15-ounce can of red kidney beans. Package, label, and store as directed.

To Use: Follow the basic directions, adding the undrained can of kidney beans to the skillet along with the squeezed tomatoes. Makes 4 or 5 servings.

SPAGHETTI-MAC

Omit the entire seasoning packet as well as the can(s) of tomatoes; replace these with a 15½-ounce jar of your favorite commercially made spaghetti sauce (1⅔ cups). Package this sauce along with the macaroni as directed.

To Use: Sauté and drain the meat as directed; pour in the spaghetti sauce plus 1⅔ cups of water; bring to a boil, then stir in the macaroni. Cover, lower the heat, and simmer for 15 minutes. Uncover and simmer for 5 more minutes, or until thickened to your liking. Makes 3 or 4 servings.

MACARONI AND CHEESE SKILLET MIX

Makes 1 pre-packaged mix to serve 2 or 3

1½ cups uncooked elbow macaroni
1 envelope (1¼ ounces) commercial cheese sauce mix
1 sandwich bag

Measure the macaroni into the sandwich bag. Slip the envelope of cheese sauce mix into the sandwich bag along with a piece of paper on which you have written pages 38 and 39; seal well and store in your cupboard until needed.

To Use: Bring 2⅓ cups of water to a boil in a skillet; stir in the macaroni; return to a boil, then cover the skillet and simmer for 10 minutes. Uncover the macaroni and stir in 4 tablespoons of butter. Measure out ¼ cup of milk; stir the cheese sauce mix into it; pour this mixture into the macaroni. Simmer, uncovered, stirring now and then, until thickened to your liking. Adjust salt and pepper to taste before serving.

MACARONI AND CHEESEBURGER

Sauté ½ pound of ground beef in a skillet; when all the pink is gone, drain off any fat. Add 2⅓ cups of water, bring to a boil and follow the basic directions given in the previous recipe.

WITH HOT DOGS

Cut 2 or 3 hot dogs into thin slices and add them to the boiling water along with the macaroni.

WITH HAM

Add 1 cup of diced, cooked ham or one 6¾-ounce can of chunk ham to the boiling water along with the macaroni. You may want to store the can of ham along with the bag of macaroni and the envelope of cheese sauce mix in your cupboard.

TUNA-RICE SKILLET MIX

Makes 1 pre-packaged mix to serve 4 or 5

1 **cup raw long-grain rice**
3 **tablespoons dried celery flakes**
½ **teaspoon dried dillweed**
½ **teaspoon salt**
1 **sandwich bag**
1 **brown paper bag, lunchbag size**
1 **can (7 ounces) tuna packed in water**
1 **(10 ¾ ounces) condensed cream of celery soup**

Combine the rice, celery flakes, dillweed, and salt in the sandwich bag; seal well. Before unfolding it, label the brown paper bag with this recipe title (or whatever variation you are using) and place the sealed rice packet, the can of tuna, and the

can of soup inside; fold down the top edges; staple them shut and store in your cupboard.

To Use: Put the undrained contents of the can of tuna into a skillet; flake the meat with your fingers. Add the soup plus 2 cups of water; stir until smooth. Bring to a boil, then stir in the rice packet. Cover and simmer for 20 to 25 minutes, or until nearly all the liquid is absorbed; turn off the heat and let the skillet stand, covered, for 10 minutes before serving.

HAM AND RICE SKILLET

Package 1 cup of rice along with 1 teaspoon dried minced onion, 1 tablespoon dried green pepper flakes, and ½ teaspoon salt. Add one 6¾-ounce can of canned, chunk ham or else add 1 cup of diced leftover ham or pork at cooking time. Add can of condensed Golden Mushroom Soup. You can also include an 8½-ounce can of peas and carrots.

To Use: Follow the same directions as for Tuna Skillet, adding the drained can of peas and carrots along with the rice packet. If you do not wish to use the small can of ham, replace it with 1 cup of diced leftover ham or pork.

SALMON KULEBIAKA SKILLET

Add ½ teaspoon dried minced onion to the rice packet ingredients. Use a 7¾-ounce can of undrained pink salmon; replace the celery soup with cream of mushroom; include a 3-ounce can of sliced mushrooms.

To Use: Prepare as for Tuna-Rice Skillet, but make sure you skin and debone all the salmon before flaking it; include the liquid from the salmon can with the skillet ingredients. Add the drained can of mushrooms along with the soup.

39

MACARONI AND CHICKEN SKILLET MIX

Makes 1 pre-packaged mix to serve 2 or 3

3 tablespoons flour
1 tablespoon granulated chicken bouillon
½ teaspoon parsley flakes
¼ teaspoon dried minced onion
¼ teaspoon celery flakes
Dash of pepper
2 sandwich bags
1½ cups uncooked elbow macaroni
1 can (5 ounces) chunk or mixing chicken
1 can (14½ ounces) regular-strength chicken broth, optional
1 brown paper bag, lunchbag size

Place the flour, bouillon, parsley flakes, minced onion, celery flakes, and pepper in a blender container and whirl into a powder; pour the powder into one of the sandwich bags (or a small envelope) and seal; this is the gravy mix. Measure the macaroni into the other sandwich bag and seal. Before unfolding the brown paper bag, label it with this recipe title (or whatever variation you are using) and this page number. Place in this bag: the gravy mix, the macaroni, the can of chicken and, if you wish, the can of chicken broth. Fold down the top edges of the paper bag, staple them shut, and store this package of mix in your cupboard until needed.

To Use: Bring 2⅓ cups of water or combined chicken broth and water to a boil in a skillet along with the entire contents of the can of chicken; flake the chicken into smaller pieces. (You can use 1 cup of leftover, cooked, diced chicken in place of the canned chicken.) Stir in the macaroni; return to a boil, then cover the skillet and simmer for 10 minutes.

Uncover the macaroni and stir in 2 to 3 tablespoons of butter. Pour the gravy mix into a shaker jar; add 1 cup cold water; shake well and pour its contents into the skillet. Simmer, uncovered, stirring now and then, until thickened to your liking. Adjust salt and pepper to taste before serving.

MACARONI AND HAM SKILLET

Make a gravy mix packet consisting of 3 tablespoons flour, 1 tablespoon granulated onion bouillon, ½ teaspoon dried minced onion, and a dash of pepper; whirl in a blender and package as directed. Replace the chicken with a 6¾-ounce can of chunk ham or 1 cup leftover, cooked, diced pork. Omit the chicken broth.

DEHYDRATED POTATOES FROM YOUR OVEN

Of all vegetables, potatoes are the easiest to dehydrate in your oven and, once dried, they will keep for up to a year at room temperature. Use the dried product in the convenient potato mixes and casseroles that follow as well as in homemade soups and stews—the dried slices take about 30 minutes to cook and can be tossed in without the bother of peeling and slicing.

Potatoes
Metal vegetable blanching basket, or French-fry basket, or heat-proof colander
Paper towels
Several cookie sheets
Vegetable oil cooking spray

Peel desired amount of potatoes and slice into rounds ⅛-inch thick. Bring a large pot of lightly salted water to a rolling boil; use a generous amount of water. Put potato slices into a vegetable basket; plunge the basket into the boiling water and wait for the water to return to a boil. Once this happens, start counting off 8 to 9 minutes of blanching time. While potatoes are blanching, set up a large mixing bowl in your sink and fill it with ice water. When the 8 to 9 minutes are complete, plunge the basketful of potatoes immediately into the ice water; chill 15 minutes.

Spread the blanched potato slices in a single layer between paper towels to dry out a bit. If you are using regular rimless cookie sheets for oven drying, spray them with vegetable oil cooking spray (do not use regular cooking oil); if you are using rimmed baking pans, spray and use only the upside-down bottoms of these pans to prevent scorching near the pan's raised rim; if you have good Teflon cookie sheets, there is no need for spray. Spread potato slices on the prepared sheets or pans as close together as possible but in a single layer. Place cookie sheets on oven racks and turn the oven on to its very lowest temperature—somewhere between "low" and "off." Keep the oven door ajar so that the air can circulate freely and let moisture escape. Make sure that the temperature never gets so hot that your hand feels uncomfortable when held in the oven: this is necessary for thorough drying.

After 1 hour, turn all the slices over; then turn the slices over every 30 minutes or so. Drying time will depend largely on your own oven, but you might start checking for doneness at 3 hours. The potatoes are done when they become brittle, somewhat translucent, and are not at all pliable. Their color should be pale white with a tinge of yellow; do not let them become brown or even dark amber in color. Some potato slices will dry faster than their neighbors, so check every 30 minutes for new removals.

Let the dried potatoes cool thoroughly, then store for up to a year in plastic bags at room temperature.

SCALLOPED POTATO MIX

Makes 3 cups or four ¾-cup servings

SAUCE MIX:

2 tablespoons nonfat dry milk
2 tablespoons flour
2 tablespoons cornstarch
1 teaspoon salt
½ teaspoon onion powder
⅛ teaspoon pepper

Combine the above ingredients to make 1 package of Sauce Mix and seal it in a small envelope. For extra convenience, multiply the Sauce Mix ingredients by 4 or 8 and store in a jar at room temperature. Use 6 tablespoons Sauce Mix to equal 1 package.

41

SCALLOPED POTATOES

3 cups Dehydrated Potatoes from previous recipe
1 package (6 tablespoons) Sauce Mix, from previous recipe
3 tablespoons butter
2⅓ cups boiling water
⅔ cup milk

Pour the potatoes into a medium-size ungreased casserole and sprinkle the Sauce Mix atop. Dot with butter; stir in the boiling water, then the milk. Bake at 400° for 30 to 35 minutes, or until tender. If you are cooking something else at a lower temperature in your oven, adjust the baking time: at 350°, bake 40 to 45 minutes; at 325°, bake 50 to 55 minutes.

QUICK HAM CASSEROLE

Before baking, add 1½ cups of cooked, diced ham to the casserole mixture. Makes four 1-cup servings.

SKILLET MEAT AND POTATOES CASSEROLE

Brown 1 pound of ground beef in a skillet until all the pink is gone from the meat; drain off excess fat, then stir in ¼ teaspoon salt plus pepper to taste. Stir in 2½ cups water, ⅔ cup milk, 1 package (6 tablespoons) Sauce Mix, and 3 cups Dehydrated Potatoes. Heat to boiling, reduce heat, cover, and simmer, stirring now and then, for about 25 minutes or until the potatoes are tender. Make four 1-cup servings.

SKILLET HOT POTATO SALAD

In a skillet, fry 6 slices of bacon over medium heat until crisp; drain the bacon on paper towels; pour ¼ cup of the bacon fat into a heat-proof measuring cup and set it aside; discard the remaining bacon fat. Into the skillet, stir 3¼ cups water, 3 cups of Dehydrated Potatoes, and 1 package (6 tablespoons) Sauce Mix. Heat to boiling, then reduce heat, cover, and simmer, stirring now and then, for about 25 minutes, or until the potatoes are tender.

Stir 1½ tablespoons of white distilled vinegar into the reserved bacon fat, then pour it evenly atop the finished potatoes. Crumble the bacon strips over the potatoes; stir gently. Briefly heat the mixture through and serve. Makes four ¾-cup servings.

AU GRATIN POTATO MIX

Makes 3 or 4 cups

AU GRATIN POTATOES USING DRY MIX:

3 cups Dehydrated Potatoes from previous recipe
2 envelopes commercial Cheese Sauce Mix (each envelope should contain about 1⅛ ounces or enough to make 1 cup of sauce)
1½ tablespoons butter
2 cups boiling water
⅔ cup milk

Assemble and bake potatoes as directed for Scalloped Potatoes in the previous recipe. Baking time adjustments are also the same. Makes 3 cups.

AU GRATIN POTATOES USING CHEDDAR CHEESE SOUP:

4 cups Dehydrated Potatoes from previous recipe
2 tablespoons butter
1 can (10¾ ounces condensed Cheddar cheese soup)
2 cups water
2 cups milk

Place potatoes in a medium-size casserole; dot with butter. In a saucepan, blend soup, water, and milk until smooth; bring to a boil, then pour over potatoes. Bake at 400° for 25 to 30 minutes or until potatoes are tender. Makes 4 cups.

PIZZA POTATOES

Makes 3 cups or four ¾-cup servings

**3 cups Dehydrated Potatoes from previous
    recipe**
1 can (16 ounces) peeled tomatoes, undrained
1½ cups water
**1 package (6 tablespoons) Sauce Mix for
    Scalloped Potatoes, previous recipe**
⅓ cup grated Parmesan cheese
¾ teaspoon oregano
One dash hot red pepper flakes
2 tablespoons butter

Pour potatoes into a medium-size casserole. Pour
tomatoes into a saucepan; use your hands to
squish them into small pieces; add water and
bring to a full boil. Stir all the remaining ingredients except the potatoes and butter into the saucepan, then stir this saucepan mixture into the casserole of potatoes. Dot with butter. Bake at 400°
for 30 to 35 minutes or until the potatoes are tender and the sauce is thickened.

PACKAGED RICE MIXES

Each method makes 4 servings

Home-packaged rice mixes will taste just like
commercial rice mixes but will cost a great deal
less. Each rice mix can be made in your choice of
four different methods—Pilaf, Rice-A-Noodle,
Standard, or Oven-Baked. Directions for each
method are followed by a list of Flavor Packets
that apply in exact measurements to all four.

To package your own dry mixes, measure the 1
cup of raw rice or rice-noodle mixture listed
under each method into a sandwich bag and set
aside. Securely seal the crushed bouillon and
whatever flavoring ingredients are called for in a
packet made from aluminum foil. Drop this
Flavor Packet into the bag of rice; seal and label
with this page number; store at room temperature
for up to 1 to 2 years.

PILAF METHOD:

1 cup long-grain, converted rice
Flavor Packet
2 tablespoons butter
2½ cups hot water

Melt the butter in a heavy saucepan over medium
heat. Sauté the rice, stirring constantly, until it
takes on a translucent quality; do not let the kernels pop. Slowly stir in the water, then the Flavor
Packet; bring to a full boil; cover and lower heat.
Simmer 20 to 25 minutes, or until nearly all of the
liquid is absorbed and the rice looks just a bit too
moist to serve. Turn off heat and let stand for 10
minutes before uncovering and serving.

RICE-A-NOODLE METHOD:

Thin egg noodles
¾ cup Carolina rice
Flavor Packet
2 tablespoons butter
2½ cups hot water

Put a handful of noodles in a bowl and crush,
repeatedly, with your fingers until they are in
small flat pieces ¼- to ¾-inch long; measure and
repeat until you get ¼ cup crushed noodles. Mix
with rice and package with a Flavor Packet.

Melt butter in a saucepan; add rice-noodle mixture; sauté, stirring, until rice begins to turn whit-
ish. Slowly stir in water, then the Flavor Packet.
Cover and simmer 12 to 14 minutes, or until
nearly all the liquid is absorbed and the rice mixture looks just a bit too moist to serve. Turn off
heat and let stand 10 minutes before uncovering
and serving.

STANDARD RICE METHOD:

1 cup long-grain converted rice
Flavor Packet
2½ cups water
1 tablespoon butter

Bring water to a boil; stir in rice, Flavor Packet,
and butter. Cover and simmer 20 to 25 minutes.
Turn off heat and let stand for 10 minutes before
uncovering and serving.

For short-grain rice: combine all ingredients; heat to a vigorous boil; cover and simmer 12 to 14 minutes. Let stand 10 minutes before uncovering and serving.

OVEN-BAKED METHOD:

1 cup long-grain, converted rice
Flavor Packet
1½ tablespoons butter
2½ cups boiling water

Preheat oven to 350°. Put the rice, Flavor Packet, and butter in a 1½-quart saucepan with a tight-fitting lid. Pour the boiling water over all; stir briefly to melt butter. Cover and bake, untouched, for 45 minutes.

For unconverted rice: preheat oven to 325°. Follow above directions using 1 tablespoon butter and only 2 cups boiling water. Cover and bake, untouched, for 25 minutes.

FLAVOR PACKETS

• *A Note About Bouillon:* The following Flavor Packets use bouillon cubes that are meant to be mixed with an 8-ounce cup of water. If you want to substitute bouillon cubes or powdered bouillon packets that require a 6-ounce cup of water, figure the differences accordingly: Three 8-ounce bouillon cubes equal four 6-ounce bouillon cubes or packets.

CHICKEN:

3 chicken bouillon cubes, crushed
¼ teaspoon parsley flakes
3 dashes pepper

BEEF:

3 beef bouillon cubes, crushed
3 dashes pepper

ONION:

3 onion or beef bouillon cubes, crushed
2 teaspoons dried minced or chopped onion
3 dashes pepper

MUSHROOM:

3 chicken or beef bouillon cubes, crushed
2 tablespoons dried mushroom slices, in bits
3 dashes pepper

CELERY:

3 chicken bouillon cubes, crushed
3 tablespoons dried celery flakes
3 dashes pepper

CURRY:

3 chicken bouillon cubes, crushed
1 teaspoon curry powder

SAFFRON:

3 chicken bouillon cubes, crushed
1 pinch saffron
1 pinch turmeric

ORIENTAL:

2 chicken bouillon cubes, crushed
1 onion bouillon cube, crushed
2 teaspoons dried celery flakes
2 teaspoons dried mushroom slices, in bits
1 teaspoon dried minced onion
Dash of powdered ginger
• **Add several dashes soy sauce to cooking water**

SPANISH:

3 chicken bouillon cubes, crushed
2 tablespoons dried green pepper flakes
2 tablespoons dried minced onion
Dash of chili powder
• **Add 2 tablespoons tomato paste to cooking water**

SEASONED BARLEY CASSEROLE MIX

Makes 6 servings

5 chicken or beef bouillon cubes, crushed
¼ to ½ cup dried mushroom slices, in bits
¼ cup instant minced onion
¼ teaspoon garlic powder
½ teaspoon pepper
1½ cups pearl barley

Measure every ingredient except barley into a sandwich bag; seal airtight with either a twist-tie wire or tape; put this sealed bag in yet another sandwich bag. Pour the barley into the open, outer bag; seal well and label with this page number or the following directions. Store at room temperature.

Directions: Bring 5 cups of water to a boil in a large saucepan; stir in barley, the inner bag of flavorings, plus 2 tablespoons butter and 2 tablespoons fresh lemon juice. Return to a boil, lower heat, cover, and simmer 45 minutes, or until barley is tender.

PACKAGE-YOUR-OWN OVEN-TOP STUFFING MIXES

Each makes six ¾-cup servings

For convenience's sake, package these stuffing mixes and store them in your cupboard. They can be prepared and ready to serve in 15 minutes.

2 chicken bouillon cubes, crushed
3 tablespoons dried celery flakes
1 tablespoon finely crushed parsley flakes
2 teaspoons dried onion flakes or instant minced onion
¼ teaspoon poultry seasoning
¼ teaspoon crushed sage
Pepper to taste
3½ cups plain stuffing cubes

Combine everything but the cubes in a small envelope or sandwich bag and seal. Measure 3½ cups cubes into a plastic bag; put in the Seasoning Envelope you have just made; seal bag with a wire twist. Store at room temperature.

Oven-Top Directions: In a saucepan, combine the contents of the Seasoning Envelope with ⅞ cup water and 5 tablespoons butter; bring to a boil; cover and simmer for 8 minutes. Add stuffing cubes, stirring quickly just to moisten, then cover, remove from heat, and let stand for 5 minutes. Fluff with a fork before serving.

Oven-Baked Directions: In a saucepan, combine ⅞ cup water, the contents of the Seasoning Envelope, and 5 tablespoons butter; simmer gently, covered, for 8 minutes. Place stuffing cubes in a casserole; pour saucepan mixture atop and toss to coat. Cover and bake at 350° for 20 minutes.

STUFFING WITH RICE

Make the Seasoning Envelope described above. Place it in a plastic bag along with 3 cups of plain stuffing crumbs (not cubes) and ½ cup Minute Rice; label and store. Follow the Oven-Top directions, using 1⅔ cups of water.

STUFFING FOR PORK

Make the Seasoning Envelope as described above, using onion bouillon. Use 2 tablespoons toasted, instant minced onion and decrease the celery flakes to 1 tablespoon. Pack this Seasoning Envelope in a plastic bag along with 3½ cups plain stuffing cubes.

TO USE STORE-BOUGHT HERB-SEASONED STUFFING CUBES

Omit the poultry seasoning, sage, and pepper from the Seasoning Envelope.

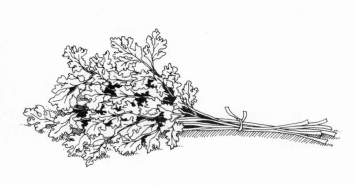

1 teaspoon parsley flakes, crumbled
½ teaspoon dry mustard
½ teaspoon salt
¼ teaspoon pepper
Pinch of paprika
Pinch of sugar

OLD-FASHIONED FRENCH:

1 teaspoon parsley flakes
½ teaspoon onion powder
½ teaspoon sugar
½ teaspoon dry mustard
½ teaspoon salt
¼ teaspoon pepper
¼ teaspoon garlic powder
⅛ teaspoon crushed celery seed

RIVIERA FRENCH

1 tablespoon sugar
½ teaspoon paprika
½ teaspoon onion powder
½ teaspoon dry mustard
½ teaspoon salt
¼ teaspoon pepper

SALAD DRESSING MIXES

Each list of ingredients makes 1 envelope of mix
yielding 1 cup of dressing

Combine the recipe ingredients listed here for 1 package, each, of dry salad dressing mix. After combining, whirl the ingredients in a blender or food processor until powdered. Package the powdered mix in a small envelope, then store the envelope in a plastic sandwich bag; you can also package the mix in squares of aluminum foil. Label the packages along with the directions that follow and store indefinitely in your cupboard.

ITALIAN

½ teaspoon sugar
½ teaspoon dry mustard
½ teaspoon salt
¼ teaspoon *each:* pepper, oregano, onion powder, garlic powder, sweet red pepper flakes
Pinch of paprika

ONION OR GARLIC

1 teaspoon onion powder or ½ teaspoon garlic powder

HERB

2 teaspoons dried dillweed or chives
1 teaspoon parsley flakes
½ teaspoon dry mustard
½ teaspoon salt
¼ teaspoon pepper

Directions: In a jar or cruet, place ¼ cup vinegar, 2 tablespoons water, and the contents of 1 package of mix; shake to blend, then set aside for at least 30 minutes in order to release the flavors. Add ¾ cup oil, shake well, and serve over salad.

WHITE SAUCE MIX

Makes about 1⅓ cups mix yielding 8 cups white sauce

1 **cup flour**
1 **tablespoon salt**
¼ **teaspoon pepper**
4 **tablespoons vegetable shortening**

Sift flour, salt, and pepper into a mixing bowl; cut in the shortening until the mixture has the look of coarse meal. Label with this page number or the following directions and store at room temperature in a tightly closed jar or container for several months.

Directions: Place 2½ level tablespoons of mix in a small saucepan; add ¼ cup milk and blend with a fork or whisk. Add 1½ tablespoons butter that has been cut into bits; heat over very low heat. When the butter has melted, gradually add ¾ cup more milk; stir constantly until the sauce thickens. Use any of the following flavor variations.

RICH CREAM SAUCE

Use heavy cream for half of the milk or else replace the milk with an equal amount of half-and-half.

CHEESE SAUCE

Stir into the thickened sauce: ¾ cup (about ¼ pound) tightly packed, grated sharp Cheddar or Swiss cheese or ¼ cup grated Parmesan.

DEVILED CHEESE SAUCE

Add to the above cheese sauce: ½ teaspoon dry mustard, ½ teaspoon Worcestershire sauce, and ⅛ teaspoon onion powder.

MUSHROOM SAUCE

Sauté 1 cup of sliced fresh mushrooms in a few pats of butter; add to the thickened sauce.

À LA KING SAUCE

To the thickened sauce add: 2 tablespoons finely minced and sautéed green pepper and 1 small minced pimiento.

SAUCE FOR MEAT OR POULTRY

Replace the milk with beef or chicken broth or use half milk and half broth.

CURRY SAUCE

Add ½ to 1 teaspoon of curry powder to the mix in the saucepan.

HERB SAUCE

To the thickened sauce, stir in your choice of: 1 tablespoon minced parsley (or 1 teaspoon dried) or 1 teaspoon snipped dillweed (or ¼ teaspoon dried).

NEWBURG SAUCE

Use ¾ cup milk mixed with ¼ cup dry sherry. Add ¼ teaspoon onion powder and a dash of Worcestershire.

SOUP MIX SAUCES

Convenient sauces for casseroles or for leftover meats and vegetables.

1 **package Cream of Leek, Cream of Mushroom, or Onion Soup Mix**
Milk
Butter, optional

Empty the package contents into a saucepan. Where the package directions call for the addition of water, add only half the amount called for, using milk instead of water. Cook according to directions, adding several pats of butter to your taste; do not add salt. Serve hot.

SHAKE-YOUR-OWN ITALIAN FLAVOR COATING MIX FOR CHICKEN OR VEAL

Makes 4½ cups mix, enough to coat four to five 2½ to 3-pound chickens or 6 sets of 8 to 10 veal chops

1½ cups dry breadcrumbs
1 cup flour
⅓ cup parsley flakes
1½ teaspoons garlic powder
1 teaspoon sweet red pepper flakes
1 teaspoon onion powder
1 teaspoon pepper
½ teaspoon salt
6 tablespoons cornmeal
6 tablespoons vegetable shortening
1½ cups finely grated Parmesan cheese, the kind that needs no refrigeration

Combine all ingredients except cornmeal, shortening, and cheese. Whirl to a powder in a blender, ¼ cup at a time, or in a food processor. Pour into a mixing bowl; mix in cornmeal, then thoroughly cut in shortening with your fingers. Stir in cheese until blended. Pour into a jar, cover, and label with this page number or the following directions. If you have used fresh cheese, store in the refrigerator; if you have used room-temperature, supermarket-shelf cheese, you can store the mix at room temperature.

Cooking Directions for One Chicken: Pour 1 cup of mix into a plastic or paper bag. Moisten chicken pieces in either water or milk; shake off excess liquid. Place 1 or 2 chicken pieces at a time in the bag and shake until coated. Place in an ungreased baking pan. Bake at 400° for 45 to 55 minutes.

Cooking Directions for Veal Chops: Use ¾ to 1 cup of mix for 8 to 10 veal chops weighing a total of about 2½ pounds; coat as for chicken. Broil on both sides until done. Use the following non-blender mix to coat veal cutlets.

TO MAKE THE MIX WITHOUT A BLENDER

Do not whirl the dry mix in a blender. Use 1¼ cups of mix per chicken or 8 to 10 veal chops or cutlets.

SHAKE-IT-AND-BASTE-IT BARBECUE COATING MIX FOR CHICKEN

Makes enough to coat one 2½- to 3-pound chicken

½ cup flour
1 chicken, cut-up
Barbecue sauce
Oregano, optional
Liquid Smoke, optional

Put flour in a plastic or paper bag. Pat chicken dry and shake, 1 or 2 pieces at a time, in the bag of flour until coated. Place these pieces on a rack in a shallow pan. Brush both sides of each piece with barbecue sauce; sprinkle with oregano, if desired. Bake at 350° for 30 minutes, then brush the tops with more barbecue sauce; bake 30 minutes more. If you want an outdoor grilled taste to your chicken, add a few drops of Liquid Smoke to the barbecue sauce.

HOT DOG WRAPPERS

BISCUIT WRAPPERS

Buy ordinary, ready-to-bake biscuits sold in cardboard cylinders in your supermarket's refrigerated section. Count on 1 biscuit per hot dog and look for 50% savings by buying the supermarket's own brand. Open the biscuit container and, on a clean surface, use your fingertips to press each biscuit out into a circle about 4 inches across. Roll 1 biscuit around each hot dog, placing them a few inches apart, seam side down, on a baking pan. (If the package directions tell you to grease the pan, do so.) Bake according to package directions, plus about 5 minutes.

For extra-biscuity hot dog wrappers, use 2 biscuits per hot dog, overlapping their edges before pressing into a circle.

FLAVORED BISCUIT WRAPPERS

Before rolling the biscuits around the hot dogs, spread over the biscuit dough your choice of: mustard; ketchup; grated Cheddar or American cheese; crumbled, cooked bacon; sautéed onions; relish. Bake as directed.

CRESCENT ROLL WRAPPERS

For an extra-flaky wrapper that still saves you money, buy a refrigerated cylinder of crescent rolls, counting on one roll per hot dog; again, save further with supermarket brand. Unroll the dough and separate it into the perforated triangles. Roll the dough around the hot dog, starting at the edge opposite the triangle's point. If you need more coverage, gently press or roll out the dough atop a very lightly floured surface. Bake, point side down, according to package directions, plus about 5 minutes.

BEEF-MUSHROOM SOUP MIX

Makes 1 envelope mix, yielding four 1-cup servings

½ **cup dried mushroom slices (available in supermarkets in the gourmet or Chinese foods section; or from the recipe on page 182 (STOCKING UP/Easy Home-Dried Foods/ Air-Dried Vegs.)**
4 **beef bouillon cubes, crushed; see note on page 44**
2 **teaspoons cornstarch (this chapter/Side-dish Mixes/Packaged Rice Mixes)**

Put ¼ cup of the mushrooms in a blender container; very briefly, whirl at lowest speed to break mushrooms into ⅛-inch bits; repeat for the remaining mushrooms. Combine these bits with the other ingredients in an envelope or sandwich bag. Seal well, label with this page number, and store in your cupboard.

Cooking Directions: Empty the contents of 1 envelope into a pot; gradually stir in 4 cups of cold water and 1 tablespoon of butter. Bring to a boil, reduce the heat, then cover and simmer 20 minutes, or until the mushrooms are tender.

BEEF MUSHROOM GRAVY

Empty the contents of 1 envelope into a pot; stir in 3 cups of cold water; simmer, covered, 15 minutes. Combine 5 tablespoons of flour and 1 cup of cold water in a jar; cover, shake well, and stir into the soup. Simmer, uncovered, about 5 minutes or until the gravy thickens; stir frequently. Add water, a few tablespoons at a time, for thinner gravy. Makes 2½ cups.

DIP RECIPE

Blend 1 envelope of mix with 2 cups of sour cream; chill before serving.

MUSHROOM BURGERS

Stir together 1 envelope of mix and ¾ cup water; let stand for 10 minutes. Mix in 2 pounds of ground beef; shape the beef into 8 to 10 hamburger patties. Grill or broil.

ONION-MUSHROOM SOUP

Replace the beef bouillon with onion bouillon.

VEGETABLE MUG-OF-SOUP MIX

Makes 1 envelope mix, yielding 1 cup of soup

Buy freeze-dried vegetables at camping and sporting goods stores. The money you'll save over commercially made instant vegetable soup will still be substantial while your soup will be deliciously fresh-tasting and nutritious.

1 **beef, chicken, or vegetable bouillon cube, crushed**
3 **tablespoons freeze-dried vegetables. Choose from or combine: green beans, peas and carrots, corn**

Combine the ingredients in an envelope or sandwich bag, label with the following directions, and seal well.

Directions: Pour the contents of 1 envelope in a cup; stir in 1 cup of boiling water; wait 8 minutes until the vegetables are tender; serve.

WITH RICE

Add 1 tablespoon Minute Rice to the envelope.

WITH PASTINA

Add 2 teaspoons egg pastina to the envelope.

WITH MEAT

Add 1 tablespoon freeze-dried chicken or beef (also available at camping and sporting goods stores) to the envelope.

BRAN MUFFIN MIX

Makes 1 package of mix, yielding 1 dozen muffins

2 cups flour
¾ cup whole bran cereal
½ cup nonfat dry milk
4 teaspoons baking powder
1 teaspoon salt
½ cup vegetable shortening
½ cup sugar
½ cup chopped walnuts

Combine the flour, bran, dry milk, baking powder, and salt in a large bowl; stir well to combine. Use a pastry blender or your fingertips to cut in the shortening until the mix looks like coarse meal. Blend in the sugar, followed by the chopped nuts. Pour this bran mix into a plastic bag or a jar and seal well. Label with this page number or the following directions and store in your cupboard for up to 2 months.

To Use: Put 1 egg and 1 cup of water in a mixing bowl; beat lightly, then stir in the bran mix. Briefly beat by hand to just blend and moisten the ingredients; do not overbeat. Spoon the mixture into 12 well-greased muffin tins. Bake at 400° for 15 to 20 minutes, or until the tops spring back when lightly pressed. Serve warm.

BANANA BRAN MUFFINS

Use 1 egg, ¼ cup of water, and ¾ cup mashed, very ripe banana along with the mix; be sure to add ½ teaspoon baking soda to the dry ingredients.

BRAN BREAD

Turn the prepared batter into a well-greased 9-by-5-by-3-inch loaf pan. Bake at 350° for 45 minutes, or until a knife inserted at the center comes out clean. Let the bread stand for 10 minutes before removing it from the pan, then let it cool on a rack. Wrap and store overnight before serving.

The above banana variation and the following whole wheat variation can be used in bread form.

WHOLE WHEAT BRAN MUFFINS

Make this mix using 1¼ cups all-purpose flour and ¾ cup whole wheat flour.

APPLEBREAD MIX

*Makes 1 package of mix,
yielding one 9-by-5-inch loaf*

2¼ cups sifted flour
1 tablespoon nonfat dry milk
1 tablespoon baking powder
1 teaspoon cinnamon
¾ teaspoon salt
¼ teaspoon nutmeg
⅛ teaspoon ground cloves
⅛ teaspoon allspice
½ cup vegetable shortening
½ cup sugar
½ cup chopped walnuts
1 brown paper bag, lunchbag size
1 jar (15 ounces) applesauce

Combine the flour, milk, baking powder, salt, and spices; stir well, then resift into a bowl. Use a pastry blender or your fingertips to cut in the shortening until the mix looks like coarse meal. Blend in the sugar, then the chopped nuts. Pour this mix into a plastic bag or a jar and seal well.

Label the brown paper bag with this recipe title and page number. Place the bag of mix within, along with the jar of applesauce. Fold down the bag's edges; staple shut and store in your cupboard for up to 2 months.

To Use: Lightly beat 1 egg in a mixing bowl; stir in the contents of the jar of applesauce. Add the mix and briefly stir to moisten and blend, but do not beat. Turn the batter into a well-greased 9-by-

5-by-3-inch loaf pan. Bake at 350° for 1 hour, or until a knife inserted at the center comes out clean. Let the loaf stand for 10 minutes before removing it from the pan to let it cool on a rack. To improve texture and flavor, wrap and store the cooled loaf overnight before serving.

FRESH FRUIT BREAD

When you are ready to use the mix, replace the jar of applesauce with 1½ cups of homemade fresh fruit purée.

CHOOSE-A-FRUIT BREAD

Replace the jar of applesauce with two 7½- or 7¾-ounce jars of junior-size baby food fruit. The price is comparable to the jar of applesauce and the range of flavors is extraordinary. You can choose from peach, peach melba, pears and pineapple, mixed fruit, banana-pineapple, apples, cherries, and many more; do not use cobblers or flavors containing tapioca.

WHOLE WHEAT PANCAKE MIX

*Makes 1 package of mix,
yielding 1 dozen 4-inch pancakes*

2 cups all-purpose flour
½ cup whole wheat flour
¼ cup nonfat dry milk
4 teaspoons baking powder
1 tablespoon sugar
¾ teaspoon salt
½ cup vegetable shortening

In a large bowl, sift together all the ingredients except the shortening. Use a pastry blender or 2 knives or your fingertips to cut in the shortening until the mix looks like coarse meal. Put the mix into a plastic bag; label with this page number; seal and store at room temperature for up to 2 months; freeze for longer storage.

To Use: In a mixing bowl, combine 2 eggs and 1½ cups of milk. Add the pancake mix and stir to blend all the ingredients; don't overbeat; let the batter rest about 10 minutes.

Lightly grease a heavy skillet or griddle and set it over medium heat. Pour the batter on the skillet in ¼ cup measures to make 4-inch round pancakes. Cook until golden on each side, turning once.

BLUEBERRY PANCAKES

Fold ¾ cup fresh (or canned and drained) blueberries into the batter.

APPLE PANCAKES

Fold 1 cup thinly sliced apples into the batter; add a dash of cinnamon.

BACON PANCAKES

Fold ¾ cup crisp bacon bits or very finely chopped, cooked ham into the batter just before cooking.

OATMEAL BREAKFAST-BISCUIT MIX

*Makes 1 package of mix,
yielding 6 large pull-apart biscuits*

1 cup flour
1 tablespoon baking powder
¼ teaspoon salt
4 tablespoons vegetable shortening
1 cup quick-cooking rolled oats

In a bowl, sift together the flour, baking powder, and salt. Use a pastry blender or your fingertips to cut in the shortening until the mix looks like fine crumbs; stir in the oats. Place the mix in a plastic bag; label with this page number and store at room temperature for up to 2 months, or freeze for longer storage.

To Use: Break 1 egg into a mixing bowl and beat; stir in ⅓ cup of milk, 2 tablespoons of either maple syrup or honey, and ½ cup your choice of raisins, or dried, mixed fruit bits, or shredded coconut. Add the mix and stir very quickly—only a few strokes—until just moistened; do not beat—the dough should be lumpy.

Use, roughly, half of the dough mixture to make 6 mounds of dough on a well-greased baking sheet; the mounds should each contain about 3 tablespoons of dough and they should be spaced 2 inches apart; use a spoon to gently pat down the top of each mound. Distribute the remaining dough equally atop the 6 mounds. Bake at 375° for 10 to 15 minutes, or until the tops are lightly browned and the bottoms are golden. Serve these pull-apart biscuits along with butter and jam.

DINNER ROLL MIX

Makes 1 package of mix, yielding 1 dozen rolls

1½ cups sifted flour
½ teaspoon salt
⅓ cup vegetable shortening
1 sandwich bag
1 package active dry yeast

Combine the flour and salt; stir well, then resift into a bowl; use a pastry blender or your fingertips to cut in the shortening until the mix looks like coarse meal. Pour the mix into the sandwich bag and seal. Label with this recipe title and page number and store in your cupboard for up to 4 months. Store the package of yeast in your refrigerator.

To Use: Pour half the mix into a bowl; mix in the yeast. Bring ½ cup of milk to the boiling point, remove from heat, and stir in 2 tablespoons sugar and 2 tablespoons cold water; stir to dissolve the sugar, then let the milk mixture cool down to a just-warm to lukewarm 115° to 120°. Pour this mixture into the bowl containing the mix; add 1 egg. Beat at low speed with an electric mixer for 30 seconds, scraping the sides of the bowl, then beat 2 to 3 minutes at high speed. By hand, stir in the remaining half of the mix to make a stiff batter; beat this batter until smooth.

Cover and let rise in a warm place until bubbly,

about 1 hour. Stir down the batter. Drop by spoonfuls into 12 greased muffin cups. Let rise until double, about 30 or 40 minutes. Bake at 375° for 15 to 20 minutes. Remove the rolls from their pan while still hot. Serve warm.

GRAHAM CRACKER PIECRUST MIX

Makes 2 packages of mix,
yielding 1 piecrust each

About 19 graham cracker squares
½ cup sugar
2 teaspoons cinnamon
2 sandwich bags

Put several squares of broken graham crackers in a blender container; whirl at highest speed until the crackers are fine crumbs; repeat until you have 3 cups. Whirl the sugar, cinnamon, and ½ cup of the crumbs until the sugar is superfine; blend this mixture into the graham crumb mixture. If you are using a food processor, you can whirl more graham squares at a time.

When the crumbs and sugar are well mixed, pour them equally between the two sandwich bags; seal well, label with this recipe title and page number and store, indefinitely, in your cupboard.

To Make One Crust: Pour 1 bag of mix into a bowl. Stir in 6 tablespoons melted butter and continue stirring until all mixture has been moistened by the butter. Reserve 2 tablespoons of the mixture and pat the rest evenly into the bottom and sides of a 9-inch or similar size pie pan. Bake the crust at 375° for 6 to 8 minutes, then cool and fill as desired. Use the reserved crumb mixture as a garnish.

COOKIE CRUMB CRUST

Omit the sugar and whirl or process enough vanilla or chocolate wafers to make 3 cups. Package and use as directed above.

MIX-IT-IN-THE-PAN CHOCOLATE CAKE AND FROSTING MIX

Makes 1 package of mix,
yielding one 8-by-8-by-2-inch cake

1¼ cups all-purpose flour
1 cup sugar
½ teaspoon baking soda
½ teaspoon salt
2 squares (1 ounce each) unsweetened chocolate
1 small package (6 ounces) semisweet chocolate morsels
⅓ cup chopped nuts

Sift together the first 4 ingredients and seal in a small plastic bag. Place this small bag within a slightly larger plastic bag along with the squares and package of chocolates and the chopped nuts. Seal, label with this page number, and store at room temperature.

Directions: Preheat oven to 350°. Break up the 2 squares of unsweetened chocolate and place, along with ⅓ cup of oil, in an 8-by-8-by-2-inch square baking pan; heat in the oven until melted, about 3 or 4 minutes; remove the pan from the oven. Add the contents of only the small plastic bag plus 1 cup of water, 1 egg, and 1 teaspoon vanilla; beat with a fork until smooth and creamy, about 1 minute. Use a rubber spatula to scrape the sides of the pan and to spread the batter evenly. Sprinkle with the semisweet chocolate morsels and the nuts. Bake for 40 minutes, or until a knife inserted in the center comes out clean; cool and serve. Goes well with ice cream.

COFFEE CAKE MIX

Makes 1 package of mix, yielding one 8-inch cake

1½ cups sifted flour
3 tablespoons granulated sugar
2 teaspoons baking powder
½ teaspoon salt

⅓ cup vegetable shortening
2 sandwich bags
⅓ cup packed brown sugar
½ cup raisins
¼ teaspoon cinnamon
Several dashes of nutmeg
1 brown paper bag, lunchbag size

Combine the flour, granulated sugar, baking powder, and salt; stir well, then resift into a bowl. Use a pastry blender or your fingertips to cut in the shortening until the mix looks like coarse meal. Pour the mix into a sandwich bag and seal.

Combine the brown sugar, raisins, cinnamon, and nutmeg in the other sandwich bag and seal. Label the brown paper bag with this recipe title and page number. Open the bag and place the 2 mix packets within. Staple shut and store in your cupboard for up to 2 months.

To Use: In a bowl, lightly beat together 1 egg and ½ cup of milk. Add the packet of flour and shortening mix and beat by hand just until the ingredients are thoroughly blended; do not overbeat. Spread half of the batter in a greased, 8-inch round cake pan. Spread ½ cup any flavor jam or preserves or marmalade over the batter. Spread the raisins and brown sugar from the remaining packet over the layer of jam. Use a teaspoon to drop the remaining batter around the edge but not in the center of the pan. Bake at 350° for 35 to 40 minutes.

HOW TO MAKE COOKIES FROM ANY CAKE MIX

A 2-layer cake mix yields about 4 dozen cookies

Choose any kind and any flavor of two-layer cake mix—your own homemade mixes from *Make Your Own Groceries* or commercial varieties including those that contain pudding in the mix—and you can easily use it as a cookie mix.

2 eggs
⅓ cup vegetable oil
1 teaspoon vanilla extract or other flavor to match the cake mix
1 package 2-layer cake mix

Lightly beat together the eggs, oil, and extract in a mixing bowl. Add about half of the cake mix and beat by hand until smooth. Stir in the remaining cake mix until well blended. Drop the cookie dough by teaspoonfuls onto ungreased cookie sheets; place the cookies about 2 inches apart from each other.

Bake at 375° for 10 to 12 minutes, or until the bottoms begin to brown; the centers will remain soft. Let the cookies cool briefly before transferring them to racks.

CHOCOLATE CHIP COOKIES

Add a 6-ounce package of semisweet chocolate morsels to the dough when you add the second half of the cake mix. Makes 4½ dozen.

OTHER ADDITIONS

When you stir in the second half of the cake mix, you can also add ½ to ¾ cup your choice of: chopped nuts, shredded coconut, or raisins.

CHEWY CHOCOLATE BAR MIX

Makes 1 package of mix, yielding 1 dozen bars

1½ cups sifted flour
¾ cup sugar
⅓ cup cocoa
2 teaspoons baking soda
½ teaspoon salt
1 small package (6 ounces) semisweet chocolate morsels
⅔ cup coarsely chopped walnuts

Combine the flour, sugar, cocoa, baking soda, and salt; stir well, then sift into a bowl. Mix the remaining ingredients, then pour the entire mix into a plastic bag or a jar and seal well. Label with this recipe title and page number. Store in your cupboard for up to 2 months.

To Use: Pour the mix into a large bowl. Add 12 tablespoons (1½ sticks) of melted butter and 1 lightly beaten egg. Stir just enough to moisten the ingredients, but do not overbeat. Spread the batter into a greased 8-inch-square baking pan.

Bake at 350° for 30 minutes, or until a sharp knife tip inserted at the center comes out clean. Set the pan on a rack and let it cool. Cut into twelve 2-by-2⅔-inch bars.

GINGERSNAP COOKIE MIX

Makes 1 package of mix, yielding 10 dozen small cookies

1¾ cups all-purpose flour
1 cup packed brown sugar
1½ teaspoons ground ginger
½ teaspoon salt
¼ teaspoon baking soda
⅛ teaspoon allspice

Combine all the ingredients; stir well, then sift into a bowl. Pour the mix into a plastic bag or a jar and seal well. Label with this recipe title and page number. Store in your cupboard for up to 2 months.

To Use: Pour the mix into a large bowl. Heat together ½ cup molasses and 4 tablespoons butter; pour this into the mix and beat until the dough becomes well blended. Form the dough into a ball; wrap it in plastic wrap and chill for 1 hour.

Divide the dough into 4 equal portions; rewrap and return all but one of them to the refrigerator. Use a rolling pin to roll out the dough as thinly as possible. Use a small cookie cutter or the floured rim of a juice glass to cut the dough into 1½-inch rounds. Place these rounds fairly close together on a lightly greased cookie sheet and bake at 350° for 6 to 8 minutes. Repeat this procedure with the remaining refrigerated dough portions.

BANANA COOKIE MIX

Makes 1 package of mix, yielding 3½ dozen cookies

This cookie mix is the answer to what to do with overripe bananas. The chewy, cake-like cookies are made with an easily assembled mix and a quick whirl of the blender.

1¾ cups flour
⅔ cup packed brown sugar
1 tablespoon cornstarch
1¼ teaspoons baking powder
½ teaspoon baking soda
¾ teaspoon salt
½ teaspoon cinnamon
¼ teaspoon nutmeg
Dash of ground cloves

Combine all the ingredients in a bowl; stir well until uniform, then pour the mixture into a plastic bag or a jar; seal well. Label with this recipe title and page number. Store in your cupboard for up to 2 months.

To Use: Pour the mix into a large bowl. Place in a blender container the following ingredients in the order listed: ⅓ cup corn oil, 2 eggs, 2 or 3 ripe bananas cut in chunks (about 1 to 1½ cups). Whirl the blender ingredients until liquefied. Pour the contents of the blender container into the bowl of mix; stir with a spoon until just moistened and still lumpy. The batter should not be smooth.

Drop the batter by tablespoonfuls 2 inches apart onto ungreased cookie sheets. Bake at 325° for 10 minutes, or until the cookies are slightly browned at the edges. Immediately remove the cookies from their sheets and cool on racks.

BANANA BREAD

To turn the recipe to make Banana Bread, omit the cornstarch. Pour the batter into a greased 9½-by-5½-inch loaf pan. Bake at 350° for 1 hour, or until a knife inserted in the center comes out clean.

Chapter 3:

FROZEN, NO-THAW SOUP CONCENTRATES

Section:

☐ Frozen, No-Thaw Soup Concentrates

HOW TO MAKE FROZEN, NO-THAW SOUP CONCENTRATES

Make any of the broths as directed in the following recipes. When the broth has reached what you consider to be normal strength, strain it through a muslin or cheesecloth-lined strainer into a clean pot. Add about 1 to 1½ teaspoons salt for every quart of strained broth, then adjust to taste. Cover and refrigerate overnight. Next day, skim off the fat that has congealed on the surface.

Wrap a ruler in aluminum foil; seal seams with clear tape. Heat the pot just enough to liquefy the jelled broth (except Vegetable Broth). Use the ruler to measure the depth of the broth in the pot, then mark that spot with a strip of masking tape—the bottom edge of the tape will be the mark. Clean and dry the ruler, then mark the spot that is one quarter distance from the ruler's bottom tip to the masking tape mark. Mark the one-quarter mark with a strip of masking tape as before. See Illustration.

Boil the broth, uncovered, until it measures up to the one-quarter mark. If too much broth boils away and measures below the one-quarter mark, add enough cold water to meet it. Let broth cool to room temperature. Measure once more, just in case more broth has evaporated during cooling. Use 8-ounce waxy paper cups or small, lidded plastic containers (such as cleaned yogurt, sour cream or margarine containers). Fill each with ¾ cup of broth concentrate. Cover, label, and freeze. One ¾-cup container of frozen concentrate plus 2¼ cups water will yield 3 cups of regular strength broth. This is about ⅓ cup more broth than you get in commercial diluted soup cans and will serve 2 or 3 people. The later addition of rice or noodles will not affect the volume of soup, but the addition of vegetables and meats will increase the number of servings to 3 or 4.

To Cook and Dilute: Bring 2¼ cups water to a boil. Add 1 frozen soup block (¾ cup concentrate); return to a boil, then cover and simmer until thawed and hot. Add any of the flavor variations listed under each soup recipe and cook according to those directions.

MARKING A RULER FOR FROZEN, NO-THAW, SOUP CONCENTRATES

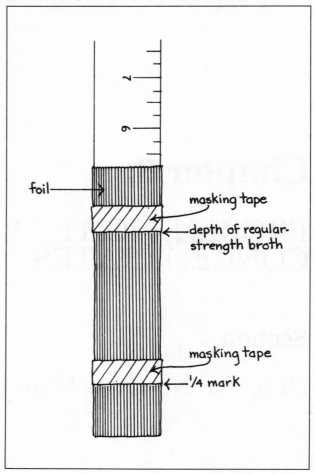

INDIVIDUAL-SERVING SOUPS

Pour ⅓ cup of the cooled broth concentrate into 3-ounce or 5-ounce waxy paper cups; cover with a square of plastic wrap and secure with a rubber band; label and freeze. Cook exactly as described above, but reduce water to 1⅛ cups. Halve any of the meats or flavor variations listed under each soup recipe and cook according to those directions. Makes 1½ cups broth.

SOUP CONCENTRATES WITH MEAT

Many soups require meat; it is best added to the container after the broth concentrate is solidly frozen. This prevents the meat from becoming stringy and also enables you to make good use of leftovers at a later date. Refer to the following list and add ¼ to ⅓ dup diced cooked meat to the container holding the ¾ cup of already-frozen concentrate.

REQUIRES DICED CHICKEN OR TURKEY MEAT:

CHICKEN NOODLE
CHICKEN ALPHABET
CHICKEN RICE
CHICKEN VEGETABLE
CHICKEN GUMBO
CHICKEN BARLEY
CHUNKY CHICKEN (Use big chunks)

REQUIRES DICED BEEF:

MINESTRONE
BEEF NOODLE
BEEF ALPHABET
BEEF BARLEY
VEGETABLE BEEF
OLD-FASHIONED VEGETABLE
TOMATO BEEF NOODLE
CHUNKY VEGETABLE BEEF (Use big chunks)

REQUIRES SAUTÉED GROUND BEEF:

GROUND BEEF NOODLE
TOMATO BEEF NOODLE

REQUIRES DICED COOKED HAM:

SPLIT PEA WITH HAM
CHUNKY SPLIT PEA WITH HAM (Use big chunks)

REQUIRES SLICED COOKED HOT DOGS:

HOT DOG BEAN

SOUPS THAT DO NOT REQUIRE MEAT:

TOMATO RICE
ONION
CREAMY ONION
ALL THE CREAM OF VEGETABLE SOUPS
LENTIL SOUP
ALL THE VEGETARIAN SOUPS

CHICKEN SOUP CONCENTRATES

*Makes about 2 quarts
regular-strength broth*

**8 or 9 pounds chicken necks and backs or 2
cut-up fowl, about 4 pounds each
2 or 3 onions, peeled and quartered
2 to 4 large carrots, scrubbed
2 to 4 large celery ribs
Celery leaves from whole stalk
6 to 8 peppercorns
1 tablespoon parsley flakes
6 thin lemon slices**

Combine all ingredients in your largest kettle or pot. Add 3 to 4 quarts of cool water or enough to cover the chicken pieces plus 1 inch. Bring the kettle to a boil and remove any surface scum. Cover kettle, reduce heat, and simmer very gently for 3 or 4 hours, adding water if it boils away too rapidly. When the broth tastes strong enough to you, refer to How to Make Frozen, No-Thaw Soup Concentrates on page 58 and continue with those directions. The following list of variations on chicken soup applies to one ¾-cup container of frozen soup concentrate. These variations apply equally to Turkey Soup Concentrate.

Cooking Directions: Bring 2¼ cups water to a boil. Add 1 frozen soup concentrate block (¾ cup) along with any frozen meat also in the container. Return to a boil, then cover tightly and simmer until thawed and hot. Makes 3 cups broth. Add any of these following flavor variations:

CHICKEN NOODLE

When broth boils, stir in ⅓ cup "kluski" noodles and ¼ cup water; cover and simmer for 20 minutes, stirring occasionally; or when broth boils, stir in ⅓ cup medium egg noodles or ½ cup thin egg noodles, cover, and simmer about 5 to 10 minutes or as noodle package directs.

CHICKEN ALPHABET

When broth boils, stir in ¼ cup alphabet macaroni; simmer, covered, 10 minutes.

CHICKEN RICE

When broth boils, stir in 3 tablespoons long-grain rice; cover and simmer 12 to 14 minutes (20 to 25 minutes for converted rice). With Minute Rice, stir ¼ cup into boiling broth, cover, remove from heat, and let stand 5 minutes.

CHICKEN BARLEY

Make as for Beef Barley on page 63 and stir in 1 or 2 teaspoons tomato paste or sauce to taste.

CHICKEN VEGETABLE

When broth boils, stir in ¾ to 1 cup frozen mixed vegetables (about half a 10-ounce package), 1 small potato cut in ¼-inch dice, and 1 or 2 teaspoons of tomato paste or sauce. Cover, return to a boil, and simmer about 10 minutes, or until all vegetables are tender. Instead of potato, you can also use the noodles, alphabets, or rice described above; but halve the amounts.

CHICKEN GUMBO

Sauté ¼ cup diced green pepper, ¼ cup chopped onion, and 1 cup fresh, canned, or frozen cut-up okra in 3 tablespoons butter for 10 minutes. Stir in hot chicken broth and a 1-pound can of well-squished tomatoes. Boil gently for 10 to 15 minutes, or until vegetables are tender. Add salt and pepper to taste.

TOMATO RICE

See directions for Chicken Rice and blend in 2 or 3 teaspoons tomato paste along with the rice. Do not use Minute Rice.

CHUNKY CHICKEN

Use chicken or turkey meat cut into 1-inch chunks. When broth boils, stir in ½ cup wide egg noodles, cover, and simmer as the noodle box directs. You can also stir in half of a 4-ounce can (¼ cup) mushroom pieces and a tablespoon of their juice. If you want a thick soup like the commercial kind, stir in a bit of cornstarch combined with cold water.

COUNTRY-STYLE GREEN BEAN AND BACON SOUP

When broth boils, turn off heat and set it aside. In a soup pot, sauté ¼ pound of bacon pieces until barely crisp; discard all fat except 1 tablespoon. Add ½ bunch chopped scallions and 1 cup trimmed fresh green beans (or half a frozen-and-thawed 9-ounce package) and sauté until scallions are soft, but not brown. Add the broth along with 1 cup diced raw potatoes, about 1 teaspoon tomato paste, 1 teaspoon salt, and pepper to taste. Cover loosely and simmer for 20 to 30 minutes, or until beans and potatoes are tender. Makes 4 servings.

TURKEY SOUP CONCENTRATES

*Makes about 2 to 3 quarts
regular-strength broth*

Turkey broth is one of the cheapest, richest, and fastest broths you can make.

3 turkey drumsticks (3 to 4 pounds total)
3 onions, peeled and quartered
4 large carrots, scrubbed
4 celery ribs
Celery leaves from the whole stalk
6 to 8 peppercorns
2 tablespoons parsley flakes
4 thin lemon slices

Combine all the ingredients in a large pot. Fill with enough water to cover, about 3 quarts, plus 1 inch. Bring the pot to a boil and remove any scum. Cover and simmer gently for 2 to 3 hours, or until the turkey is no longer attached to the bone. When the broth is done, refer to How to Make Frozen, No-Thaw Soups Concentrates on page 58 and continue with those directions. The cooking directions and list of flavor variations in the previous Chicken Soup Concentrates recipe apply exactly to Turkey Broth.

CREAM OF VEGETABLE SOUPS

*Makes about 5 cups,
serves 3 or 4*

Any Cream of Vegetable Soup can be made from this recipe as well as Cream of Chicken Soup. Use frozen chicken or turkey broth concentrates, unless instructed otherwise, along with your choice of fresh, frozen, canned, or leftover vegetables.

1 **frozen chicken or turkey broth concentrate block (¾ cup)**
2¼ **cups boiling water**
Your choice of vegetable, below
3 **tablespoons butter**
3 **tablespoons onion, finely minced or grated**
3 **tablespoons flour**
1½ **teaspoons salt**
Pepper to taste
1 **cup milk**
⅓ **cup cream, optional**

Combine the frozen broth concentrate and the 2¼ cups boiling water in a covered pan and simmer until warm and defrosted; set aside. Choose the vegetable you want from below and cook it as directed. When the vegetable is tender, place it in a blender or food processor container along with enough of its own cooking liquid to measure 2 cups. Whirl until well puréed; set the 2 cups of purée aside.

Heat butter in a soup pot; add onion and simmer about 5 minutes, or until soft but not brown; remove from heat and blend in flour, salt, and pepper. Gradually stir in 2 cups of the chicken broth and 1 cup of milk. Return to lowest heat and cook until thick and smooth, stir continuously. Stir the 2 cups vegetable purée into the thickened mixture; slowly heat through. Stir in cream if you wish. Ladle soup into bowls; sprinkle each with chopped parsley or chives or a dash of paprika; serve.

CREAM OF ASPARAGUS

Combine 2 pounds asparagus trimmed and cut into 1-inch lengths and ¾ cup of the chicken broth; simmer, covered, until tender, about 8 to

10 minutes, and purée as directed. Increase both butter and flour in recipe to 4 tablespoons each. You can also use one 10-ounce package of frozen asparagus or one 1-pound can asparagus spears.

CREAM OF BROCCOLI

Cook 2 cups coarsely chopped fresh broccoli or one 10-ounce package frozen broccoli pieces, covered, in 1 cup of the chicken broth until tender, about 10 to 15 minutes. Purée as directed.

CREAM OF CARROT

Cook 3 cups finely shredded carrots in 1 cup of the chicken broth, covered, for 5 to 10 minutes. No need to purée if carrots have been shredded; or, you can cook 2 cups thinly sliced carrots, as above, and purée.

CREAM OF CELERY

Gently simmer 2 cups peeled chopped celery in 1 cup of the chicken broth, covered, until tender, about 10 minutes. Purée as directed.

CORN CHOWDER

Cook 2½ cups fresh corn or one 9-ounce package of frozen corn kernels in 1 cup of milk or chicken broth until tender; purée as directed. You can also use a 16-ounce can of cut or cream-style corn, puréed.

CREAM OF MUSHROOM

Chop fine ½ to 1 pound mushrooms. Simmer them for 15 minutes in 4 tablespoons butter and 1 teaspoon grated onion; stir in 1 teaspoon fresh lemon juice. Purée with chicken broth as directed.

GOLDEN MUSHROOM

Same as Cream of Mushroom, above, but use beef broth in the recipe instead of chicken broth.

GREEN PEA

Cook 2 cups fresh or one 9-ounce package frozen peas in 1 cup of the chicken broth, covered, until tender. Purée as directed. You can also use a 16-ounce can of peas.

CREAM OF POTATO

Cook 1½ cups sliced potatoes and ½ cup chopped leeks or onions in 1 cup of the chicken broth, covered, for 15 minutes. Purée as directed.

CREAM OF SPINACH

Cook, covered, 1 pound spinach or 1 package frozen chopped spinach in ¼ cup of the chicken broth. Purée as directed. Increase both butter and flour to 4 tablespoons each.

CREAM OF TOMATO

Combine 3 cups canned stewed or home-cooked tomatoes (all crushed) with 1 tablespoon chopped onion, ¼ teaspoon celery seed, ¼ bay leaf, 1 whole clove, and a pinch of sugar. Simmer, uncovered, until reduced to 2 cups. Purée as directed and strain through a sieve. Increase both butter and flour to 4 tablespoons each. Make sure the strained tomato purée is hot before slowly stirring it into the broth. Serve at once; this soup does not reheat well.

CREAM OF CHICKEN

Omit the vegetable purée and use 1 cup chicken broth, instead. This creamed soup is nice with the addition of diced cooked chicken and cream.

CREAM OF LEFTOVERS

Almost any leftover cooked vegetable can be turned into a cream soup. Use 1 to 1½ cups cooked vegetable plus enough chicken broth to measure 2 cups. Purée in a blender or food processor.

BEEF SOUP CONCENTRATES

*Makes about 2 quarts
regular-strength broth*

3 or 4 pounds beef shin, ribs, shank, or other beef soup meat, cut in chunks
1 pound or more beef marrow bones, cracked
2 medium onions, each studded with a clove
2 large carrots, scrubbed
2 large celery ribs with leaves
Celery leaves from whole stalk
4 or 5 peppercorns
A 1-inch piece bay leaf
1 tablespoon parsley flakes
3 quarts cool water

In your largest kettle or pot, brown the chunks of beef on all sides; add all the other ingredients; bring to a boil and skim off scum as it rises. Cover and simmer very gently for 4 hours. Add water if it boils away too rapidly and skim the scum from time to time. If the broth is still not strong enough for your liking, add 1 pound ground beef (frozen is okay) and continue simmering. Don't think that your broth is too weak because it doesn't match the deep brown color of canned beef broth. Commercial broth is made brown by either roasting the uncracked marrow bones at 400° for 2 hours before boiling them and/or adding a few drops or spoonfuls of Gravy Master or Kitchen Bouquet to the broth.

When broth reaches regular strength, refer to How To Make Frozen, No-Thaw Soup Concentrates on page 58 and continue with those directions. The following list of variations on beef soup applies to one ¾-cup container of frozen soup concentrate.

Cooking Directions: Bring 2¼ cups water to a boil. Add 1 frozen soup concentrate block (¾ cup) along with any frozen meat also in the container. Return to a boil, then cover tightly and simmer until thawed and hot. Add any of these flavor variations:

VEGETABLE BEEF

When broth boils, stir in ¾ to 1 cup frozen mixed vegetables (about half a 10-ounce package), 1 small raw potato cut in ¼-inch dice, and 1 or 2 teaspoons of tomato paste or sauce. Cover, return to a boil, and simmer about 10 minutes or until vegetables are tender. Instead of potato, you can use the noodles, alphabets, or rice described in the following variations; but halve the amounts.

OLD-FASHIONED VEGETABLE

This is the same as Vegetable Beef, above, only no tomato sauce or paste is added.

BEEF NOODLE, BEEF ALPHABET

Follow the same directions under Chicken Noodle and Chicken Alphabet on page 59.

GROUND BEEF NOODLE

Either add ¼ to ⅓ cup cooked and drained ground beef to any Beef Noodle soup, above, or freeze the sautéed ground beef in the soup concentrate container.

TOMATO BEEF NOODLE, TOMATO GROUND BEEF NOODLE

Begin to make any of the above Beef Noodle, Beef Alphabet, or Ground Beef Noodle soups, and blend in half an 8-ounce can of tomato sauce. Cover and simmer for 15 minutes.

MINESTRONE

When broth boils, stir in the following: ½ cup frozen mixed vegetables or peas (half a 10-ounce package); ⅛ cup broken thin egg noodles; 1 small raw potato cut in ¼-inch dice; ½ cup canned or cooked kidney beans and their liquid; 1 or 2 teaspoons tomato paste or tomato sauce (or ½ cup canned tomatoes); and a dash of garlic powder. Cover and simmer about 10 minutes, or until vegetables are tender. Serve with grated Parmesan cheese sprinkled atop.

BEEF BARLEY, MUSHROOM BARLEY

Boil ⅓ cup pearl barley in 2½ cups water in a covered pot for 1 hour, or until tender. Add enough water to measure 2¼ cups; add frozen soup concentrate block along with any frozen meat also in the container. Cover and cook until hot.

For Mushroom Barley, stir in one 4-ounce can mushroom pieces and a few tablespoons of mushroom juice.

CHUNKY VEGETABLE BEEF

Use cooked beef stew meat cut into 1-inch chunks. When broth boils, stir in 1 cup frozen mixed vegetables (half a 10-ounce package) and ½ to ¾ cup raw potatoes also cut into 1-inch chunks. Cover and simmer for 10 to 15 minutes, or until potatoes are tender. If you wish, blend in 1 or 2 teaspoons of tomato paste or sauce.

ONION SOUP

Sauté 1 or 2 sliced medium onions in 1½ to 2 tablespoons butter until limp but not brown. Lower heat; sprinkle onions with 1 teaspoon flour and stir briefly until onions are golden. Pour in 3 cups hot diluted beef broth plus ¾ cup hot water. Simmer, uncovered, for 20 minutes.

CREAMY ONION SOUP

Sauté onions as described above. Lower heat and sprinkle with 1 tablespoon flour; stir until golden. Pour in 3 cups hot diluted beef broth and ½ cup hot water. Simmer, uncovered, for 20 minutes, then stir in ¼ cup hot milk.

63

VEGETABLE SOUP CONCENTRATES

*Makes about 2½ quarts
regular-strength broth*

These soups are flavorful, filling, and very low in calories.

4   tablespoons butter, margarine, or corn oil
4   large onions, coarsely chopped
4   large carrots, coarsely sliced
4   celery ribs with leaves, coarsely chopped
4   parsnips, coarsely sliced
2   medium turnips, cut in chunks
1   cup fresh snipped parsley or ⅓ cup dried
    flakes
Celery leaves from whole stalk
1   bay leaf, crumbled
1   teaspoon fresh basil (¼ teaspoon dried)
1   teaspoon peppercorns
1   tablespoon salt
3   quarts water

Melt butter in a large kettle or pot. Add onions, carrots, celery, parsnips, and turnips, and sauté until almost tender, about 15 to 20 minutes. Add all remaining ingredients; bring to a boil; cover, reduce heat, and simmer for 3 hours. When the broth tastes strong enough to you, refer to How to make Frozen, No-Thaw Soup Concentrates on page 58 and continue with those directions. If you don't like the color of your strained broth, stir in just a bit of Gravy Master or Kitchen Bouquet. The following variations on Vegetable Soup apply to one ¾-cup container of frozen soup concentrate.

Cooking Directions: Bring 2¼ cups water to a boil. Add 1 frozen soup concentrate block (¾ cup); return to a boil; cover and simmer until thawed and hot. Add any of these flavor variations:

VEGETARIAN VEGETABLE

Follow the same directions given under Vegetable Beef on page 63.

VEGETABLE NOODLE, VEGETABLE ALPHABET, VEGETABLE RICE

Refer to the recipe for Chicken Soup Concen-trates on page 59. Follow the instructions under Chicken Noodle, Chicken Alphabet, and Chicken Rice. To make soup heartier, blend a few tea-spoons of tomato paste or sauce into the broth along with macaroni or rice.

VEGETABLE BARLEY, VEGETABLE MINESTRONE, CHUNKY VEGETARIAN VEGETABLE

Refer to the Beef Soup Concentrates recipe on page 62. Follow the instructions under Mine-strone, Beef Barley, and Chunky Vegetable Beef.

QUICK SPLIT PEA WITH HAM SOUP CONCENTRATE

This hearty soup is well worth the making and will provide many handy lunches and dinners.

3   medium onions, chopped
Bacon fat
1   or 2 pounds diced cooked ham or 1 pound
    bacon
2   pounds split peas
Salt and pepper

In your largest kettle, sauté the onions in a gener-ous amount of bacon fat until soft. Add and sauté the ham or bacon. Remove from heat and stir in 1 quart very cold water. Whirl the split peas in a blender or food processor until powdered—do this 1 cup at a time if using a blender. Very slowly, stir the powder into the kettle. Add enough additional cold water, if necessary, to cover the mixture plus 2 inches. Simmer over lowest heat for several hours until peas are very, very mushy and onions seem to have dis-appeared. Stir the mixture frequently to pre-vent sticking at the bottom and add water as necessary.

When the soup is tender and has the consistency of thick oatmeal, remove from heat and let cool to room temperature. Add salt and pepper to taste. Divide the soup concentrate among 2-cup or 4-cup plastic containers, label, and freeze.

Cooking Directions: Let the frozen containers

thaw at least halfway. Place in a soup pot and add enough milk to dilute to desired consistency. Heat to serve.

CHUNKY SPLIT PEA WITH HAM

When diluting the concentrate, add extra milk and some water plus 1-inch chunks of raw potato and either cooked ham or uncooked hot dog slices. Cover and simmer until potatoes are done, about 15 minutes.

BEAN SOUP CONCENTRATES

Makes about 2 quarts
ham broth concentrate

3 medium onions, coarsely chopped
Bacon fat or bacon trimmings
4 pounds pork neck bones, smoked, if possible,
or 2 meaty ham bones
4 peppercorns
Salt

In a large kettle, sauté the onions in a generous amount of bacon fat or trimmings until soft. Add the pork neck or ham bones, the peppercorns, and about 3 quarts of water, or enough to cover everything plus 2 inches. Cover and simmer 3 to 4 hours; add water if it boils away too rapidly and skim off any surface scum. When broth reaches a flavorful strength, strain it into a clean pot and add salt to taste. Pick off any extra ham meat from the bones, being careful of the small, stray pieces in the pork neck bones. Set the ham meat aside.

Refer to How to Make Frozen, No-Thaw Soup Concentrates on page 58, and reduce the same stock to one quarter of its original volume. Do not refrigerate the broth beforehand to remove any fat. Package as directed, then divide the ham meat among the containers. Label and freeze.

BEAN AND BACON SOUP

Bring 2¼ cups water to a boil. Add 1 frozen ham broth block (¾ cup concentrate plus any ham meat in the container) and return to a boil; cover and simmer until thawed and hot.

Open two 16-ounce cans (about 4 cups) of beans—choose from pork and beans in sauce, or plain, undrained navy, black, or pinto beans, etc. Stir the beans and their liquid into the hot broth and crush some of the beans with a potato masher so as to thicken the soup. Gently simmer, uncovered, for about 10 to 15 minutes, then serve. Makes about 6 cups soup; serves 4 to 5.

HOT DOG BEAN SOUP

Dilute and cook Bean and Bacon Soup as described above. Add several sliced hot dogs along with the canned beans. Simmer until hot dogs are cooked.

LENTIL SOUP

Bring 8½ cups water to a boil. Add 2 frozen ham broth blocks (¾ cup concentrate plus any ham meat in the container) and return to a boil; cover and simmer until thawed. Stir in 1 pound (2 heaping cups) washed lentils; bring to a boil; skim off foam and simmer, covered, 20 to 30 minutes or until tender. Blend in one 6-ounce can tomato paste, 1 tablespoon fresh parsley, and salt and pepper to taste. Cover and simmer 10 more minutes before serving. Serves 4 to 6.

BEAN AND BEEF

Instead of using ham broth concentrate, you can substitute beef broth concentrate or canned beef broth in any of the above bean soup recipes.

Chapter 4:

CONDIMENTS

Sections:

☐Reduced-Calorie Salad Dressings
☐Sauces and Seasonings
☐Refrigerator-Cured Pickles and Relishes

REDUCED-CALORIE MAYONNAISE DRESSING BASE

Makes 2 cups

A tasty mayonnaise substitute at less than half the price of commercial with a fraction of the oil and with only 58 calories per tablespoon. Use this mayonnaise as the creamy base for any of the Reduced-Calorie Salad Dressings that follow.

3 tablespoons cornstarch
½ cup cold water
¾ cup water
2 tablespoons white distilled vinegar
1 tablespoon lemon juice
2 fresh egg yolks, at room temperature
1 teaspoon dry mustard
½ teaspoon salt
½ teaspoon lemon juice
⅓ cup corn oil

Put the cornstarch into a small jar; add ½ cup cold water and shake well to mix. In a non-aluminum saucepan, bring the ¾ cup water, 2 tablespoons vinegar, and 1 tablespoon lemon juice to a boil; reduce the heat to a low simmer. Gradually pour the cornstarch liquid into the saucepan mixture, stirring immediately and constantly until well thickened and clear. Remove from heat and quickly cool by placing the pan in cold water; stir now and then to prevent a top-film from forming; set aside.

Warm a mixing bowl in hot water and dry it. Use an electric mixer on medium speed to beat the yolks until thick and lemon colored; beat in mustard, salt, and the remaining ½ teaspoon lemon juice. Beginning with no more than half a teaspoon at a time, beat in the oil. Beat continuously; don't rush; make sure every bit of oil is absorbed before adding any more. When only half the oil is left, you can add it a teaspoon at a time. When the beaten mixture is smooth and thick, gradually stir in the cooled cornstarch mixture, using a wire whisk to blend the ingredients thoroughly. Pour this finished mayonnaise into a container to chill before using.

DIET SALAD DRESSING BASE

Makes 1½ cups

This oil-free salad dressing counts 18 calories per tablespoon. Use it as the base for any of the Reduced-Calorie Salad Dressings that follow or spice it up with one more teaspoon of dry mustard and use it plain.

2 tablespoons flour
2 tablespoons sugar
¾ teaspoon dry mustard
½ teaspoon salt
1½ cups skim milk
2 fresh egg yolks, at room temperature
¼ to ⅓ cup white distilled vinegar

Combine the flour, sugar, mustard, and salt in a non-aluminum saucepan; blend in the milk, then simmer, stirring frequently, over low heat until the mixture bubbles and thickens; this will take about 5 to 10 minutes. Lightly beat the 2 egg yolks in a medium-size bowl. Very gradually, stir half of the hot mixture into the yolks, then stir the hot yolk mixture gradually back into the saucepan. Slowly simmer this new mixture, stirring constantly, for 2 or 3 minutes more.

Remove the saucepan from the heat and directly cover the surface of the sauce with plastic wrap so that no film can form. Let the mixture cool for about 20 minutes or until lukewarm. Stir in ¼ cup of the vinegar; taste the dressing before deciding to add the rest. Pour the finished dressing into a clean jar or bottle and refrigerate.

DAIRY SALAD DRESSING BASE

Makes 1⅓ cups

Use this creamy, dairy salad dressing plain or as the base for any of the Reduced-Calorie Salad Dressings that follow. Count 17 calories per tablespoon if you are using regular creamed cottage cheese; count 11 calories per tablespoon if using lowfat cottage cheese.

1 cup creamed or 1 cup lowfat cottage cheese
⅓ cup buttermilk
Salt and pepper to taste

Whirl all the ingredients in a blender or food processor until smooth. Lacking these machines, you can use an egg beater or an electric mixer.

REDUCED-CALORIE SALAD DRESSINGS

Makes 1 cup each

Choose the flavor you want, combine all the listed ingredients, then refrigerate overnight or at least several hours before using. Where the ingredients list states "Dressing Base," you will use your choice of the preceding: Reduced-Calorie Mayonnaise Dressing Base for a thick salad dressing; or Diet Salad Dressing Base for a more liquid salad dressing; or Dairy Salad Dressing Base for a creamy salad dressing. The flavors will be similar but the textures and calories will vary according to your choice.

CREAMY ITALIAN

¾ cup Dressing Base
1 tablespoon vinegar
1 tablespoon fresh lemon juice
1 tablespoon oil, optional
1 or 2 tablespoons water
2 garlic cloves, put through a garlic press
1 teaspoon Worcestershire sauce
1 teaspoon sugar
½ teaspoon dried oregano, powdered between the heels of your hands

THOUSAND ISLAND

½ cup Dressing Base
⅓ cup chili sauce
2 or 3 tablespoons milk
1 tablespoon sweet pickle relish

RUSSIAN

½ cup Dressing Base
¼ cup chili sauce
2 tablespoons milk
1 teaspoon Worcestershire sauce
1 teaspoon grated onion
½ teaspoon prepared horseradish
Snipped fresh parsley to taste

CREAMY GARLIC

¾ cup Dressing Base
1 tablespoon oil, optional
1 tablespoon vinegar
1 tablespoon fresh lemon juice
1 tablespoon water or dry white wine
2 or 3 garlic cloves, put through a garlic press

CREAMY ROQUEFORT, BLUE, OR GORGONZOLA CHEESE

¾ cup Dressing Base
¼ cup (or more) crumbled Roquefort, blue, or Gorgonzola cheese
¼ cup milk
1 teaspoon Worcestershire sauce
Dash of pepper

CREAMY DILL

1 cup Dressing Base
¼ cup fresh dillweed (or 1 tablespoon dried)
2 or 3 tablespoons milk

CREAMY FRENCH

¾ cup Dressing Base
1½ tablespoons fresh lemon juice
1 tablespoon sugar
1 tablespoon oil, optional
1 teaspoon paprika

¼ teaspoon dry mustard
Salt and pepper to taste
3 tablespoons ketchup, optional

YOGURT SALAD DRESSINGS

Makes 1¼ cups

1 cup plain yogurt
2 tablespoons regular mayonnaise
1½ tablespoons fresh lemon juice
½ teaspoon paprika
½ teaspoon salt
¼ teaspoon garlic powder
Dash of Tabasco sauce

Mix the ingredients until smooth. Just 8 calories per tablespoon.

BLUE CHEESE-YOGURT DRESSING

Add 2 tablespoons crumbled blue, Roquefort, or Gorgonzola cheese to the ingredients; omit the paprika and garlic. Count 24 calories per tablespoon.

YOGURT-DILL DRESSING

Replace the paprika, garlic, and Tabasco with ¼ cup snipped fresh dillweed (or 1 tablespoon dried dillweed).

CUCUMBER-LEMON SALAD DRESSING

Makes 2 cups

1 cup finely chopped seeded cucumber
Salt
1 cup plain yogurt
2 tablespoons fresh lemon juice
1 teaspoon minced fresh parsley

Place cucumbers in a bowl and sprinkle with salt to taste plus a little extra; let stand for 10 minutes, then drain off excess water. Mix in the remaining ingredients. Chill before using.

RANCH-STYLE BUTTERMILK SALAD DRESSING

Makes 1 cup

¾ cup buttermilk
4 heaping tablespoons lowfat cottage cheese
3 tablespoons chopped onion
1 tablespoon minced fresh parsley
1 tablespoon snipped fresh (or freeze-dried) chives
¼ teaspoon dry mustard
¼ teaspoon salt

Whirl all ingredients in a blender or food processor until smooth. Count 8 calories per tablespoon.

STRICT-DIET SALAD DRESSINGS

Makes about 1 cup each

The following dressings lack much substance but they also lack oil, starches, and calories. These dressings can sometimes be sneaked into a non-medical, strict-menu diet to make a plain bowl of lettuce more appealing.

SWEET-AND-SOUR DRESSING

⅔ cup water
⅓ cup strained fresh lemon juice
1 teaspoon sugar
¼ teaspoon paprika
¼ teaspoon salt

Combine all the ingredients; refrigerate overnight and shake before using. Count 2 calories per tablespoon.

TOMATO-LEMON DRESSING

1 cup tomato juice
⅓ cup strained fresh lemon juice
1 tablespoon grated onion
1 teaspoon finely minced parsley
¼ teaspoon salt
⅛ teaspoon pepper

Combine all the ingredients; refrigerate overnight

and shake before using. Count 2 calories per tablespoon.

TOMATO-HERB DRESSING

1 small can (8 ounces) tomato sauce
2 tablespoons white distilled vinegar
1 teaspoon Worcestershire sauce
½ teaspoon grated onion
1½ teaspoons fresh minced basil (or ½ teaspoon dried and crushed)
1½ teaspoons fresh snipped dillweed (or ½ teaspoon dried and crushed)
½ teaspoon salt

Whirl all the ingredients in a blender or shake well in a covered jar or cruet. Refrigerate overnight and shake before using. Count 4 calories per tablespoon.

DUXELLES

Makes 2 cups

Duxelles, or mushroom concentrate, is a good seasoning to have on hand whenever you want the quick addition of buttery, fresh mushrooms to your cooking. Duxelles has long been used in gourmet, French cuisine but it can also be used to enhance ordinary casseroles, soups, gravies, and dips; it can be used as a garnish for steak or broiled fish or plain vegetables; it makes an excellent omelet or crêpe filling; and it can serve as the base for various soups and sauces.

1 pound fresh mushrooms
4 tablespoons butter (not margarine)
4 tablespoons very finely minced onions
Salt and pepper to taste

Wash and trim the mushrooms; use a sharp knife to mince them finely; if you have a food processor, use it in short bursts to avoid chopping too finely. Several handfuls at a time, place the minced mushrooms in a clean non-terrycloth towel or in several doubled paper towels; twist the mushrooms in the towel to extract any juices; repeat for all the minced mushrooms.

In a skillet, heat the butter to bubbling over medium-high heat; add the mushrooms and onions and cook, stirring, until the mushroom pieces begin to separate from each other and any extra liquid has evaporated; this will take about 5 or more minutes; do not overcook the mushrooms. Remove from heat; add salt and pepper to taste; let cool to room temperature.

Pour half the duxelles into a 1-cup container, cover and store in your refrigerator for up to 1½ weeks. Line a cookie sheet with wax paper; spoon out 8 well-spaced mounds of the remaining duxelles on the sheet, using 2 tablespoons per mound; gently press each mound into a thin disc.

Freeze the discs, uncovered, until solid, then transfer them to a plastic bag and return them to the freezer; thaw briefly before using.

MUSHROOM SAUCE

Add 4 to 6 tablespoons duxelles to 1 cup of any white sauce; heat through and serve. Makes 1¼ cups.

TANGY MUSHROOM SAUCE

Melt 1½ tablespoons of butter in a saucepan; stir in, but do not brown, 2 tablespoons flour followed by ½ cup chicken broth; 1 tablespoon strained fresh lemon juice; 2 to 4 tablespoons duxelles; and ⅛ teaspoon dried dillweed. Cook and stir until thickened; adjust salt and pepper to taste. Serve, hot, over broiled fish, chicken cutlets, cooked green beans, or boiled potatoes. Makes ¾ cup.

DUXELLES DIP

Combine ½ cup duxelles with ½ cup sour cream; mix well; add salt and pepper to taste. Refrigerate for several hours before serving at room temperature. Use as a dip for raw vegetable sticks or serve over baked potatoes. Makes 1 cup.

QUICK MUSHROOM SOUP

Melt 2 tablespoons of butter in a soup pot; stir in 2 tablespoons flour and ½ cup duxelles. Slowly stir in 1⅛ cups chicken broth followed by 1⅛ cups milk; continue stirring until thickened. Adjust salt and pepper to taste. Makes 2¾ cups of soup.

CREAMED DUXELLES

Serve this elegant form of duxelles over broiled fish or as a main course sauce for veal scaloppine or chicken breasts.

Gently heat ½ cup duxelles in a saucepan; stir in a pinch of either dried tarragon or dillweed. Stir in 1 tablespoon of flour until completely absorbed, followed by 2 tablespoons dry white wine; let simmer briefly. Stir in ¼ cup heavy cream and simmer, stirring constantly, until thickened to your liking. Adjust salt and pepper to taste. Serve hot.

MS. MARINADE

*Makes 2 cups, enough to marinate
4 pounds of meat*

Keep this marinade on hand for a variety of charcoal-grilled or broiled meats, including beef kebabs, all manner of steaks, London broil, and lamb chops.

1½ cups dry red wine
½ cup strained fresh lemon juice
⅓ cup corn oil (not vegetable or olive oil)
4 medium-size garlic cloves, peeled, smashed, and minced
2 teaspoons salt
2 teaspoons pepper
1 teaspoon oregano, crushed between the heels of your hands

Combine all the ingredients in a pint-size container, cover, label with this page number or the following directions, and store in your refrigerator for up to 3 months.

Directions: Shake the container well before each use and measure out ½ cup of marinade for every pound of meat you are using. Marinate cubed meat in a bowl and steaks or chops fitted snugly in a shallow pan, turning them once. Meat should marinate in the refrigerator overnight or for 6 to 8 hours at room temperature; reduce this time by a few hours if room temperature exceeds 80°. Baste with the marinade as you charcoal-grill or broil the meat.

ORIENTAL COOKING SAUCE

Makes 4 cups

This handy stir-fry seasoning sauce keeps well in your refrigerator and goes well with beef, pork, chicken or shrimp.

4 tablespoons cornstarch
1 teaspoon garlic powder
½ teaspoon powdered ginger
¼ teaspoon pepper
1 can (13¾ or 14½ ounces) regular-strength beef broth
⅔ cup dark corn syrup
⅔ cup soy sauce
⅓ cup dry sherry
⅓ cup white distilled vinegar
Water

Pour 4 cups of water into a quart-size or slightly bigger jar; mark the 4-cup line with a piece of tape; pour out the water. Put the cornstarch, garlic powder, ginger, and pepper in this jar; add the can of beef broth; cover the jar and shake until the cornstarch is dissolved. Open the jar and add the corn syrup and the soy sauce; cover and shake to blend. Re-open the jar; add the sherry, vinegar, and enough water to meet the 4-cup line. Cover and refrigerate for up to 1 month. Always shake or stir the contents of the jar before using.

STIR-FRY BEEF

Cut about ¾ pound flank or sirloin steak, slanting and across the grain, into very thin strips; set aside. Have ready 1 package frozen pea pods, completely thawed; 1½ cups sliced fresh mushrooms; and 1 cup Oriental Cooking Sauce. Heat 2 tablespoons of oil in a wide skillet over medium-high heat; sauté and stir the meat until only a little pink remains; add both the pea pods and the mushrooms; stir and sauté until just tender; do not overcook. Stir in the Oriental Cooking Sauce and continue cooking until the sauce thickens. Serve over rice or Chinese noodles.

Variations on this recipe are endless: you can use sliced pork or chicken or whole shrimp along with your choice of a 3-cup total of bean sprouts, or try water chestnuts, green pepper strips, thinly sliced zucchini, shredded bok choy, or frozen Chinese vegetables.

DIJON MUSTARD

Makes 2 cups

Here's a fresh-made mustard whose flavor is so much better than any heat-processed commercial variety that you can even give it as a gift. You can buy dry mustard in cup quantities at spice and herb stores; it is sometimes called mustard flour. Less economical but widely available are the larger cans of hot, English dry mustard sold in all supermarket spice aisles.

1 cup dry mustard
½ cup cold water
1¼ cups good dry white wine
1¼ cups white distilled vinegar
1 small onion, chopped (or ½ cup chopped shallots or scallion bulbs)
3 large garlic cloves, peeled, smashed, and very finely minced
2 teaspoons sugar
2 teaspoons salt
6 allspice berries
2 medium bay leaves
1 to 3 teaspoons dried tarragon

Put the dry mustard into the top part of a non-aluminum double boiler; stir in the cold water until smooth; set aside for at least 20 minutes to release the mustard's full flavor. In the meantime, pour the wine and the vinegar into an enamel or tempered glass or stainless steel cooking pot; do not use anything made of aluminum or any chipped enamelware in this recipe. Put all the remaining ingredients (except the mustard paste) in the pot and simmer, uncovered, about 10 to 15 minutes, or until the level of the cooking liquid is reduced by half. An easy way to correctly gauge the halfway mark is to vertically dip a wooden spoon handle in the pot before simmering; lightly pencil the liquid's level on the spoon, then pencil in the halfway mark. After simmering, use the halfway mark as your reduced-by-half measure. If you prefer a medium-to-hot mustard, simmer for up to 20 minutes, or until the liquid is reduced by a little more than half.

Pour the halved liquid mixture through a fine-mesh strainer into the mustard paste; gently press our any extra juices; blend the liquid and mustard-paste until smooth. Place the top part of the double boiler over its partner pot of simmering water; cook and stir the mustard mixture until it thickens to the consistency of heavy cream; this will take from 10 to 12 minutes and you should remember that the mixture, like gravy, will thicken even more upon cooling.

Remove the top part of the double boiler from the bottom part; let the mustard cool to room temperature, stirring occasionally. Pour the mustard into attractive jars; cover and store in your refrigerator for up to 1 year. If, upon first tasting it, the mustard is too hot, let it mellow for 3 or 4 weeks before using it.

SWEET AND SPICY GERMAN MUSTARD

Makes 2 cups

Both dry mustard and white mustard seeds, sometimes called yellow, can be purchased at supermarkets or spice and herb stores.

⅔ cup white mustard seeds
½ cup dry mustard
1 cup cold water
2 cups cider vinegar
1 medium onion, chopped (or ¾ cup chopped scallion bulbs)
4 medium garlic cloves, peeled, smashed, and finely minced
¼ cup packed brown sugar
2 teaspoons salt
1 teaspoon cinnamon
½ teaspoon allspice
½ teaspoon dill seeds
½ teaspoon dried tarragon
¼ teaspoon turmeric
2 to 4 tablespoons honey

Put the mustard seeds and the dry mustard in a glass or ceramic bowl; stir in the cold water until smooth; cover and set aside for 4 to 6 hours to soften the seeds and release the mustard's full flavor.

Pour the vinegar into an enamel or tempered glass or stainless steel cooking pot; do not use anything made of aluminum or any chipped enamelware in this recipe. Mix all the remaining ingredients except the honey into this pot and simmer, uncovered, for about 10 to 15 minutes, or until the level of the cooking liquid is reduced by half. An easy way to correctly gauge the halfway mark is to vertically dip a wooden spoon handle in the pot before simmering; lightly pencil the liquid's level on the spoon, then pencil in the halfway mark. After simmering, use the halfway mark as your reduced-by-half measure. If you prefer a medium-to-hot mustard, simmer for up to 20 minutes, or until the liquid is reduced by a little more than half.

After letting it cool slightly, pour the halved liquid mixture through a strainer into the mustard mixture; stir to blend, then pour this combined mixture into a blender or food processor container. Whirl or process until smoothly puréed.

Pour the mixture into the top part of a non-aluminum double boiler; place this top part over its partner pot of simmering water. Cook and stir the mustard mixture until it thickens to the consistency of heavy cream; this will take from 10 to 12 minutes and you should remember that the mixture, like gravy, will thicken even more upon cooling.

Remove the top part of the double boiler from the bottom and stir in 2 to 4 tablespoons of honey, depending on your taste. Let the mustard cool to room temperature, stirring occasionally. Pour the finished mustard into attractive jars and refrigerate for 5 to 7 days before using. This mustard can be stored, refrigerated, for up to 1 year. If, upon first tasting it, the mustard is too hot, let it mellow an additional 2 or 3 weeks before using it.

HANDY GARLIC

Makes about 1 cup

Jars of minced garlic preserved in oil can usually be found in the produce section of a supermarket. The idea of keeping ready-made, minced garlic on hand is an excellent one. This recipe furthers the good idea by using fresh rather than rehydrated garlic for better flavor without a trace of chemicals.

About 8 large bulbs (not cloves) fresh garlic
Corn oil (not vegetable or olive oil)

Remove the cloves from all the bulbs and peel them. Use the flat side of a chef's knife to smash each clove flat. Use a small sharp knife to mince each smashed clove as finely as possible. If your food processor can effectively handle 1 cup, use it instead of mincing with a knife. Process the peeled garlic cloves in short bursts to mince; make sure you don't purée the garlic.

Put the minced garlic in a glass jar with a 1-cup capacity. Slowly drizzle in enough oil to cover the garlic; stir well to remove all air bubbles. Cover the jar and store in your refrigerator for up to 1 year. Use in any recipe calling for garlic: ½ teaspoon minced garlic equals 1 medium clove.

PRESERVED HERBS

• You can preserve fresh summer herbs like parsley, dill, chives, or basil by salting rather than drying or freezing them. This method will retain both color and texture enough to use them even in salads.

Choose a widemouth glass jar and line the bottom with the washed and dried herb. Cover the herb with a layer of kosher or pickling or sea salt and repeat this layering until the jar is full. Cover and store in your refrigerator for a whole winter season. To use, rinse off the desired amount of herb in a strainer under running water and use as you would fresh herbs.

• A quick way to dry green leafy herbs like basil, parsley, oregano, mint, dill, sage, or chives is to use a microwave oven. This method retains better flavor than air-dried herbs and it also retains the herbs' green colors.

Place the herb sprigs on a paper towel and cover with another paper towel; put this arrangement in a microwave oven for 1 minute. Take the herbs out of the oven and let cool; if they are not completely dry and brittle, cover again and put them back in the oven for a few more seconds.

SALAD HERBS

Makes 1 cup

½ cup dried parsley flakes
1 tablespoon dried thyme
1 tablespoon celery seeds
1 tablespoon dried onion bits (sold near dried soup greens)
1 tablespoon dried green pepper flakes
2 teaspoons dried oregano
1 teaspoon dried marjoram
3 tablespoons onion powder
1 teaspoon dill seeds

Combine everything except onion powder and dill seeds in a blender or food processor container; whirl to a powder, then add onion and dill seeds. Sprinkle on salads, hot vegetables, and cottage cheese.

POULTRY SEASONING

Makes ½ cup

3 tablespoons dried thyme
2 tablespoons dried marjoram
2 tablespoons dried rosemary
1 tablespoon dried sage
1 tablespoon dried savory
2 teaspoons celery seeds
½ teaspoon ground allspice
½ teaspoon dried oregano
¼ teaspoon pepper

Whirl the ingredients in a blender or food processor until powdered. Use in poultry stuffings and in gravies, sauces, and stews.

Section: REFRIGERATOR-CURED PICKLES AND RELISHES

QUICK PICKLES AND RELISHES FROM YOUR REFRIGERATOR

None of the following pickle recipes require canning, processing in water baths, or fermenting in crocks. Simply follow these traditional recipes, put the pickles in any glass jar or plastic container you may have, and let them cure in your refrigerator. Your pickles will turn out fresher, crisper, and more flavorful than canned and you won't have to bother with equipment or special processing. Covered and refrigerated, these pickles will keep well for at least three months.

THINGS TO KNOW BEFORE MAKING PICKLES

• Never use pots or utensils made of aluminum, iron, zinc, or brass; instead, use unchipped enamel, glass, or stainless steel.

• Use only pure, uniodized salt without any additives, or else use pickling salt.

• Sizes of jars and containers will depend on the amount in the recipe. Although less appealing, plastic containers are a bit safer than glass which can sometimes crack. If using plastic containers, choose a sturdy kind—like the kind you would use in the freezer. Do not heat these. You can use jars made of thick-gauge glass so as to prevent cracking when hot liquid is added; peanut butter, mason, pickle, and similar thick glass jars are fine to use; mayonnaise jars are not. If re-using a store-bought jar that has a piece of cardboard inserted in the jar's lid, make sure you remove the cardboard before cleaning the jar thoroughly; cardboard can harbor bacteria which could ruin your pickles.

• Heat all glass jars before pouring in any hot vinegar mixture; do this by repeatedly filling them with very hot tap water. Let the jars stand, filled with hot water, right up to the point when they are packed with ingredients. Pour the hot pickling solution into the jars very slowly. This should prevent the jars from cracking.

• Do not store or let the pickles come in contact with any kind of metal container or lid. Always use a doubled piece of plastic wrap to protect pickles from a lid that is not plastic or enameled metal.

• Give the refrigerated pickles a chance to get pickled. Do not open the jars for 2 to 4 weeks.

BREAD AND BUTTER PICKLES

Makes 4 pints

These sweet-and-sour pickles are easily made with ordinary cucumbers. They remain extra crisp because they are never cooked.

10 to 12 medium-size, not too ripe, unwaxed cucumbers
3 or 4 large onions
⅔ cup salt
3 cups cider vinegar
3 cups sugar
2 teaspoons celery seeds
½ teaspoon turmeric
¼ teaspoon mustard seeds
¼ teaspoon cayenne pepper

Read "Things to Know Before Making Pickles," above.

Wash the cucumbers; cut off and discard the bitter tips; cut into ¼-inch slices. Peel the onions and slice them into very thin rings. Put the cucumbers and onions into your largest ceramic, glass, or stainless steel bowl; pour the salt atop and toss with your hands to thoroughly coat the vegetable mixture in salt. Let this mixture stand at room temperature for 3 hours, then transfer to a large plastic colander to drain for up to 1 more hour. Rinse the vegetable mixture repeatedly with cold water to remove all the salt; set aside in the colander to drain again.

When the cucumbers and onions are well

drained, heat 4 pint-size (or 2 quart-size) jars by running very hot tap water into them (don't heat if you are using plastic containers). Make a pickling solution by combining the remaining ingredients in a non-aluminum cooking pot; bring to a boil; simmer, uncovered, for 2 minutes; remove from heat and set aside.

Pack the cucumber-onion mixture into the heated jars. Slowly pour in the pickling solution right up to the jars' brims. Cover the jars; let them cool to room temperature, then refrigerate.

FREEZER PICKLES

Makes 4 cups

Pack these sweet dills into small plastic containers, freeze them, and defrost as needed.

1 **pound gherkins or baby pickling cucumbers, each about 3 inches long, sliced ⅛-inch thick (about 4 cups, packed)**
1½ **pounds small onions sliced ⅛-inch thick (about 2 cups packed)**
¼ **cup salt**
⅛ **cup water**
⅔ **cup sugar**
½ **cup cider vinegar**
3 **tablespoons chopped fresh dillweed (or 1 tablespoon dried)**

Read "Things to Know Before Making Pickles," on page 77.

Mix cucumbers, onions, salt, and water in a large bowl; let stand at room temperature for 2 or 3 hours; drain thoroughly in a colander, but do not rinse. Return the vegetables to the empty bowl and mix in the remaining ingredients; let stand, stirring now and then. When the sugar is completely dissolved and the liquid covers the vegetables, pack the mixture into small 1- or 2-cup plastic freezer containers, leaving 1-inch headspace. Label and freeze. To use, defrost in refrigerator.

SPICY PICKLED GREEN BEANS

Makes 3 pints

2 **pounds fresh green beans**
1⅔ **cups white distilled vinegar**
1⅔ **cups water**
¾ **cup sugar**
2 **medium garlic cloves, peeled and smashed**
1 **tablespoon peppercorns**
1 **tablespoon mustard seed**
1 **tablespoon salt**
4 **inches of stick cinnamon**
3 **medium onions, peeled and sliced into thin rings**

Read "Things to Know Before Making Pickles," on page 77

Wash and trim the ends off the green beans, leaving them whole. Cook the beans in boiling water for 8 to 10 minutes, or until they are just tender; set aside to drain. Make a pickling solution by combining all the remaining ingredients except the onions in a large cooking pot; heat to boiling, then add the onions and beans. Return to a boil and simmer, uncovered, for 15 minutes.

Heat 3 pint-size jars by running very hot tap water into them (don't heat if you are using plastic containers); when the jars are well heated, use a slotted spoon to fill them with the beans and onions. Slowly pour in the pickling solution, using a strainer so that the spices do not get into the jars; fill right up to the jars' brims. Cover the jars; let them cool to room temperature, then refrigerate.

DILLED GREEN BEANS

Makes 4 pints

3 **cups white distilled vinegar**
1 **cup water**
1 **cup light corn syrup**
½ **cup sugar**
2 **tablespoons dill seeds**
1 **tablespoon dried dillweed (or 3 tablespoons fresh)**

1 **tablespoon salt**
½ **teaspoon hot red pepper flakes**
1 **cup thinly sliced onion rings**
3 **pounds fresh green beans**

Read "Things to Know Before Making Pickles" on page 77.

Heat 4 pint-size jars (or 2 quart-size jars) by running very hot tap water into them (don't heat if you are using plastic containers). Make a syrup by combining everything except the green beans in a non-aluminum saucepan; bring to a boil; cook for 3 minutes, then remove from heat and set aside.

Wash and trim the ends off the beans, leaving them whole. Cook the beans in boiling water for 8 to 10 minutes, or until they are just tender. Drain the beans and pack them, still hot, into the heated jars. Slowly pour the hot syrup into the jars along with the onion rings; fill right up to the brim; make sure the spices are equally dispersed among the jars. Cover each of the jars; let them cool thoroughly to room temperature, then refrigerate.

PICKLED BEETS

Makes 4 pints

About 26 small, fresh beets (4 pounds)
2 **cups white distilled vinegar**
1 **cup sugar**
1½ **tablespoons salt**
7 **whole cloves**
4 **inches of stick cinnamon**
3 **whole allspice berries**
3 **medium onions, peeled and sliced into thin rings**

Read "Things to Know Before Making Pickles" on page 77.

Cut off the beet tops leaving 3 inches of stem and roots. Wash the beets carefully without breaking their skins and put them in a large pot with cold water to cover. Cover and cook just until tender, about 30 to 40 minutes. Drain, reserving 1 cup of the cooking liquid, then plunge the beets into cold water. Either slip off the beet skins or peel with a vegetable peeler; trim tops and roots. Slice the beets or cut them into quarters; set them aside.

Heat 4 pint-size jars (or 2 quart-size jars) by running very hot tap water into them (don't heat if you are using plastic containers). In a non-aluminum cooking pot, combine the 1 cup of reserved beet liquid, the vinegar, sugar, salt, and spices; heat to boiling, then add both the beets and onions; simmer, uncovered, for 5 minutes. Use a slotted spoon to pack the beets and onions into the jars. Slowly pour the pickling solution over the beets, using a strainer so that the spices do not get into the jars; fill right up to the jars' brims. Cover the jars; let them cool to room temperature, then refrigerate.

PIMIENTOS

Makes 2 quarts

8 **large sweet red peppers**
Boiling water
2½ **cups white distilled vinegar**
2½ **cups water**
1 **cup sugar**
8 **garlic cloves, peeled**
4 **teaspoons corn oil**
2 **teaspoons salt**

Read "Things to Know Before Making Pickles" on page 77.

Remove seeds and all inner white membranes from the peppers; cut them lengthwise into 1- or 2-inch strips. Place the strips in a large bowl; add boiling water to cover; let stand 5 minutes, then drain. Heat 2 quart-size jars with very hot running water (don't heat if using plastic containers). Bring the vinegar, water, and sugar to a boil in a non-aluminum saucepan; simmer for 5 minutes. Into each empty jar put: 4 garlic cloves, 2 teaspoons oil, and 1 teaspoon salt. Pack the pepper strips into the jars; pour the hot vinegar solution slowly over the peppers, filling the jars to the brim. Cover, let cool to room temperature, and refrigerate.

COCKTAIL ONIONS

Makes 3 pints

3 pounds small white pearl onions (2 quarts)
½ cup salt
2 cups white distilled vinegar
3 tablespoons whole allspice berries
2 tablespoons black peppercorns
3 small hot red peppers

Read "Things to Know Before Making Pickles" on page 77.

Peel the onions; sprinkle them with salt; cover with cold water and let stand in the refrigerator for 24 hours. Drain and rinse the onions thoroughly. Heat 3 pint-size jars with very hot running water (don't heat if using plastic containers). Slowly heat the vinegar to a boil along with the allspice and peppercorns tied into a cheesecloth bag; add the onions and return to a boil. Pack onions into hot jars; discard the spice bag; place 1 hot pepper in each jar and slowly pour the hot vinegar up to the brim. Cover, let cool to room temperature, and refrigerate.

INSTANT TOMATO RELISH

Makes 1 cup

2 tomatoes, finely chopped
½ medium onion, finely chopped
½ medium green pepper, seeded and finely chopped
¼ cup cider vinegar
1 teaspoon sugar
Salt and pepper to taste
2 tablespoons chopped fresh basil leaves, optional

Combine all the ingredients; chill and drain before serving with sandwiches or burgers. If you have a food processor, use it to chop the first 3 ingredients together.

FOUR-HOUR GARDEN RELISH

Makes 2 cups

2 cups sliced radishes
½ cup sliced scallions
½ cup white distilled vinegar
2 tablespoons water
2 teaspoons soy sauce
2 teaspoons sugar
½ teaspoon Tabasco sauce
½ teaspoon salt

Place radishes and scallions in a small crock or attractive jar. Combine the remaining ingredients, blending them to dissolve the sugar and salt; pour the liquid over the vegetables and let marinate in the refrigerator for 4 hours or more before serving. Stir the relish now and then as it marinates.

Chapter 5:

DAIRY PRODUCTS

Sections:

☐ Dairy Products
☐ Five Easy Cheeses

EGG SUBSTITUTE

Makes the equivalent of 2 eggs

Use this low-cholesterol egg substitute in cooking and baking. You can halve these ingredients if your recipe calls for only one egg.

2½ tablespoons nonfat dry milk
2 teaspoons corn or sunflower seed oil
4 egg whites at room temperature

Stir together the milk and oil in a small mixing bowl. Add one of the egg whites (do not beat it) and gently stir to combine it with the other ingredients; add the remaining 3 egg whites and stir to form a smooth paste. Use in place of 2 eggs in any recipe.

USE FOR YOLKS

Turn to page 209 in *Make Your Own Groceries* for an array of recipes which depend on many yolks.

WHIPPED BUTTER

Makes 1½ cups

Stretch 1 cup of butter into an easy-to-spread, 1½ cups while you save over commercial whipped butter.

2 sticks (or half of a 1-pound block) salted or unsalted butter (not margarine)
1 tray of ice cubes

Let the butter soften completely to room temperature. Place the softened butter in the top part of a metal double boiler; use an electric mixer to beat the butter smooth; lacking a double boiler, you can put the butter in either a stainless steel bowl or an aluminum pan. Fill the bottom part of the double boiler with the ice cubes and enough cold water to almost surround the top part of the double boiler; if using a metal bowl or pan, set it in a large bowl filled with the ice water. Use an electric mixer to beat the butter while it is surrounded by the ice water; beat at high speed, scraping down the sides, until it begins to look like cake frosting. Continue beating and scraping until the butter begins to stiffen and get whiter. When the butter begins to resist beating and starts to form lumps and sticks to the inside of the beaters, stop. Use a rubber spatula to scrape the whipped butter into a small crock or attractive container. Cover and refrigerate immediately. Let the whipped butter chill and firm for several hours before using.

FLAVORED BUTTERS

Makes ½ cup or 8 tablespoons, each

Have several of these butters on hand for a wide range of uses. You can also double the recipe ingredients, pack the flavored butter into an attractive, ceramic crock and give it as a dinner party gift.

Directions: Combine 1 stick (8 tablespoons) of softened butter with your choice of the ingredients that follow. Blend thoroughly and refrigerate until ready to use. Let the flavored butter soften slightly before serving.

CHIVE BUTTER

Add 4 tablespoons snipped chives and 1 teaspoon strained fresh lemon juice. Use on fish, poultry, and potatoes.

CHILI BUTTER

Add 1 teaspoon chili powder, ¼ teaspoon garlic salt, and a pinch of ground cumin. Use on crusty French bread, corn, and popcorn.

CURRY BUTTER

Add 1 teaspoon curry powder and 1 teaspoon strained fresh lemon juice. Use on poultry, lamb, green vegetables, and rice.

DILL BUTTER

Add 2 tablespoons snipped fresh dillweed and 1 teaspoon strained fresh lemon juice. Use on seafood, lamb, potatoes, rice, and spinach.

HONEY-ORANGE BUTTER

Add 2 tablespoons honey, 1½ teaspoons grated fresh orange peel, ½ teaspoon strained fresh orange juice, and ¼ teaspoon ground cardamon. Use on sweet potatoes, acorn squash, carrots, raisin bread, or any other fruit bread.

HORSERADISH BUTTER

Add 3 tablespoons horseradish and 1 teaspoon strained fresh lemon juice. Use on roast beef and corned beef sandwiches.

LEMON BUTTER

Add 1 tablespoon strained fresh lemon juice and ¼ teaspoon grated fresh lemon peel. Use on seafood, poultry, green vegetables, and potatoes.

MUSHROOM BUTTER

Add 3 tablespoons duxelles from page 000 and 1 teaspoon strained fresh lemon juice. Use on green vegetables, roasts, and poultry.

MUSTARD BUTTER

Add 2 tablespoons prepared Dijon-style mustard. Use on ham or beef sandwiches and spinach.

PAPRIKA BUTTER

Add 1 teaspoon paprika and ¼ to ½ teaspoon dry white wine or strained fresh lemon juice. Use on poultry and potatoes.

PARSLEY BUTTER

Add 3 tablespoons finely minced fresh parsley; a dash of Tabasco sauce; and 1 teaspoon strained fresh lemon juice. Use on poultry, seafood, green vegetables, and potatoes.

ROQUEFORT BUTTER

Add ¼ to ½ cup crumbled Roquefort cheese and 1 teaspoon Worcestershire sauce. Use on baked potatoes and crusty French bread.

YOGURT DRINKS

Any of the following methods for making yogurt drinks costs lots less than buying the ready-made, supermarket variety, while the yogurt drink you make yourself is better than or at least the same as its commercial counterpart.

FRESH FRUIT METHOD:

⅓ to ½ cup milk
⅓ cup peeled, coarsely diced, fresh fruit
1 cup plain yogurt
2 teaspoons sugar or honey

Combine all the ingredients in a blender container in the order listed; whirl until the fruit is puréed. Some fruit suggestions are: strawberries, blueberries, peaches, apricots, pitted cherries, banana slices, or whatever combination strikes your fancy. Makes about 1¾ cups.

PRESERVES METHOD:

½ cup milk
4 level tablespoons any fruit preserve
1 cup plain yogurt

Combine all the ingredients in a blender container in the order listed; whirl until the preserves are free of lumps. Makes 1⅔ cups.

COMMERCIAL METHOD:

½ **cup milk**
1 **container (1 cup) any flavor, commercial
   yogurt**

Combine the ingredients in a blender; whirl until smooth. Makes 1½ cups.

COEUR À LA CRÈME

Makes 9 servings, ⅓ cup each

The French have long served this unflavored, heart-shaped, dessert cheese. It was once made by placing clabbered milk in a heart-shaped, straw or wicker basket mold and allowing the whey to drain out so as to form a creamy cheese that was then unmolded, sprinkled with sugar, and served with either heavy cream or crème fraîche.

Coeur à la Crème is now made from a combination of ready-made, creamy cheeses which are packed into a heart-shaped, perforated, ceramic mold, and left to drain overnight. The unmolded cheese is usually garnished with whole, sweetened strawberries or else fruit sauce or preserves. Lacking a Coeur à la Crème mold, you can either use a clean, small, (3- or 4-cup capacity) shallow, non-laquered bread basket; or else you can make a mold by hammering sizeable nail holes into the bottom, business-side of a 9-inch cake pan; large nails like mortar or flooring nails work well but smaller nails are fine if they are spaced more frequently. You can also use a disposable, aluminum cake pan with similar puncture holes. If you don't mind performing a more delicate unmolding, you can also use a shallow colander.

CHEESECLOTH

8 **ounces cream cheese (1 cup), at room
   temperature**
1 **cup cottage cheese**
½ **cup sour cream**
A well-chilled mixing bowl
½ **cup heavy whipping cream**

Dampen the cheesecloth and line whatever mold you are using with it; let the cheesecloth edges overlap the rim of the mold. Combine the cream cheese, cottage cheese, and sour cream in a large mixing bowl. Use an electric mixer to beat these ingredients until they are smoothly blended; set the bowl aside.

Clean and dry the mixer beaters; pour the heavy cream into the chilled mixing bowl and beat at medium speed until the cream is whipped and can hold soft peaks; do not overbeat it into stiff peaks. Use a rubber spatula to gently but thoroughly fold the whipped cream into the cheese mixture. Spoon this combined mixture into the mold; pack it in firmly so that there are no air pockets. Fold the overlapping cheesecloth onto the top of the mixture in the mold. Place a cake rack on a deep plate; place the mold atop the cake rack so that it can drain; cover the whole arrangement with plastic wrap and refrigerate overnight.

When ready to serve, remove the plastic wrap; open up the cheesecloth and, very carefully, invert the mold onto the center of a chilled platter. Carefully, peel off the cheesecloth. Garnish as described above. *Make Your Own Groceries* has a recipe for Crème Fraîche on page 135 and Fresh Fruit Sauce recipes on page 210.

INSTANT CRÈME FRAÎCHE

Makes 2 cups

Crème fraîche is a rich, less tart version of sour cream which is usually dolloped on top of fresh fruits and berries. The traditional French version of crème fraîche is a dairy product that is incubated much like yogurt, but this similar-tasting version is simply a blend of ready-made ingredients.

½ **cup heavy whipping cream**
½ **cup sour cream**
½ **cup plain yogurt**

In a chilled bowl, whip the heavy cream only until it is thickened and droopy, soft mounds can be formed; do not whip it to the point of holding soft peaks. In a storage bowl or container, stir the sour cream until smooth; drain off any liquid from the yogurt and stir it into the sour cream. Thoroughly blend the whipped cream into this mixture. Cover and refrigerate for 24 hours. Stir before using. Use over fruits or as a salad dressing base or in any recipe calling for traditional crème fraîche.

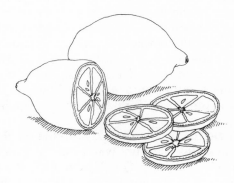

PASHKA

Makes 10 to 12 servings

Pashka, a homemade, fruited, lightly sweetened cheese is a traditional Russian Easter dessert. You can make one without having to make your own cheese by using the following no-cook method.

3 **egg yolks, at room temperature**
⅔ **cup sugar**
1 **cup heavy whipping cream**
2 **teaspoons vanilla extract**
½ **teaspoon almond extract**
1 **package (8 ounces) cream cheese, at room**

temperature
8 **tablespoons (1 stick) sweet (unsalted) butter (not margarine) at room temperature**
2 **containers (12 ounces each) pot cheese, at room temperature**
1 **cup chopped, mixed, candied fruits, including citron**
½ **cup slivered almonds, well broken**
¼ **cup light raisins**
1 **teaspoon freshly grated lemon peel**
1 **teaspoon freshly grated orange peel**
Cheesecloth
1 **clean dry clay flower pot, 6 inches deep and 6 inches across at the rim with a drainage hole at the bottom**

Begin by making a custard: In a medium bowl, use an electric mixer to beat the egg yolks and sugar together until fluffy and light. Pour the cream into a medium-size saucepan; heat slowly to boiling. Gradually pour the hot cream into the yolk mixture, beating constantly as you do this. Pour the mixture back into the saucepan and cook over medium heat, still stirring constantly, until the mixture becomes thickened enough to coat a tablespoon. Remove from heat, stir in the vanilla and almond extracts, and allow the custard to cool; be sure to stir it now and then to prevent a skin from forming on top.

Beat the softened cream cheese and butter together in a large mixing bowl; set aside. Press the pot cheese through a sieve or a food mill so that it is free of lumps. Stir the smoothed pot cheese into the cream cheese-butter mixture and beat until smooth and blended. Stir in the cooled custard, followed by ¾ cup of the candied fruits, and all of the almonds, raisins, and lemon and orange peel.

Line the flower pot with a dampened double layer of cheesecloth; leave 4 inches of cheesecloth overhanging the rim. Spoon the cheese mixture into the pot, then fold the extra cheesecloth atop to form a cover. You now need a flat plate or saucer or a bowl or saucepan whose bottom will just fit inside the flower pot rim to press against the cheese mixture without allowing any to escape. Place the plate directly on top of the cheesecloth, then place a heavy weight atop; the weight might be a brick or a tower of heavy cans or books or a 5-pound canister of sugar or flour. Once weighted, set the flower pot arrangement on a rack that has been set over a shallow pan. Place the whole arrangement in the refrigerator for 24 hours so that any excess liquid can drain out through the pot's drainhole.

When the pashka is firm, unmold it: Unwrap the cheesecloth from the top, then invert the flower pot onto a serving plate; gently loosen the pot from the cheesecloth, then slowly peel off the cheesecloth. Press the remaining ¼ cup of candied fruits into the pashka in an attractive border decoration. Serve with fresh strawberries or with a fruit sauce atop each serving, or spread the pashka on crisp vanilla or lemon cookies, then top each cookie with a strawberry half.

EASY PASHKA

Makes 6 servings

This softer version of pashka is not quite as impressive as the previous recipe but it's easily assembled, quickly set, and the flavor is very close to the real thing. It makes a nice, shared dessert.

⅔ **cup sugar**
½ **cup cold water**
1 **envelope (1 tablespoon) unflavored gelatin**
1 **cup heavy whipping cream**
1½ **cups sour cream, at room temperature**
½ **teaspoon vanilla extract**
¼ **teaspoon almond extract**

Combine the sugar and water in a small saucepan; sprinkle the gelatin atop and let it soak for 5 minutes without stirring. Stir well and bring to a full, rapid boil, stirring constantly; remove from heat. Mix in the heavy cream and set aside. In a medium-size bowl, stir the sour cream until it is smooth; add the extracts. In a thin stream, gradually stir the hot sugar and cream mixture into the sour cream; beat continuously until smooth. Pour this mixture into a 4-cup bowl or mold; cover and refrigerate for 6 hours or overnight.

To unmold the pashka, quickly dip the bowl up to its rim in a sinkful of hot water only just until the edges begin to liquefy. Quickly dry the bowl's outside, then invert the bowl onto a serving dish. The pashka will slowly slip out; if it doesn't, return the bowl to the hot water for a few more seconds. If the unmolded surface has become mushy, refrigerate until firm. Serve this pashka as a dip for fresh hulled strawberries or spread on plain vanilla or lemon cookies, then top each cookie with a strawberry half or sugared blueberries.

EASY CREAM CHEESE

Makes 1 pound or 2 cups

This surprisingly easy to make cheese costs half the price of commercial cream cheese and contains half the calories.

2 **quarts whole milk, at room temperature**
2 **cups cultured buttermilk, at room
     temperature**
A candy or deep-fat thermometer
Cheesecloth
½ **teaspoon salt**

Combine the milk and buttermilk in a heavy cooking pot; attach the thermometer. Heat over medium-low heat, stirring frequently, until the thermometer reads 170°; at that point, reduce the heat enough to maintain a temperature of 170° to 175°; do not let the milk get any hotter than this. Maintain this temperature for 30 to 60 minutes, or until the mixture separates into thick, lumpy curds (which is the cheese) and yellowish whey.

While you wait for the curds to appear, line 2 colanders or strainers each with 4 layers of dampened cheesecloth; set 1 colander inside a bowl that allows for good drainage; set the other colander in your clean kitchen sink.

When the curds have completely separated out, immediately spoon them into the colander that was set inside the bowl; use a slotted spoon to do this and spoon lightly: the more delicately you lay the curds into the colander, the lighter your cheese will be in texture. When you can no longer gather any more curds with the slotted spoon, go to the colander that was set in your sink and gradually pour in all the remaining curds and whey. Allow both colanders to drain at room temperature for 2 or 3 hours; drain the bowl of whey now and then.

Place the 2 lumps of drained cheese in a blender or food processor container, add the salt, then whirl or process until the cheese is smooth and velvety to your liking. Scrape the cream cheese into an attractive container, cover, and refrigerate for up to 1 week. Use just as you would commercial cream cheese; as a spread, in omelets, or pressed into celery ribs.

IN QUANTITY

If you prefer to make a lot of cream cheese, especially if you have no other uses for the extra 2 cups of buttermilk, double the recipe to make 4 cups. Use a large cooking pot and when you use the blender to smooth the cheese, do so only 2 cups at a time (a food processor will handle the full load). Pack the cream cheese into 1-cup containers and freeze for future use. To use, let the container of cheese thaw, then beat the cheese smooth with an electric mixer, blender, or food processor; do not re-freeze.

EASY COTTAGE CHEESE

Makes about ¾ pound

This is the farmhouse version of cottage cheese, sometimes called clabbered milk. It's fast and easy to make and it's lots tangier than the commercial cottage cheese you're probably used to. If it's too sour for your taste, make the more involved cottage cheeses in Chapter 12.

1 **quart whole milk**
1 **quart skim milk**
An oral fever thermometer
2 **tablespoons fresh cultured buttermilk, at
     room temperature**
Cheesecloth
½ **to 1 teaspoon salt**
Several tablespoons milk or cream

Pour the whole and skim milks into the top part of a non-aluminum double boiler (you may have to improvise one), then set the top part over hot water. Very gradually, warm the milk over medium-low heat until it reaches no higher than 72° to 82° on the thermometer. Remove the top part of the double boiler from the bottom and, if necessary, allow the milk to cool to 72°.

Stir in the buttermilk; cover and let the mixture stand in a warm place (anywhere from 72° to 80°) for 10 to 18 hours, or until a soft curd forms. Do not jiggle the container or disturb it at all during this clabbering period. The curd will have some whey on its surface and will look a bit like yogurt. If you don't see these signs after 10 hours, keep checking every 2 hours until you do.

Line a sieve or colander with enough dampened cheesecloth to overlap the edges; set it in your kitchen sink. Pour the clabbered mixture into the sieve and let the whey drain out for a few minutes. Stir the curd with a fork occasionally and lift the cloth to roll the cheese from side to side to help the draining.

When all the whey has drained out, discard the cheesecloth and put the cottage cheese in a plastic container. Stir in salt to taste, then moisten the cheese by stirring in several tablespoons of milk or cream. This cottage cheese will become firmer in texture after 24 hours in the refrigerator. Homemade cottage cheese contains no preservatives so it will keep no more than 1 week in your refrigerator. You can turn this particular cottage cheese into mock sour cream by whirling it smooth in a blender.

GREEK FETA CHEESE

Makes ¾ pound

This is an easily-made cheese, but you will need a candy thermometer and dessert-type rennet tablets. Rennet tablets for making custard are sold in most supermarkets under the brand name "Junket"; the small boxes are found next to the pudding and gelatin mixes.

2½ rennet tablets
1 tablespoon lukewarm, 90° water
1 package of cheesecloth

2 quarts whole milk, at room temperature
A candy or deep-fat thermometer
1 tablespoon salt
2 cups cold water

Crush the rennet tablets; put them in a small cup, then let them dissolve in the tablespoon of 90°, barely lukewarm water; you can gauge the water's temperature by remembering that your own body temperature is around 98°, so the water should feel neither warm nor cool to your fingers; set the rennet aside. Line a large sieve or colander with some dampened cheesecloth; set the lined sieve inside a bowl that allows for good drainage and set this arrangement aside. Unroll the remaining package of cheesecloth and cut 4 separate squares, each measuring about 6 to 10 inches. Dampen each square and set these aside for later.

Pour the room-temperature milk into a 3-quart enamel pot; stir in the dissolved rennet mixture and set a candy thermometer in place. Set the pot over medium-high heat and stir frequently for 8 to 10 minutes, or until the milk coagulates and separates into curds leaving a clear liquid whey. It is important that the milk's temperature never goes above 205°, so adjust the heat accordingly as you stir and wait for the curds to form.

Dip as much whey out of the cooking pot and into the cheesecloth-lined sieve as possible; let it drain completely through, then gently and gradually dip the curds into the sieve. Let the curds drain for about 5 minutes, or until they are just warm enough to handle. Use your hands to form the curds into 4 equal balls. Place each ball on 1 square of the pre-cut cheesecloth; wrap each up, dumpling style, so that the 4 cheesecloth corners meet, and twist the ends tightly to squeeze out any excess whey. Place the wrapped feta cheese balls on a cake rack and set them aside to cool completely. In the meantime, dissolve the tablespoon of salt in 2 cups of cold water and set aside.

When the feta cheese balls are cool, remove and discard the cheesecloth; place the feta balls in a ceramic or glass-covered casserole or mixing bowl and pour the salt solution atop. If the cheese balls are not completely covered by the salt solution, make enough salt solution to accomplish this. Cover the casserole and refrigerate the feta for 24 hours before serving. The feta balls will keep for about 3 weeks in your refrigerator if you change the salt solution every week. To serve, rinse the cheese ball under cold running water before slicing; return any unused portions or slices to the salt solution.

EASY SWEET CHEESE

Makes about 1½ pounds,
or 3 cups

Serve slices of this light-textured, somewhat sweet cheese for breakfast or with fruits for dessert.

A 4-cup mold, described below
Cheesecloth
2 quarts whole milk, at room temperature
5 large fresh eggs, at room temperature
2 cups cultured buttermilk, at room
**   temperature**
1 tablespoon sugar
½ teaspoon salt

Line your choice of cheese mold with a single layer of dampened cheesecloth; let the cheesecloth edges overlap the rim of the mold. Your mold can be a perforated, ceramic coeur à la crème heart or a clean 1-pound coffee can in which you have hammered 12 holes in the bottom and 4 vertical lines of 4 holes each up the rimmed sides at the noon, 3, 6, and 9 o'clock positions; use large nails, such as mortar or flooring nails. Another choice for a mold is a disposable aluminum pan—the 9-inch round, the 8-inch square, or the 9-by-5-inch loaf pan sizes will all work—in which you have punctured from 20 to 28 holes. Set the lined mold aside.

Slowly warm the milk in a large heavy pot; the milk should be warm but not hot: when you can dip your pinky finger into the milk and then slowly count to 10, the milk is at the proper temperature; if the milk becomes too hot for your finger to withstand, let the milk cool somewhat and re-test it.

In a mixing bowl, beat the eggs until fluffy then, just briefly, beat in the buttermilk, sugar, and salt. Very gradually, pour the egg mixture into the finger-tested, warm milk. Cover the pot with its lid and let the mixture stand on low heat for 2 minutes; stir now and then. Turn off the heat; remove the lid and wait for the mixture to separate out into curds and whey. As soon as the separation seems complete, use a slotted spoon to lightly place the curds in the cheesecloth-lined mold. Do this delicately and in small, gently placed amounts; the more delicately you lay the curds into the mold, the lighter your cheese will be in texture. When you can no longer gather any more curds with the slotted spoon, use a small strainer to complete the job.

Cover the mold and allow it to drain atop a rack-over-a-bowl arrangement for about 3 hours at room temperature (only 1 hour if room temperature is above 82°), then refrigerate the whole arrangement for another 8 hours, or until well chilled and completely drained. Unmold the cheese onto a dish, slice, and serve.

SOYBEAN CHEESE (TOFU)

Makes 1 pound or 2 cups

This homemade tofu is a little less dense than the commercial variety, but that is the only difference.

1 cup (½ pound) dry soybeans
Cold water
Clean unbleached muslin, at least 12-inches
**   square (or a non-terrycloth dish towel)**
2 tablespoons white distilled vinegar
Cheesecloth

Soak the soybeans either 12 hours or overnight in enough cold water to cover them. Drain and rinse the beans repeatedly until the rinse water becomes clear. Put 2 cups of cold water in a blender container followed by 1 cup of the soaked soybeans; whirl at high speed until the mixture becomes a smooth purée; pour the purée into a large mixing bowl. Repeat this puréeing process for the remaining 2 or 3 cups of beans, using 2 cups of cold water per cup of soaked soybeans; continue to pour the purée into the large mixing bowl.

When all the beans have been puréed, thoroughly dampen the muslin and line a large sieve or colander with it. Set the lined sieve over a large non-aluminum cooking pot. Pour a manageable amount of bean purée into the lined sieve; quickly gather up the four corners of muslin, dumpling-style, and twist the ends of the cloth together. Squeeze the muslin bundle to extract the soy milk. When you have squeezed the bean purée as dry as possible, discard the pulp and re-use the muslin to squeeze the next batch of bean purée.

When all the soy milk has been extracted from the bean purée, set the pot over low to medium-low heat and slowly bring it to a full boil; let it simmer gently for 1 minute, then remove from the heat. Stir in the vinegar with a non-aluminum spoon

and let the soy milk stand, undisturbed, for about 5 minutes, or until it curdles. While you are waiting for the soy milk to curdle, line your sieve or colander with several layers of dampened cheesecloth.

Pour the curds into the cheesecloth, gather the corners; twist the unfilled cheesecloth right up to the curds, then tie a string around the twisted cheesecloth to form a snug ball of cheese. Rinse the cheese ball in cold water, then hang it over a kitchen faucet arm or on a shish kebab skewer set over a deep pot so that it drains for 6 to 12 hours, or until it feels firm to the touch and has no excess liquid.

Remove the cheesecloth and place the tofu in a small mixing bowl; fill the bowl with enough water to cover the tofu and refrigerate. If you change the water every day, the tofu will keep for a week.

Chapter 6:

FROM THE DELICATESSEN

Section:

☐Luncheon Meats and Sausages
☐Delicatessen Specialties

GROUND BEEF SALAMI

Makes 3 pounds

This salami is easily made from ordinary ground beef, it's quite inexpensive, and it tastes exactly like commercial Thuringer-style salami. The salami keeps for 3 weeks in your refrigerator or can be frozen without any loss of taste or texture. The only special ingredient you will need is Morton's Curing Salt. The salt is sold in 2-pound, navy blue boxes and can be bought in some suburban and most rural supermarkets across the country; butchers who carry sausage casings usually have curing salt; you can also check the Yellow Pages under Butcher's Supplies or Feed Stores.

Instead of traditional casings, you will use 1¾ yards (36 inches wide) of white nylon netting or enough to make four rectangles, each roughly 14 by 18 inches. Get the strong, inexpensive kind with large holes. It is sold at fabric stores.

4½ pounds ground chuck, at room temperature
⅓ cup curing salt
1¾ teaspoons garlic powder
1½ teaspoons pepper
2 tablespoons Liquid Smoke
4 pieces nylon netting, each 14 by 18 inches
Strong string

Put the ground beef in your largest mixing bowl; the reason it should be at room temperature is so your fingers won't cramp from mixing the cold meat. Stir together the curing salt, garlic powder, and pepper in a measuring cup; measure the Liquid Smoke into a small container. Sprinkle a little of the salt mixture over the meat, then follow this by a little of the Liquid Smoke; use your hands to mix in the seasonings; repeat until all the seasonings have been thoroughly and evenly mixed in. Cover and refrigerate the mixture for 24 hours.

Remove the meat mixture from the bowl and cut it into 4 equal parts. Shape each part into a round

log about 9 inches long. Place each log on a piece of nylon netting; snugly roll up the log with the netting, leaving the 2 side ends open; tie the ends tightly with string so that you now have what looks like a meat-filled party favor. Place the wrapped logs, not touching, on a broiler pan or any rack-over-pan arrangement that will allow fat to drip out. Bake the salami logs at 225° for 4 hours.

Remove the netting from the salami logs while they are still hot, then allow them to cool. Wrap each salami individually, then refrigerate and/or freeze. Cut each log into slices and serve either plain or in sandwiches.

DUTCH LOAF

*Makes two 9-by-5-by-3-inch loaves,
each about 2½ pounds*

If you pack a lot of lunch boxes, this loaf will save you some money, count on 68 sandwich-size (⅛-inch thick) slices per loaf. You can freeze the second loaf for future use or turn it into the Pickle and Pimiento Loaf as described in the variation that follows.

3 pounds ground beef
2 pounds ground pork
1 cup soy flour (available at health food stores, sometimes called soya flour)
1 cup nonfat dry milk
2 tablespoons salt
1 tablespoon sugar
1 teaspoon pepper
½ teaspoon ground ginger

Ask your butcher to grind the beef and pork together twice through a meat grinder or do this with your own meat grinder using a fine blade; a food processor will also do the job, but be careful not to purée the meat. Place the combined ground meats in a large mixing bowl; sift together the remaining ingredients and gradually work this dry mixture into the meat; knead well, using your hands. Divide the loaf mixture between two 9-by-5-by-3-inch or similar size loaf pans. Press out the air pockets in each loaf; put a piece of plastic wrap on top of the meat and press firmly all around so that the meat becomes pressed and packed; remove the plastic wrap. Bake at 275° on the center oven rack for 2½ hours.

Just before the loaves are done, fill the kitchen sink with ice water; upon removal, set the loaf pans in the ice water for 20 to 30 minutes. Cover the cooled loaves and refrigerate. Remove both loaves from their pans to slice and serve; wrap the unmolded loaves for either refrigerator or freezer storage.

PICKLE AND PIMIENTO LOAF

Add to the uncooked loaf mixture: ½ cup drained pickle relish and a 4-ounce jar of drained, diced pimientos. Cut the relish and pimiento amounts by half if adding to just one loaf.

GROUND BEEF BREAKFAST SAUSAGE

Makes 1 pound, or 14 patties

These spicy, lean sausage patties are a nice change from fatty pork sausage. They complement both eggs and hash brown potatoes.

1 **pound lean ground beef**
2 **tablespoons grated onion**
2 **beef bouillon cubes, crushed**
½ **teaspoon allspice**
¼ **teaspoon marjoram**

¼ **teaspoon nutmeg**
⅛ **teaspoon cayenne pepper**
¼ **cup ice cold water**

Put the ground beef in a large mixing bowl; sprinkle the seasonings evenly atop followed by the ice cold water; mix well with your fingers. Shape the meat into a log about 7 inches long and wrap it in plastic wrap. Refrigerate overnight to use for tomorrow's breakfast.

Use a sharp knife to cut the sausage log into ½-inch slices. Sauté the slices in a non-stick skillet until nicely browned on both sides, then serve.

GROUND TURKEY BREAKFAST SAUSAGE

Makes 1 pound, serves 4

These breakfast sausage patties taste very much like their pork sausage cousins except that they cost less and contain practically no fat. One-pound chubs of ground turkey can be found in the frozen meats section of most supermarkets.

¼ **cup fine dry breadcrumbs**
1 **teaspoon salt**
¼ **teaspoon ground sage**
⅛ **teaspoon ground ginger**
1 **tablespoon fresh lemon juice**
½ **cup chicken broth**
A 1 pound chub of ground turkey, thawed

Combine the breadcrumbs, salt, sage, ginger, and lemon juice in a mixing bowl; stir in the chicken broth and allow the mixture to soak for 15 minutes. Mix in the ground turkey and form into patties about 2½ inches round and ¾-inch thick. Sauté the patties in a non-stick skillet until nicely browned on both sides, then serve.

MARINATED MUSHROOMS

Makes 1½ cups

¾ cup salad oil
¼ cup olive oil
½ cup strained fresh lemon juice
1 medium onion, very finely minced
3 whole bay leaves
1 tablespoon chopped fresh parsley (or 1
    teaspoon flakes)
1 teaspoon salt
¼ teaspoon pepper
3 small cans (4 ounces each) whole button
    mushrooms

Combine all the ingredients except the mushrooms in a 3- or 4-cup lidded plastic container; secure the lid and shake vigorously until the mixture looks creamy. Drain the mushrooms well and add them to the marinade. Cover and let stand at room temperature for 8 hours or in the refrigerator from 8 hours to 2 days.

When ready to serve, let the container reach room temperature, then roll each mushroom, individually, in paper towels to remove all excess oil. Serve with toothpicks as an appetizer or as part of an antipasto platter.

MARINATED EGGPLANT

Makes 3 cups

1 pound small eggplants
⅓ cup red wine vinegar
⅓ cup olive oil
3 medium garlic cloves, smashed and finely
    minced
½ teaspoon dried oregano, crushed
½ teaspoon dried basil, crushed
½ teaspoon salt
Pepper to taste

Do not peel the eggplants, but cut off and discard the bitter tips at each end; cut the eggplants into 1-inch cubes. Bring a large pot of water to a rolling boil; drop in the eggplants all at once, reduce the heat, and simmer, uncovered, for 5 to 10 minutes, or until the eggplant cubes are just tender but not mushy. Drain the cubes in a colander; rinse them well under cold running water; drain again in the colander, then pat dry with paper towels. Put the cubes in a mixing bowl.

Combine the remaining ingredients in a shaker jar; fasten the lid and shake until creamy and blended. Pour this marinade evenly over the eggplant; toss to coat well, then cover and marinate in the refrigerator for 1 to 3 hours. Using a slotted spoon, remove the cubes to a serving plate and serve as an appetizer or as part of an antipasto.

PICKLED HERRING IN WINE

Makes 2 to 3 cups

3 herring, fresh or frozen and thawed
1 medium onion, sliced thinly
1 cup dry white wine
1 cup white distilled vinegar
¾ cup sugar
3 bay leaves

Wash and fillet the herring; cut it into 1-inch pieces. In a large glass jar, arrange alternate layers of herring and onion slices. In a non-aluminum saucepan, combine the remaining ingredients; heat to boiling; let cool and pour over the fish. Cover the jar and refrigerate at least 3 days before serving.

PICKLED SALT HERRING

Makes about 4 cups

Salt herring is sometimes easier to come by than fresh.

12 to 14 salt herring
Cold water
1 large sweet onion, red or white
3 tablespoons mixed pickling spices
2 medium-size bay leaves, halved
White distilled vinegar
Sugar
Water

Soak the salt herring in a bowl of cold water for 4 hours; change the water and turn the fish over every hour; let fresh water dribble into the bowl constantly; drain well. Cut each herring down the backbone and cut it into 1- or 2-inch pieces. Slice the onion thinly. In a small ceramic crock or glass jar or ceramic casserole dish, arrange alternate layers of herring and onion slices, while sprinkling the spices and bay leaves throughout.

Mix a pickling liquid of 2½ parts water to 1 part vinegar; for each cup of vinegar you use, add 1½ tablespoons sugar. Stir the pickling liquid to dissolve the sugar, then pour it over the herring layers; make sure there's enough liquid to cover the fish plus at least ½ inch. Cover well and refrigerate for at least 3 days before gently stirring and serving.

PICKLED EGGS

Makes 1 dozen

12 hard boiled eggs
1 medium onion
1 cup white distilled vinegar
About 1 cup of juice from a can of beets
1 medium garlic clove, peeled and partially
   smashed
2½ teaspoons mixed pickling spices
1 medium bay leaf
½ teaspoon salt
Cold water

Peel the eggs. Cut the onion into thin slices; separate the slices into rings. Pack the eggs into a large glass jar with the onion rings scattered in between. Lacking a large glass jar, use several

widemouth mayonnaise jars or a large plastic container or a mixing bowl, but do not use a container made of aluminum.

Combine the remaining pickling ingredients in a mixing bowl; stir until the salt dissolves, then pour the pickling mixture over the eggs. Add enough cold water to cover the eggs; cover the jar securely and gently turn the jar upside down several times to blend in the water. Refrigerate, right side up, for 2 or 3 days, or until pickled to your liking.

CHICKEN PÂTÉ SPREAD

Makes 2 cups

⅔ cup peeled thinly sliced inner celery ribs
2½ tablespoons mayonnaise
2 tablespoons dry sherry
1 tablespoon finely minced fresh parsley
1 teaspoon strained fresh lemon juice
¼ teaspoon salt
⅛ teaspoon nutmeg
2 dashes pepper
2 cups well-diced cooked chicken, both white
   and dark meat
½ cup finely chopped almonds, toasted

In a small mixing bowl, combine the celery, mayonnaise, sherry, parsley, lemon juice, salt, nutmeg, and pepper; put half the mixture into a blender container. Whirl briefly, then gradually whirl in 1 cup of the chicken until you get a smooth spread. Scrape the spread onto a clean board and set it aside. Repeat the same procedure with the remaining mixing bowl ingredients and the other cup of chicken. If you have a food processor, you can accomplish all of the above in one motion.

Shape the spread into a ball, using hands wet with water. Roll the ball in the toasted almonds to cover. Cover the ball with plastic wrap and let it ripen in the refrigerator overnight. Let the pâté reach room temperature just before serving.

CREAMY LIVERWURST SPREAD

Makes 2 cups

1 chub (8 ounces) liverwurst or braunschweiger spread
1 cup sour cream
1 tablespoon prepared horseradish

Let all the ingredients reach room temperature to make mixing easier. Discard the casing from the liverwurst, cut the spread into chunks, and put them in a mixing bowl followed by the sour cream and horseradish. Use an electric mixer to beat the mixture into a creamy smooth spread. If you have a food processor, simply whirl all the ingredients until smooth. Do not use a blender to make the spread.

Mound the spread into an attractive shallow serving bowl and serve immediately with crackers and raw vegetable sticks. Refrigerated, the spread will keep for 1 week.

SMOKED SALMON SPREAD

Makes 1 cup

1 teaspoon strained fresh lemon juice
½ teaspoon fresh snipped dillweed (or ⅛ teaspoon dried)
1 package (3 ounces) sliced smoked salmon (lox)
2 small packages (3 ounces each) cream cheese, at room temperature

Put the lemon juice and dill in a blender container. Cut the salmon into small pieces; put them into the blender, then whirl to a smooth purée. With the blender still running, add big lumps of the softened cream cheese, one at a time, until they are all part of a creamy spread. If you have a food processor, you can accomplish this entire procedure in one motion.

Scrape the spread into a small attractive bowl, and either serve immediately with crackers or cover and refrigerate for future use.

BAGELS

Makes 1 dozen

2 envelopes active dry yeast
4 tablespoons sugar
2 cups lukewarm, 110° water
About 5⅔ cups flour
1 tablespoon salt
3 quarts water
Cornmeal
1 egg yolk
1 tablespoon cold water

Dissolve the yeast and 3 tablespoons of the sugar in the 110° water; let rest 10 minutes. In a mixing bowl, stir together 3 cups of the flour and the salt. Vigorously beat the softened yeast into the salty flour until smooth; gradually add enough remaining flour to make a stiff dough.

Knead the dough for 15 minutes, adding enough flour to get a firm stiff dough. Shape the dough into a ball; place it in a large, lightly greased bowl; cover loosely and let the dough rise in a warm place for about 40 minutes. Punch the dough down; lightly knead it again, then divide it into 12 equal balls. Holding a ball with both hands, poke your floured thumbs through the center; with one thumb in the hole, work around the perimeter to form a bagel, much like a doughnut, about 3 inches across. Place the bagels on a floured board, cover, and let rise 20 minutes; the dough will not double in bulk.

In a large shallow pan, bring the water and the remaining tablespoon of sugar to a gentle and steady boil; boiling is what makes the bagels chewy. Preheat oven to 400°. Lightly grease a rimmed baking sheet and sprinkle it with cornmeal. One at a time, gently drop 4 of the dough bagels into the boiling water; simmer the bagels, 4 at a time, for 6 minutes, turning often. Remove them with a slotted spatula and drain on paper towels to cool for 5 minutes. Place the boiled bagels on the baking sheet and bake for 10 minutes. Remove them from the oven and brush each bagel with a mixture of the yolk and cold water. Return the brushed bagels to the oven and bake 25 to 30 minutes longer, or until well browned. Cool on a rack.

PUMPERNICKEL BAGELS

Replace the initial 3 tablespoons sugar with 3 tablespoons dark molasses. Use 2 cups of rye flour, 2 cups of whole wheat flour, and 1⅔ cups all-purpose flour.

ONION BAGELS

Add ⅓ cup instant toasted onion to the flour along with the salt.

OTHER FLAVORS

Immediately after brushing the bagels with the egg mixture, sprinkle them with any of the following: coarse salt, sesame seeds, poppy seeds, caraway seeds, toasted instant minced onion.

GEFILTE FISH

Makes 4 to 6 servings

3 carrots, sliced into rounds
1½ cups coarsely chopped onions
1 tablespoon salt
2 peppercorns
6 cups water
1½ pounds pike fillets, fresh or frozen and thawed
2 eggs
2 tablespoons ice water
2 tablespoons matzo or cracker meal
½ teaspoon salt
Dash of pepper

Place half the carrots, half the onions, 1 tablespoon salt, the peppercorns, and 6 cups of water in a large pot; simmer, covered, for 30 minutes.

During this time, bone and skin the raw fish. Run the fish, along with the remaining carrots and onions, through a meat or food grinder several times; or whirl in a food processor. Place the ground fish and vegetables in a mixing bowl along with the remaining ingredients. Use an electric mixer on highest speed to beat this mixture until fluffy (don't use a food processor here). Shape the mixture into ovals, using about 3 to 4 tablespoons for each.

Uncover the simmering pot and return it to a gentle boil. One by one, drop the ovals into the pot; cover and simmer for 20 minutes. Remove the fish and carrots from the cooking water; place them on a dish; cover and chill. Serve the chilled gefilte fish on lettuce with the carrots sprinkled atop.

RICE PUDDING, GREEK STYLE

Makes 6 servings

1 quart whole milk, at room temperature
⅓ cup sugar
⅓ cup uncooked rice
½ teaspoon salt
½ cup cream, light or heavy
½ teaspoon vanilla extract
½ cup raisins
Cinnamon

In a heavy saucepan, gradually heat the milk to a simmer; stir in the sugar, rice, and salt; simmer, uncovered, for 45 minutes, stirring occasionally. Remove the saucepan from the heat; stir in the cream, vanilla, and raisins. Pour the pudding into 6 custard cups and allow them to cool at room temperature. Sprinkle lightly with cinnamon and serve.

Chapter 7:

SNACKS

Sections:

- Freezer-to-Oven Appetizers
- Crackers, Chips, and Snacks
- Nutritious Goodies

PASTRY FOR FREEZER-TO-OVEN APPETIZERS

Makes 1 recipe

Use this pastry recipe in the following three recipes. You can choose to make the basic pastry, below, or try your hand at the variation for puff pastry. While the puff pastry variation makes for extra-flaky appetizers, either pastry will work nicely.

The watchword for making any pastry is "work quickly." The faster you form and roll the dough, the cooler the butter will stay so that it remains separate between the dough and makes a flaky pastry.

2 cups sifted flour
1 teaspoon salt
12 tablespoons butter, well chilled
About 6 tablespoons ice water

Sift the flour and salt together into a chilled mixing bowl. Use your fingers to quickly cut in 6 tablespoons of the butter until the mixture looks like coarse meal. Quickly cut in the remaining butter until the mixture looks like small peas. Sprinkle 1 tablespoon of the ice water over the mixture; gently toss with a fork, then push the mixture to the sides of the bowl. One at a time, incorporate 4 or 5 more tablespoons of ice water into the mixture in the same manner until the mixture becomes moistened, but not sticky. Form the dough into a ball; roll the ball into a cylinder about 10 inches long; wrap and refrigerate for 1 hour or more before using.

PUFF PASTRY

Make the above pastry and refrigerate it for 1 hour. In the meantime, let 4 tablespoons of butter soften enough to be spreadable but still somewhat firm. On a floured surface, roll the chilled dough cylinder into an 8-by-21-inch rectangle, then cut in into 3 equal parts, each 8 by 7 inches. Leaving

a ½-inch margin on all sides, spread one of the thirds with 1 tablespoon of the butter. Stack the next third squarely atop the first; spread it with another tablespoon of the butter. Stack the last third on top; wrap and refrigerate the stack for 15 minutes.

Cut the stacked chilled dough lengthwise into 2 halves; stack one atop the other. Roll this dough stack into another 8-by-21-inch rectangle then cut it into equal (8-by-7-inch) thirds. Using the remaining 2 tablespoons of butter, butter and stack the thirds just as before; wrap and refrigerate for 1 hour.

Repeat the procedure described in the above paragraph (i.e.: halve, stack, roll, third, stack, and refrigerate) two more times with a 15-minute refrigeration period in between; omit the butter. End by, once more, cutting the dough lengthwise into 2 halves and stacking one atop the other. Wrap and refrigerate for 1 hour or overnight or until ready to use.

FREEZER-TO-OVEN CRESCENT ROLL-UPS

Makes 4 dozen 3-inch crescents

2 recipes Pastry or Puff Pastry from the
**   previous recipe**
Choice of filling, recipes follow
1 egg, optional
1 tablespoon cold water, optional

Makes 2 separate batches of Pastry or Puff pastry as directed and refrigerate when complete for 1 hour or longer. Cut each stacked batch into 3 equal parts so that you get 6 small stacks; wrap and refrigerate all but 1 stack. On a floured surface, roll the dough stack into a circle that will be 9 inches across after trimming off the ragged edges. Spread the dough circle with the specified amount of the filling of your choice leaving ½-inch margins around the circle's edges. Cut the circle into 8 equal slice-of-pie-shaped wedges. Beginning at the circle edge, roll 1 wedge loosely toward its point; form a crescent out of the rolled-up wedge by bending in the tips with the point face-down. Place the crescent on a wax-paper-lined cookie sheet. Roll up the remaining wedges in the same manner. If you want a golden glaze on the crescents, lightly beat together the egg and water, then brush over the crescents with a pastry brush.

Place the first batch of crescents, uncovered, in your refrigerator or freezer while you roll out and shape the remaining stacks of dough. For a flaky pastry, be sure to refrigerate or freeze each batch as soon as you make it. Place the cookie sheets of completed crescents in the freezer; when they are solidly frozen, transfer them to a plastic bag; label with cooking directions or this page number and return to the freezer.

Cooking Directions: Place frozen crescents, point-down, on an ungreased cookie sheet. Bake in a preheated 400° oven for 20 to 25 minutes, or until golden.

CHOICE OF FILLINGS

Each of the following fillings covers 6 dough circles and makes enough to fill four dozen crescents. If you want several filling flavors, divide the ingredient proportions accordingly.

LIVERWURST FILLING

Mash until blended: ½ pound high quality liverwurst and 2 teaspoons water or dry sherry. Use 2 tablespoons of this filling per 9-inch circle.

CHEDDAR CHEESE FILLING

Spread each circle with 1 teaspoon mayonnaise, then sprinkle it with 2 tablespoons shredded Cheddar cheese.

HAM, CHICKEN, OR BEEF FILLING

Use one 4½-ounce can of deviled ham and, if necessary, blend in a few drops of water to make a spreading consistency. Other flavors include a 4½-ounce can of chicken spread or corned beef spread or roast beef spread. Use 1 heaping tablespoon per 9-inch circle.

SHRIMP FILLING

Mix together ⅔ cup very finely chopped, small, cooked shrimp; a 3-ounce package of cream cheese; and celery salt or crushed celery seed to taste. Use 2½ tablespoons of filling per 9-inch circle.

FREEZER-TO-OVEN CHEESE TWISTS

Makes 5 dozen

2 recipes Pastry or Puff Pastry from the previous page
1 cup grated sharp Cheddar cheese
2 eggs, beaten
Choice of: caraway, poppy, or sesame seeds, or coarse salt

Make two separate batches of Pastry or Puff Pastry as directed and refrigerate. Yet again, roll batch number one into an 8-by-21-inch rectangle; cut that rectangle into 3 equal parts, each 8 by 7 inches. Leaving no margins, sprinkle 1 of the dough thirds with ¼ cup of the cheese. Stack the next dough third atop the first; apply some pressure to embed the cheese within. Sprinkle the top dough layer with ¼ cup of cheese; cover with the remaining dough third; press to embed. Cut the stacked dough lengthwise into 2 halves; stack one atop the other; wrap and refrigerate for 30 minutes. Repeat this procedure for the second batch of Pastry or Puff Pastry.

Turn 1 dough package onto a lightly floured surface, keep the other refrigerated until ready to use. Working fast, use a rolling pin to roll the dough package into a 4-by-15-inch strip. Brush the strip with the beaten egg; sprinkle with seeds or salt. Cut across the dough to make 4-by-½-inch strips. Holding each strip at the ends, twist in opposite directions to make a spiral; place on a wax-paper-lined cookie sheet. When the sheet is full, place it, uncovered, in the freezer. When the

101

twists are frozen, transfer them to a plastic freezer bag; label with cooking directions or this page number and return to the freezer.

Cooking Directions: Place frozen twists on a greased cookie sheet. Bake in a preheated 400° oven for 10 to 15 minutes, or until golden.

FREEZER-TO-OVEN CURRIED TURNOVERS

Makes about 2 dozen

½ pound ground lamb
1 medium onion, finely chopped
2 garlic cloves, smashed and finely minced
2 tablespoons curry powder
1 teaspoon salt
⅓ cup water
½ cup diced potato in ½-inch dice
1 recipe Pastry or Puff Pastry from page 100.
1 egg, beaten

Sauté the lamb in a small skillet or saucepan just until no pink remains; drain off all excess fat. Add the onion and garlic, stir and sauté until the onion is limp. Stir in the curry powder and salt, followed by the water and the diced potatoes. Cover and slowly simmer about 20 minutes, or until the potatoes are tender and the water has been absorbed; stir now and then, and adjust water if necessary. Let the filling cool completely.

On a lightly floured surface, roll the chilled pastry or puff pastry dough ⅛- to ⅟₁₆-inch thick. Cut it into circles 3 inches in diameter using a cookie cutter, a glass tumbler, or a clean tuna can which has been opened on both top and bottom. Place a rounded teaspoon of the cooled filling on the right half of each circle. Fold each circle of dough over itself and its filling to make a half circle. Moisten the inside edges with a little bit of water; flute the edges or press them with a fork to seal.

Place the turnovers slightly apart on ungreased cookie sheets; brush each turnover top with egg, then gently prick each one with a fork. Bake at 400° for about 20 minutes, or until lightly browned. Let the turnovers cool on their cookie sheets, then place the sheets, uncovered, in the freezer. When the turnovers are frozen, transfer

them to a plastic bag; label with the following cooking directions or this page number and return them to the freezer.

Cooking Directions: Preheat oven to 350°. Place the desired number of frozen turnovers slightly apart on an ungreased cookie sheet. Bake 15 to 25 minutes, or until hot throughout. Serve immediately.

PIZZA TURNOVERS

Make the following turnover filling: In a small saucepan, sauté 3 tablespoons finely chopped green pepper, 3 tablespoons finely chopped onion, and 1 small minced garlic clove in 1 tablespoon of olive oil. Blend in 5 tablespoons of tomato paste, 2 tablespoons of water, ½ teaspoon crushed oregano, and ¼ teaspoon salt, stirring until smooth. Cover and simmer gently for 10 minutes. Remove the pan from the heat and let it cool to lukewarm before stirring in ½ cup (about 2 ounces) shredded skim-milk mozzarella cheese.

On a lightly floured board, roll one recipe of chilled Pastry or Puff Pastry into circles and fill, fold, and seal as directed above. Place the turnovers on cookie sheets, brush with 1 beaten egg, and prick with a fork. Bake at 450° for 10 to 12 minutes then cool, freeze, and package as described. Follow the same cooking directions to heat the frozen turnovers.

FREEZER-TO-OVEN APPETIZER CRÊPES

Makes 3½ dozen

3 large eggs
1 cup whole milk
⅔ cup flour
About 5 tablespoons butter
Choice of filling, recipes follow
Toothpicks

Place eggs and milk in a blender or food processor container; whirl briefly to mix. Add the flour and whirl until the mixture is a smooth batter; set aside. Heat a 10-inch frying pan over medium heat (or set an electric frying pan at 350°); when hot, add ½ teaspoon of butter, swirling it around to coat the pan's bottom. Slowly pour 1 tablespoon of the batter into the frying pan; spread it into a 3½-inch circle either with a spatula or by tilting the pan around. When the surface looks dry, in about 30 seconds, turn the crêpe with a spatula and lightly brown the other side. Continue making crêpes, pouring in enough batter to make 4 crêpes at a time, adding ½ teaspoon of butter to the pan after each batch. Remove the crêpes from the pan; stack them on a plate; continue until you have used all the crêpe batter.

To make roll-up appetizers: Place about 1 heaping teaspoon of filling on the center of each crêpe; fold the right and left sides of the crêpe over the filling, then roll up and enclose the filling entirely; secure with a toothpick. When all the crêpes have been filled, place them on a cookie sheet; cover loosely with wax paper; freeze the sheet of crêpes until solid. Transfer the crêpes to a plastic freezer bag; label with cooking directions or this page number and return to freezer.

Cooking Directions: Preheat oven to 375°. Place the frozen crêpes, slightly apart and seam side down, in a shallow ungreased casserole that is at least 2 inches deep. Cover with foil and bake for 15 minutes; uncover and bake 5 minutes more, or until heated through. Remove all the toothpicks and serve warm on a platter.

SHRIMP FILLING

Beat until smooth: one 8-ounce package cream cheese; 12 ounces tiny, cooked shrimp, chopped; 1 tablespoon fresh lemon juice; a dash of Tabasco.

BACON AND MUSHROOM FILLING

Fry 8 slices of bacon until very crisp; drain the bacon on paper towels and pour off all but ¼ cup of the fat. Chop 1 medium onion and 1 pound of mushrooms; add them to the pan of hot bacon fat and sauté briefly. Cover the pan and let the contents cook over medium heat until limp; uncover and cook until mushroom juices have evaporated. In a small jar, shake together 2 tablespoons flour and ¼ cup dry sherry or dry vermouth; stir this into the mushrooms. Stir until thick and bubbly; remove from heat; add salt and pepper to taste. Let cool completely before using.

FREEZER-TO-OVEN CHINESE SHRIMP TOAST

Makes about 32 triangles

½ **pound raw shrimp, thawed if frozen, shelled and deveined if fresh**
⅓ **cup finely minced water chestnuts**
1 **tablespoon finely minced onion**
1 **egg white**
2 **teaspoons dry sherry**
2 **teaspoons cornstarch**
½ **teaspoon salt**
Several dashes of white pepper
Dash of ground ginger
About 8 slices white home-style bread, such as Pepperidge Farm Sandwich Bread
Oil for frying

Using your sharpest knife, mince the shrimp as finely as possible; if you are using a food processor to mince, be really careful not to overprocess the shrimp into mush. Combine shrimp, water chestnuts, and onion and set aside. In a mixing bowl, use a wire whisk to beat the egg white until it is foamy but not stiff. In a small bowl, blend the sherry, cornstarch, salt, pepper, and ginger until smooth; pour this mixture into the foamy egg white and stir to blend. Add the minced shrimp, water chestnuts, and onion to the bowl of ingredients and mix well to coat uniformly.

Remove the crusts from the bread. Evenly spread about 2 tablespoons of the shrimp mixture atop each slice; press the mixture into the bread with the bottom of a spoon. Pour enough oil in a frying pan to reach a depth of 1 to 2 inches; heat the oil over medium-high heat until hot but not smoking. Fry several slices at a time, shrimp side down, until golden brown, then turn the slices over and continue frying until the bread is golden and the shrimp mixture is well set. Drain the slices on paper towels; repeat for all the slices.

Let the fried shrimp toasts cool to room temperature, then place them in 1 layer on cookie sheets; place the cookie sheets, uncovered, in your freezer overnight, then stack and store the frozen toasts in plastic bread bags. Seal, label with page numbers 103 to 104 or the following cooking directions, and return them to the freezer.

Cooking Directions: Preheat oven to 350°. Place the frozen slices directly on the middle oven rack and bake for 10 to 20 minutes, or until hot and crisp. Cut an "X" in each slice to make 4 triangles and serve hot.

CRABMEAT TOASTS

Replace the shrimp with ½ pound fresh, canned, or frozen-and-thawed crabmeat; the crabmeat should be shredded and well drained; the water chestnuts are optional. Replace the ginger with a dash or two of cayenne pepper; omit the white pepper.

FREEZER-TO-OVEN TUNA HORS D'OEUVRES

Makes almost 7 dozen

1 can (7 ounces) tuna or salmon, drained and well flaked
1 small package (3 ounces) cream cheese, at room temperature
2 tablespoons minced fresh dillweed (or 2 teaspoons dried)
Pepper to taste
16 slices fresh spongy supermarket-type bread
6 tablespoons butter, at room temperature

Mix together the tuna, cream cheese, dillweed, and pepper until smooth and well blended. Trim the crusts off the bread. Place a slice of bread on your work surface; cover it with a damp, nonterrycloth towel; use a rolling pin to roll the slice out flat. Remove the towel; spread the flattened slice with about a teaspoon of butter, then spread the butter with a rounded tablespoon of the tuna mixture. Roll the slice up tightly, jelly-roll fashion; wrap it in foil; label along with cooking directions or this page number and freeze. Repeat this procedure for all the slices of bread.

Cooking Directions: Unwrap the frozen rolls, figuring on 5 appetizers per roll. Cut each roll into ½-inch slices; arrange the slices, cut side up, on a generously buttered cookie sheet. Bake in a preheated 450° oven for 10 minutes, or until hot and toasted.

FREEZER-TO-OVEN PUFF BALLS

Makes 3 dozen

8 tablespoons (1 stick) butter, cut in chunks
¼ teaspoon salt
1 cup water
1 cup flour
4 eggs, at room temperature
1 cup shredded Swiss or extra-sharp Cheddar cheese
1 teaspoon dry mustard
2 dashes Tabasco Sauce

Combine the butter, salt, and water in a 2- or 3-quart cooking pot. Stir over medium-high heat to melt the butter, then let the mixture come to a boil. In one quick motion, remove the pot from the heat, immediately dump in the flour, and proceed to beat the mixture energetically with a wire whisk until it is just smooth; don't beat past the point where the batter becomes smooth. One at a time, add the eggs, beating well after each addition so that, finally, the mixture looks smooth and satiny. Beat in the remaining ingredients.

Use a teaspoon to drop 1½-inch balls of batter about an inch apart onto greased cookie sheets. Bake in a preheated 350° oven for 20 to 30 minutes, or until puffed and golden, but do not remove the puffs from the oven; instead, turn off the oven heat, use a toothpick (or something with a sharp slender point) to prick each puff ball in 4 places, then close the oven door and allow the puff balls to dry for 15 minutes.

Let the completed puff balls cool; freeze them, uncovered and in a single layer, on a cookie sheet until solid; pack them into plastic bags; seal and label along with this page number or the following cooking directions; return to the freezer.

Cooking Directions: Preheat oven to 350°. Place the desired amount of puff balls, slightly apart, on a cookie sheet; bake for about 5 minutes, or until warm throughout.

WHOLE GRAIN PUFF BALLS

Replace the flour with ⅔ cup whole wheat pastry flour mixed with ⅓ cup all-purpose flour.

Section: CRACKERS, CHIPS, AND SNACKS

SWEDISH CRISPBREAD CRACKERS

Makes about 6 dozen

¼ cup lukewarm, 110° water
1 envelope active dry yeast
8 tablespoons butter or vegetable shortening
¾ cup milk
1 teaspoon sugar
½ teaspoon salt
1 cup rye flour
About 2 cups all-purpose flour

Pour the lukewarm water into a large mixing bowl; sprinkle on the yeast and stir to dissolve; let stand for 5 minutes. In a small pan, combine the butter, ½ cup of the milk, the sugar, and the salt; heat to melt and dissolve. Remove the pan from the heat, stir in the remaining ¼ cup of milk, then let this mixture cool to a lukewarm 110°. Stir the pan of 110° liquid into the bowl of yeast. Beat in the rye flour until smooth, then stir in enough of the remaining flour to make a medium-stiff dough. Knead the dough for 10 minutes; let it rise in a warm place for 30 minutes; punch the dough down and knead it again for another 10 minutes.

Divide the dough into 2 equal balls; roll 1 ball as thinly as you possibly can on a floured cookie sheet or upside-down baking pan. Cut the dough into 3-by-4-inch rectangles, using a pizza cutter or a ravioli wheel or a sharp greased knife; do not separate the dough after cutting. Cover loosely with plastic wrap and let rise for 30 more minutes. Repeat with the remaining dough ball. Prick the risen crackers with a fork and bake at 350° for 15 to 20 minutes, or until lightly browned; when cool, break the crackers off along the cut lines.

CARAWAY CHEESE TWISTS

Makes 4 dozen

1½ cups flour
½ cup grated Swiss cheese

1 tablespoon caraway seeds, slightly crushed
¼ teaspoon salt
5 tablespoons cold butter
3 tablespoons vegetable shortening, chilled
About 3 tablespoons ice water
1 egg, lightly beaten
2 tablespoons coarse or kosher salt

In a mixing bowl, combine flour, cheese, caraway seeds, and the ¼ teaspoon salt. Cut the butter into ½-inch chunks; quickly use your fingers to incorporate the chunks into the flour mixture. Still working fast, cut in the shortening. Sprinkle 3 tablespoons of the ice water over the mixture; toss well with a fork or your fingers until the dough is moist enough to form a ball. If the dough crumbles, add more ice water, only 1 or 2 drops at a time; the dough should not be sticky. Divide the dough into 2 balls; wrap and refrigerate them for 1 hour.

Remove 1 dough ball from the refrigerator and roll it out, on a lightly floured surface, into a 12-inch square. Using a greased sharp knife or a pizza cutter or a ravioli wheel, cut the square in half, vertically, then cut across, horizontally, to make a series of strips that are 6 inches long by ½ inch wide. Brush the strips with half of the beaten egg, then evenly sprinkle the surface with 1 tablespoon of the coarse salt. Take the 2 upper-left-hand strips and match them together on their unsalted sides so as to form a double strip with salted sides out. Use your left hand to pinch 2 of the strips together at one end; use your right hand to wind the double strip into a long, loose spiral. Place the spiral on an ungreased cookie sheet and repeat doubling-up and twisting the remaining strips. Bake for 8 to 10 minutes or until golden at 375°. While the first batch bakes, repeat the same procedure with the remaining dough ball. Store in a covered jar.

SALT STICKS

Makes 16

1 cup coarsely crushed cornflakes
1 tablespoon poppy or sesame seeds
2 teaspoons coarse or kosher salt or 1 teaspoon regular salt
2 cups flour
1 teaspoon baking soda
½ teaspoon salt
6 tablespoons vegetable shortening
¼ cup cider vinegar or white distilled vinegar
½ cup plus several tablespoons whole milk

Uniformly combine the crushed cornflakes, coarse salt, and poppy seeds; spread the mixture over a piece of wax paper and set aside. Generously grease a cookie sheet; set it aside. Blend the flour, baking soda, and salt in a mixing bowl; thoroughly cut in half the shortening, then cut in the rest. Add the vinegar and ½ cup of the milk; stir until the mixture is moistened throughout. Form the dough into a ball and knead it on a floured surface until it is smooth and satiny.

Divide the dough into 4 equal balls, then divide each ball into 4 equal pieces so that there are 16 pieces in all. Roll each piece into a stick about 6 inches long. Brush a dough stick with some of the remaining milk, then roll it over the cornflake mixture to coat and embed the crumbs into the dough. Place the stick on the greased cookie sheet. Repeat this coating procedure with the remaining dough sticks. Bake at 450° for about 15 minutes, or until golden.

SNACK STICKS

Makes 8 dozen 3-inch sticks

1½ cups lukewarm, 110° water
1 envelope active dry yeast
1 tablespoon sugar
5 to 5½ cups flour
About 6 tablespoons melted butter
Salt

Pour the water in a large mixing bowl; sprinkle the yeast atop, wait a few minutes, then stir to dissolve. Use an electric mixer on medium speed to beat in the sugar, then gradually beat in 3 cups of the flour. Continue beating until the mixture pulls away from the mixing bowl in long strands. With a strong spoon, vigorously beat in enough ½-cup measures of flour to make a soft dough. Knead the dough on a floured surface for about 10 minutes, or until smooth and blistered; knead in extra flour if the dough becomes sticky.

Form the dough into a ball, cut the ball into 8 equal pieces, then quarter each of those pieces to get 32 pieces of dough. Use your hands to roll the first piece of dough into a rope about 9 to 10 inches long; cut the rope into thirds and arrange them nearly 1 inch apart on greased cookie sheets. Repeat this procedure for all the dough pieces.

Let the dough sticks rise in a warm place for about 15 minutes, or until they appear somewhat puffy. Use a pastry brush to brush each dough stick with a little butter, then sprinkle lightly with salt. Bake at 400° for 15 minutes, or until golden. Cool before serving or packaging.

ONION OR GARLIC FLAVOR STICKS

Instead of sprinkling the unbaked sticks with plain salt, use onion or garlic salt.

WHEAT STICKS

Use 3 cups of all-purpose flour with 2 to 2½ cups of whole wheat flour.

WHOLE WHEAT CHEESE ROUNDS

Makes about 4 dozen

1 cup (about 4 ounces) grated sharp Cheddar cheese, at room temperature
7 tablespoons butter, at room temperature
1 cup whole wheat pastry flour (or ⅔ cup whole wheat flour plus ⅓ cup all-purpose flour)
Scant ¼ teaspoon salt
⅛ teaspoon cayenne pepper

Use your hands to uniformly blend all the ingredients. Lightly flour your hands and shape the mixture into a log about 1½ inches in diameter. Wrap the log in wax paper and chill it for several hours or overnight until firm; you can keep it in your refrigerator like this for up to a week.

Use a sharp or serrated knife to cut the log into thin slices between ⅛- and ¼-inch thick. Place the slices slightly apart on a lightly greased cookie sheet. Bake in a 375° oven for 8 to 10 minutes. Let cool. Store in a plastic bag.

FREEZER-TO-OVEN ROUNDS

Wrap the dough log in aluminum foil and freeze it. When unexpected guests arrive, simply unwrap, slice, and bake the frozen rounds just as previously directed; no need to defrost.

CARAWAY-RYE CHEESE ROUNDS

Replace the whole wheat pastry flour with ½ cup rye flour mixed with ½ cup all-purpose flour; prepare the dough log as directed, roll it in slightly crushed caraway seeds, pressing to embed the seeds in the dough, then wrap and refrigerate.

SODA CRACKERS

Makes about 2 dozen

2 cups flour
2 tablespoons sugar
½ teaspoon baking soda
½ teaspoon salt
4 tablespoons vegetable shortening
About 1 cup buttermilk
Kosher, sea, or table salt, optional

Sift together the flour, sugar, baking soda, and salt into a mixing bowl. Use a pastry blender or 2 dinner knives or your fingertips to quickly cut the shortening into the dry ingredients; work fast to get a coarse and crumbly mixture. Gradually pour in some of the buttermilk and toss lightly with a fork to moisten evenly. Still working quickly, continue tossing gradually, adding enough buttermilk

to just hold the mixture together; do not let the mixture become sticky. When the mixture is firm enough to handle, press it into a ball of dough.

Pinch off pieces of dough about 1½ inches round, and roll them out on a well-floured surface to circles somewhere between ⅛- and ¼-inch thick; turn and flour the circles as you roll to prevent sticking. Place the dough circles just slightly apart from each other on an ungreased cookie sheet. Sprinkle the circles with salt to taste and pat them to embed the salt. Prick each circle several times with fork tines. Bake at 400° for 3 or 4 minutes, or until slightly browned at the edges.

ONION CRACKERS

Replace the salt that is to be sifted with the flour with 1 teaspoon of onion salt or simply add ½ teaspoon onion powder to the existing ingredient list. When the dough circles are arranged on the cookie sheets, sprinkle with onion salt, pressing slightly to embed. Prick and bake as directed.

SESAME CRACKERS

When the dough circles are arranged on the cookie sheets, sprinkle them with a generous amount of untoasted sesame seeds along with some salt to taste, if desired; pat each circle to embed the seeds. Prick and bake as directed.

WHEAT CRACKERS

Use 1 cup all-purpose flour and 1 cup whole wheat flour; increase the shortening to 5 tablespoons.

RYE CRACKERS

Use 1 cup all-purpose flour and 1 cup rye flour. If you wish, add ½ teaspoon of caraway seeds to the dough mixture after cutting in the shortening.

FRESH POTATO STICKS

Makes 5 or 6 cups

4 large Idaho potatoes
Vegetable oil, peanut oil, or vegetable
    shortening for frying
About 1 teaspoon salt

Wash and peel the potatoes; drop them into enough cold water to cover. Cut the potatoes into julienne strips either with a food processor or manually. To manually cut into strips, use a very sharp knife, the slicing slot of a hand grater, or a cabbage shredder/slicer; cut the potatoes into slices ⅛-inch thick. Stack a few of the potato slices at a time and cut them into strips about ⅛-inch thick; drop the strips into a large bowl of cold water, and continue cutting until all the potatoes are in strips and in the bowl of cold water.

Pour the potatoes into a colander; rinse them well under cold running water; allow them to drain, then pat dry between several thicknesses of paper towels.

Oven-Baked Method: Preheat oven to 450°. Very generously, grease 2 or more rimmed baking sheets with vegetable shortening; use enough to make a thick white film over each sheet about ⅛-inch deep; sprinkle lightly with salt to prevent sputtering. Spread the potato strips over the sheets, touching, but in 1 layer; brush the tops of the strips with oil. Bake for 2 to 8 minutes, or until golden and crisp. Drain on paper towels; adjust salt to taste.

Saucepan Method: Pour equal amounts of oil and vegetable shortening into a large heavy saucepan to a depth of 3 inches; heat to 360° to 375° on a deep-frying thermometer. Fry the potato strips, a handful at a time, until they are golden and crisp; stir the strips after the sputtering subsides to prevent sticking. Drain on paper towels, adjust salt to taste, and repeat with the remaining strips.

Electric Frying Pan Method: This is the same as the Saucepan Method, above, but do it in an electric frying pan which will maintain the proper frying temperature without a thermometer.

Deep-Fry Method: Heat oil in a deep fryer to 360° to 375°. Place a big handful of strips in the basket and lower it into the hot oil; stand back and lift the basket out as soon as the oil bubbles up. Lower the basket again and repeat removing and lowering back in until the bubbling subsides; then lower the basket and stir the strips with a long spoon to prevent sticking. Fry until crisp and golden brown. Drain on paper towels; salt to taste; repeat with the remaining strips.

FLAVORED POTATO STICKS

After baking or frying the potato sticks, pour them immediately into a paper bag along with salt and your choice of: barbecue seasoning, chili powder, or garlic or onion powder. Shake the bag to coat, then drain the sticks on paper towels.

TORTILLA CHIPS

Makes about 8 to 10 cups

1 package of 12 corn tortillas, defrosted if
    frozen
Vegetable oil and shortening for frying
Salt

Arrange the tortillas in a stack. Cut the stack, much as you would cut a pie, into triangular wedges making 6 equal wedge-shaped stacks; if your knife isn't sharp enough, cut 2 tortillas at a time with scissors. Pour equal amounts of oil and shortening into a heavy skillet to a depth of ½ to 1 inch; heat over medium-high heat. When the oil is hot enough to make 1 tortilla triangle sizzle, add the tortilla triangles, a stack at a time. Stir them with a slotted spoon to separate them as they fry; cook until they are crisp, about 1 to 2 minutes. Drain the chips on paper towels; sprinkle with salt to taste, then repeat with the remaining stacks. Tightly covered, the tortilla chips keep well at room temperature for 2 or 3 weeks.

NACHO CHEESE CHIPS

Immediately after removing the tortilla chips from the fat, put them in a paper bag along with a few teaspoons of commercial, powdered cheese sauce mix and chili powder to taste; shake the bag

109

to coat the chips; adjust salt to taste and shake again, then drain the flavored chips on paper towels.

BARBECUE TORTILLA CHIPS

Use the same paper bag method as described above, shaking in only barbecue seasoning to taste.

PLANTAIN CHIPS

Makes 2 or 3 cups

1 large green plantain banana
4 cups cold water
2 tablespoons salt
Vegetable oil for frying

Cut the tips off the plantain and discard them; cut the plantain into 2 round halves. Much like skinning an orange, cut 4 even, lengthwise slits through the skin of each half; then, beginning at the corner edge of 1 slit, pull the skin away, diagonally rather than lengthwise. Repeat with the remaining slits until the plantain is all peeled. Cut the plantain into diagonal slices about ¾-inch thick; place the slices in a mixing bowl along with the water and the salt; stir to dissolve the salt; let stand at room temperature for 1 hour.

Take the plantain slices out of the salt water and pat dry on paper towels; save the salt water. Heat oil to 300° in a deep fryer or at a 3-inch level in a heavy saucepan or electric frying pan. Fry handfuls of slices until they are slightly amber in color; do not brown them. Spread them on paper towels, then use a metal spatula to press each slice down flat; do this while the slices are still hot. Put the flattened slices back into the salt water for 5 minutes. Heat the oil up to 360°. Drain the slices in a strainer; discard the water then refry the slices for a few minutes until they are amber and crisp; be careful to stand clear of the sputtering oil. Drain the chips on paper towels; sprinkle with salt to taste and serve hot or at room temperature.

SUGAR AND SPICE MIXED NUTS

Makes 2 to 3 cups

½ cup sugar
4 tablespoons cornstarch
1 teaspoon cinnamon
½ teaspoon nutmeg
¼ teaspoon allspice
Dash of ground cloves
Dash of ground ginger
½ teaspoon salt
1 egg white
2 tablespoons cold water
Butter
¾ cup unsalted blanched whole almonds
¾ cup unsalted walnut halves
½ cup unsalted whole filberts
1 cup raisins, optional

Into a small shallow bowl, sift together: sugar, cornstarch, the five spices, and the salt. In another small but deeper bowl, beat the egg white and water until slightly frothy. Preheat oven to 250° and grease a rimmed baking sheet with butter. Pour the almonds into the egg white; stir gently to coat. Retrieve 1 almond from the bowl with a fork; roll it gently in the sugar mixture and place it on the baking sheet. Repeat this procedure, 1 almond at a time, until all are coated; then repeat with the other nuts. Bake about 1¼ to 1½ hours, or until the coating is crisp. Cool the nuts on the baking sheet, then mix in the raisins; store in a tightly covered jar at room temperature.

ROASTED CHICKPEAS

Makes 1½ cups

1 can (16 or 20 ounces) chickpeas (also called garbanzo beans)
3 tablespoons butter
½ teaspoon salt

Open up the can of chickpeas; drain out the liquid, then repeatedly fill the can with water and empty it, using your fingers to prevent the chickpeas from falling out. Pour the chickpeas into a colander, run them under cold running water, then allow them to drain. Pat the chickpeas dry between several thicknesses of paper towels.

Melt but do not brown the butter in a skillet; turn off the heat and add the chickpeas and the salt; stir gently so that all the chickpeas become coated. Pour the mixture into a 9-by-13-inch shallow rimmed baking pan. Bake at 400° for about 30 minutes, or until the chickpeas become dry and golden; shake the pan now and then as the chickpeas bake. Cool before serving.

CHILI CHICKPEAS

Add 1 teaspoon chili powder and ½ teaspoon onion powder to the skillet when you add the salt.

SEASONED WHEATS

Makes 6 cups

6 cups spoon-size non-frosted shredded wheat
6 tablespoons melted butter
2 teaspoons your choice of seasoned salt, onion salt, hickory smoked salt, or barbecue seasoning salt

In a single layer, spread the shredded wheat in a large shallow rimmed baking pan or use 2 smaller pans. Drizzle the melted butter evenly over the shredded wheat; sprinkle evenly with the salt of your choice. Bake at 350° for 15 to 20 minutes, stirring once, until the butter is absorbed and the wheats are lightly toasted. Serve either warm or cooled.

SPICY PUMPKIN SEEDS

Makes 2 cups

¼ cup corn oil
½ teaspoon Worcestershire sauce
½ teaspoon paprika
¼ teaspoon chili powder
⅛ teaspoon ground cumin
⅛ teaspoon cayenne pepper
2 dashes Tabasco sauce
2 cups hulled pumpkin seeds

Preheat the oven to 300°. Combine everything except the pumpkin seeds in a large skillet. Heat until hot, but not smoking, then stir in the pumpkin seeds so that they become uniformly coated with oil and spices. Spread the mixture in a rimmed, shallow baking pan. Bake for about 10 minutes, or until the pumpkin seeds are crisped; stir the seeds once during this time. Cool before serving.

NUTTY POPCORN

Makes 3 quarts

3 quarts popped popcorn
1 cup cashew nuts
8 tablespoons butter
½ cup honey
1 tablespoon freshly grated orange peel

Spread the popcorn in a large baking pan; sprinkle the nuts evenly atop; set aside. Melt but do not brown the butter in a saucepan; blend in the honey and orange peel; drizzle this liquid evenly over the popcorn, then use 2 metal spatulas to mix it in. Bake at 300° for 25 minutes stirring the mixture once or twice as it bakes. Let the popcorn cool; break up the bigger chunks and serve.

NUTTY OATMEAL CARROT COOKIES

Makes 5 dozens

1 cup all-purpose flour
1 cup whole wheat flour
½ teaspoon baking soda
½ teaspoon baking powder
¼ teaspoon salt
1 cup vegetable shortening
1¼ cups packed brown sugar
2 eggs
½ teaspoon vanilla extract
¼ teaspoon orange extract
1½ cups grated carrots
1¼ cups chopped walnuts
2 cups uncooked quick oats

Put the first 5 dry ingredients in a small mixing bowl; use a wire whisk to mix thoroughly ; set the bowl aside. In a large mixing bowl, use an electric mixer to beat together the shortening, sugar, eggs, and extracts until creamy. By hand, stir in the flour mixture followed by the remaining ingredients in the order listed.

Drop rounded spoonfuls of this cookie dough 1 inch apart onto greased cookie sheets. Bake at 350° for about 20 minutes, or until lightly browned. Remove the hot cookies to racks to cool.

CARROT CUPCAKES

Makes 1 dozen

⅔ cup corn oil
¾ to 1 cup packed brown sugar
1 tablespoon orange juice concentrate
¾ teaspoon cinnamon
¾ teaspoon freshly grated orange peel (or ¼ teaspoon dried)
½ teaspoon nutmeg
Several dashes of ground cloves
2 eggs

⅔ cup all-purpose flour
⅔ cup whole wheat flour
½ teaspoon baking powder
¼ teaspoon baking soda
½ teaspoon salt
1½ cups grated carrots
½ cup chopped walnuts

Grease cupcake tins or line them with paper liners; set aside. In a large mixing bowl, use an electric mixer to cream together the oil, brown sugar, orange juice concentrate, cinnamon, orange peel, nutmeg, and cloves; beat in the eggs, 1 at a time; set the mixture aside. Mix the 2 flours, baking powder and baking soda, and salt; add half of this to the liquid ingredients and stir until well blended before stirring in the remaining half. Evenly stir in the carrots and nuts.

Spoon the batter into the prepared tins filling them ¾ full. Bake at 350° for 30 to 40 minutes, or until a sharp knife inserted at the center of a cupcake comes out clean.

CHEWY CARROT BROWNIES

Follow the ingredients list above making the following changes: Reduce oil to ½ cup and increase the brown sugar to 1½ cups; increase the flours to 1 cup of each kind; omit baking soda but increase the baking powder to 1 teaspoon; increase the grated carrots to 2 cups. Follow the directions, above; turn the batter into 2 greased 8-by-8-by-2-inch pans and bake at 350° for about 30 minutes, or until a knife inserted at the center comes out clean.

SPICY BEET CAKE

Makes 1 cake

2⅓ cups flour
4 teaspoons baking powder
2 teaspoons baking soda

1½ teaspoons allspice
1 teaspoon cinnamon
¼ teaspoon ground cloves
½ cup vegetable shortening
1¼ cups sugar
2 eggs
1 can (16 ounces) cut beets
½ teaspoon orange extract
1¼ cups chopped walnuts
Confectioner's sugar

In a medium-size mixing bowl, thoroughly combine the first 6 dry ingredients; set the bowl aside. In a large mixing bowl, use an electric mixer to beat the shortening and sugar until light and creamy; beat in the eggs, 1 at a time; set the bowl aside.

Open the can of beets and drain all the liquid into a blender container; put about 3 beet pieces in the blender and whirl into a purée. With the blender still running, slowly drop in the beet pieces, one at a time, until all the beets have been smoothly puréed. Pour the purée into the mixture, then add the orange extract; use the electric mixer to mix well. Using a strong spoon, gradually add the dry ingredients, mixing well after each addition. Fold in the walnuts.

Turn the batter into a greased and lightly floured, 9-cup Bundt cake pan. Bake at 350° for 50 to 60 minutes, or until a sharp knife inserted in the cake comes out clean. Let the cake cool in its pan for about 30 minutes before inverting it onto a serving dish. Sift some confectioner's sugar over the cooled cake top before serving.

CHOCOLATE BANANA BROWNIES

Makes one 8-inch square pan

1¼ cups flour
⅓ cup unsweetened cocoa powder
1 teaspoon salt
½ teaspoon baking soda
½ teaspoon cinnamon
⅛ teaspoon nutmeg
⅓ cup corn oil
¼ cup milk

1 egg
⅞ cup sugar
1½ cups ripe banana chunks

Combine and sift the flour, cocoa, salt, baking soda, cinnamon, and nutmeg into a large mixing bowl; set aside. In the order listed, place the remaining ingredients in a blender container and whirl until smooth and puréed; lacking a blender, use a bowl and an eggbeater or wire whisk. Mix the liquid mixture into the bowl of dry ingredients, stirring only until the batter is moist but still lumpy.

Turn the batter into a greased 8-by-8-by-2-inch pan. Bake at 350° for 25 to 30 minutes, or until the sides just begin to pull away from the pan. Allow to cool then cut into bars.

FRESH APPLE COOKIES

Makes about 5 dozen

1½ cups flour
½ cup finely chopped walnuts
½ teaspoon baking powder
½ teaspoon baking soda
½ teaspoon salt
½ teaspoon cinnamon
¼ teaspoon nutmeg
½ cup vegetable shortening
1 cup packed brown sugar
2 eggs
1 cup uncooked quick oats
2 cups firm apples, peeled, cored, and cut into small dice
⅔ cup raisins

In a medium-size bowl, thoroughly blend the first 7 dry ingredients; set aside. In a large mixing bowl, beat together the shortening and sugar until creamy; one at a time beat in the eggs, then stir in the dry ingredients. Add the remaining ingredients in the order listed, stirring after each addition.

Drop generously rounded teaspoonfuls of the cookie dough onto greased cookie sheets about 2 inches apart. Bake at 350° for 10 to 15 minutes,

113

or until the cookies become browned at the edges. Remove the hot cookies to racks to cool before serving.

WATCH-YOUR-WEIGHT APPLE CRISPS

If you enjoy the taste and appreciate the low calorie count of those small snack-time envelopes filled with crisp, dried apple bits, you can further your enjoyment by buying them for less. The contents of the supermarket-bought snack contain ½ ounce of freeze-dried, sliced apples. The identical freeze-dried apples can be bought in bigger and cheaper quantities at any camping or sporting goods store that carries freeze-dried camping foods.

HEALTHY APPLESAUCE DROPS

Makes 5 dozen

1 cup whole wheat flour
1 cup all-purpose flour
1 cup uncooked quick oats
2 tablespoons nonfat dry milk
2 tablespoons soy (or soya) flour, optional
2 teaspoons wheat germ
1 teaspoon baking soda
1 teaspoon cinnamon
½ teaspoon salt
½ cup safflower or corn oil
1 cup packed brown sugar
1 egg
1¼ cups applesauce

In a medium-size mixing bowl, thoroughly combine the first 9 dry ingredients; set the bowl aside. In a large mixing bowl, beat together the oil and sugar, then beat in the egg. Stir in the dry mixture alternately with the applesauce until blended.

Drop generously rounded teaspoonfuls of the cookie dough 2 inches apart onto greased cookie sheets. Bake at 375° for about 10 minutes, or until the cookies are golden around the edges. Remove the hot cookies to racks to cool.

BANANA-ORANGE DROPS

Replace the applesauce with ⅔ cup mashed, ripe banana; ⅓ cup frozen orange juice concentrate, thawed; and ⅓ cup water.

FRESH BLUEBERRY COBBLER BARS

Makes one 8-inch square pan

1 cup flour
1 cup quick cooking oats
⅔ cup packed brown sugar
Grated rind of 1 orange
8 tablespoons butter, softened
3 cups fresh blueberries
⅔ cup granulated sugar
2 teaspoons strained fresh lemon juice
2 teaspoons strained fresh orange juice
½ teaspoon cinnamon
⅛ teaspoon nutmeg
1 tablespoon cornstarch

Combine the flour, oats, brown sugar, and grated orange rind, then use your fingertips to quickly but thoroughly mix in the butter. Press half of the mixture into the bottom of a well-greased 8- or 9-inch square baking pan; set aside.

Put the blueberries, granulated sugar, lemon juice, orange juice, cinnamon, and nutmeg in a non-aluminum cooking pot; gently bring to a boil. Over medium heat, cook and stir the berries until they burst and the sugar dissolves; you may want to mash some of the berries to prevent sticking. Dissolve the cornstarch in 1 tablespoon of cold water and stir it into the berry mixture; continue cooking and stirring until the mixture bubbles and thickens.

Let the blueberry mixture cool somewhat, then spread it over the flour-oats crust in the baking pan. Sprinkle the blueberry mixture evenly with the remaining flour-oats mixture. Bake at 350° for about 40 minutes, or until the top crust is slightly browned. Cool completely, then cut into bars.

MAPLE-WHEAT PEANUT BUTTER COOKIES

Makes about 5 dozen

1¼ cups whole wheat flour
1¼ cups finely crushed graham cracker crumbs
½ teaspoon baking soda
½ teaspoon salt
8 tablespoons butter, softened
½ cup packed brown sugar
1 egg
½ teaspoon vanilla extract
½ cup pure maple syrup
1 cup peanut butter

In a medium-size bowl, thoroughly stir together the flour, crumbs, baking soda, and salt; set the bowl aside. Combine the butter and brown sugar in a large mixing bowl; use an electric mixer to beat them until light and creamy, then beat in the egg followed by the vanilla, syrup, and peanut butter. By hand, gradually stir in the dry ingredients to form a soft dough.

Shape generously rounded teaspoons of dough into 1-inch balls and place them about 2 inches apart on lightly greased cookie sheets. Flatten each ball with wet fork tines to make a criss-cross pattern. Bake at 350° for 10 to 12 minutes, or until the edges become lightly browned. Remove the hot cookies to racks and let them cool.

NUTTY CEREAL BARS

Makes one 8-inch square pan

2 tablespoons butter, softened
3⅓ cups unsweetened puffed wheat cereal
⅔ cups coarsely chopped peanuts
⅓ cup sugar
⅓ cup light corn syrup
⅔ cup peanut butter
1 teaspoon vanilla extract

Generously grease an 8-by-8-by-2-inch baking pan with the softened butter; set the pan aside. Combine the puffed wheat and peanuts in a mixing bowl; set the bowl aside. Combine the sugar and syrup in a saucepan; stir constantly while bringing the mixture to a rolling boil. When the sugar

is all dissolved, remove the pan from the heat and stir in the peanut butter and vanilla until smooth. Immediately, drizzle this mixture over the bowl of cereal and nuts, then quickly stir with a wooden spoon to coat uniformly. Still working quickly, use a rubber spatula to turn the mixture into the buttered baking pan. Use the spatula to pat the mixture evenly into the pan. Let the pan cool and harden completely, then cut into bars.

COTTAGE CHEESE COOKIES

Makes about 6 dozen

2 cups flour
1 teaspoon baking powder
¼ teaspoon salt
4 tablespoons butter, softened
4 tablespoons vegetable shortening
¾ cup packed brown sugar
⅓ cup granulated sugar
2 eggs
1 cup cottage cheese
3 tablespoons frozen orange juice concentrate, thawed

In a medium-size bowl, thoroughly combine the flour, baking powder, and salt; set the bowl aside. In a large mixing bowl, use an electric mixer to beat the butter, shortening, and the two sugars until light and creamy; beat in the eggs, 1 at a time, then beat in the cottage cheese and orange juice concentrate until smooth. Use a spoon to gradually stir in the flour mixture.

Drop the cookie dough by generously rounded teaspoonfuls about 2 inches apart onto lightly greased cookie sheets. Bake at 350° for 10 to 15 minutes, or until the edges become lightly browned. Remove the hot cookies to racks to cool.

PROTEIN TARTS

Makes 9

These thick, custard tarts provide a sneaky way to slip children some dairy proteins, and they are easily made in muffin tins.

2 eggs, at room temperature
2 eggs, at room temperature, separated
⅔ cup milk
⅓ cup sugar
1 teaspoon vanilla extract
¾ cup flour
3 tablespoons sugar
2 tablespoons nonfat dry milk
4 tablespoons butter, cut in chunks
Cinnamon

Put the 2 eggs and 2 egg yolks in a medium-size mixing bowl. Reserve the extra egg whites for later. Use an egg beater to beat the eggs and egg yolks until blended; stir in the milk, the ⅓ cup of sugar, and the vanilla; set the bowl aside.

In another medium-size mixing bowl, thoroughly combine the flour, 3 tablespoons of sugar, and dry milk. Use a pastry blender or your fingers to quickly cut in the butter until it looks like coarse meal. Stir in, roughly, 3 tablespoons of the reserved egg white, 1 tablespoon at a time, until the mixture becomes a moist but not sticky dough.

Divide the pastry dough into 9 equal balls (only 8 balls if the cups in the muffin tins measure more than 2½ inches across); put each dough ball into a muffin cup and press the dough out firmly so that it covers the bottom and sides in each cup. Briefly stir the egg mixture, then pour it equally among the dough-lined cups. Sprinkle the top of each tart with a dash of cinnamon. Bake, without jiggling, at 300° for 45 to 55 minutes, or until the custard has set and a sharp knife inserted at the center comes out clean. Let the tarts cool completely before removing them from their tins. Store refrigerated.

CHEESE "COOKIES"

Makes about 4 servings

Older children will recognize these as crackers, but the younger crowd will enjoy them as sugarless, cut-out cookies.

¼ cup whole wheat flour
½ teaspoon baking powder
⅓ cup gently packed, grated Monterey Jack or Muenster cheese, at room temperature
1 egg, beaten smooth

Thoroughly stir together the flour and baking powder, then use your fingers to cut in the grated cheese; gradually add enough spoonfuls of the beaten egg to moisten the mixture into a non-sticky dough. Shape the dough into a ball, wrap it, and chill for an hour or more.

On a lightly floured surface, roll the dough to about ⅛-inch thick. Use cookie cutters to cut the dough into various shapes. Place the cookies on ungreased cookie sheets. Bake at 350° for about 15 minutes, or until the cookies are lightly browned at their edges. Cool before serving.

CHEWY BRAN COOKIES

Makes 4 dozen

1¾ cups flour
½ teaspoon baking soda
½ teaspoon salt
8 tablespoons butter
¾ cup packed brown sugar
¼ cup granulated sugar
1 egg
1 teaspoon vanilla extract
¾ cup sour cream
1 cup slightly crushed bran flakes cereal

Thoroughly combine flour, baking soda, and salt in a medium-size bowl; set aside. In a large mixing bowl, use an electric mixer to beat together the butter and the two sugars until light and creamy; beat in the egg and vanilla. Use a wooden spoon to fold in the sour cream; gradually stir in the flour mixture until just moistened; then fold in the bran cereal.

Drop well-rounded teaspoonfuls of this cookie dough about 1 inch apart onto lightly greased cookie sheets. Bake at 375° for 8 to 12 minutes, or until the edges become lightly browned. Remove the hot cookies to a rack and allow them to cool.

HOMEMADE ZWIEBACK

Makes about 5 dozen

¼ cup lukewarm, 110° water
7 tablespoons sugar
1 envelope active dry yeast
¾ cup milk
4 tablespoons butter
½ teaspoon salt
2 eggs, well beaten
¼ teaspoon cinnamon
¼ teaspoon nutmeg
¼ teaspoon mace
4 to 5 cups flour

Put the ¼ cup of lukewarm, 110° water in a large mixing bowl; stir in 1 teaspoon of the sugar; sprinkle the yeast atop; wait a minute, then stir to dissolve. Set this mixture aside for about 10 minutes, or until bubbly. In the meantime, scald but do not boil the milk in a saucepan; remove it from the heat and stir in the butter, the salt, and the remaining sugar so that they melt and dissolve; set the pan aside and let it cool to a lukewarm 110°.

When the milk mixture is lukewarm, stir it into the yeast mixture followed by the eggs and the spices. Use a strong spoon or your fingertips to stir in enough flour to make a moderately stiff dough. Knead the dough on a well-floured surface for 10 to 15 minutes, or until the dough becomes smooth and blistered; work in more flour as you knead to prevent stickiness. Place the dough in a lightly greased bowl; turn the dough to grease the top, then cover loosely and let it rise in a warm place for about 1½ hours or until it is doubled in bulk.

Punch down the dough, knead it for a few turns, then cover and let it rise again for 45 more minutes, or until it is doubled. Again, punch the dough down, knead it briefly, then divide it into 4 equal pieces. Shape each piece of dough into a 12-inch-long loaf; place the loaves, apart from each other, on 2 lightly greased cookie sheets; cover loosely and let rise in a warm place for about 30 minutes, or until the loaves look puffy.

Bake the loaves on their cookie sheets at 350° for about 20 to 25 minutes, or until they are golden brown; if you are using 2 oven racks, switch the cookie sheets after 10 minutes to ensure equal baking time. Remove the loaves and let them cool on racks until warm to the touch; in the meantime, reduce the oven temperature to 225° and wash the cookie sheets.

Use a serrated bread knife to cut the loaves into ½-inch slices. Arrange the slices, cut side down and almost touching, back on the cookie sheets. Set the sheets on the middle oven rack(s); leave the oven door just slightly ajar (or prop it open with any 1-inch-deep baking pan) and bake for 1 hour. Turn the slices over and bake for another hour, or until both sides of the slices are dry throughout. Cool completely on wire racks.

WHOLE WHEAT ZWIEBACK

Increase the butter to 8 tablespoons; increase the milk to 1 cup; increase the sugar to 8 tablespoons. Use 2 cups of whole wheat flour followed by 2 to 3 cups of all-purpose flour to make the dough.

TRAIL MIXES

Makes 6 cups

Combine either list of ingredients in plastic bags.

ROASTED SALTED MIX

2 cups raisins
1 cup salted roasted almonds
1 cup salted roasted cashews
1 cup Spanish peanuts
1 cup sunflower seeds

FRUIT MIX

2 cups chopped dried apricots
1½ cups raisins
1½ cup slivered almonds
1 cup carob dots (or semisweet chocolate morsels)

Chapter 8:

SWEETS

Sections:

☐ No-Thermometer Candies
☐ Freezer Jams, Jellies, and Preserves
☐ Puddings
☐ No-Machine Ice Creams

MARSHMALLOWS

Makes 6 dozen

2 cups sugar
3 envelopes (3 tablespoons) unflavored gelatin
2 dashes of salt
1 cup cold water
1 teaspoon vanilla extract
Butter
Confectioner's sugar

Combine the sugar, gelatin, and salt in a saucepan; stir in the water. Heat the mixture over low heat so that the sugar dissolves; bring the mixture just to the boiling point but don't let it boil. Remove the pan from the heat; let it cool for 8 minutes, then stir in the vanilla. Transfer the mixture to a large mixing bowl. Using an electric mixer, beat at high speed until the mixture is fluffy and thickened and will stand in soft peaks; this will take 10 to 15 minutes of beating. Use butter to generously grease a 13-by-9-by-2-inch (or similar) pan. Pour the marshmallow mixture into the pan; spread it evenly. Set the pan aside, uncovered, until the mixture is cool. Lay a sheet of wax paper very loosely over the top of the pan and let it stand for 12 to 24 hours. Remove the marshmallow block from its pan. With scissors dipped in hot water, cut the marshmallow block into 1-inch squares; roll the squares in confectioner's sugar; if you want to get fancy, use several small cookie cutters in place of scissors. Store the marshmallows in an airtight container at room temperature.

HONEY MARSHMALLOWS

Replace 1 cup of the sugar with 1 cup of honey; reduce the water to ⅞ cup. You will have to beat the mixture for about 15 to 20 minutes in order to make it fluffy. Let the covered marshmallow block stand 24 to 48 hours before removing it from its pan.

FRUIT-FLAVORED MARSHMALLOWS

In a saucepan, combine a 3-ounce package of fruit-flavored gelatin and ½ cup boiling water. Heat over very low heat to dissolve; then stir in ¾ cup sugar. Cook and stir to dissolve, but do not let the mixture boil. Blend in 3 tablespoons light corn syrup. Transfer the mixture to a large mixing bowl and refrigerate until slightly thickened. Beat to a fluff as directed above and pour it into a greased 9-by-9-by-2-inch pan. Cool and cut as directed. Makes 4 to 5 dozen flavored and colored marshmallows.

CHOCOLATE AND CARAMEL TORTOISES

Makes about 3 dozen

3 cups (¾ pound) unbroken pecan halves
1 14-ounce bag of caramels (about 50)
1½ tablespoons milk
2½ teaspoons butter
6 ounces semisweet chocolate, in morsels (1 cup) or in a candy bar

Lightly grease a cookie sheet. Arrange 4 pecan halves on the sheet in the form of an "X"; the pecans should be placed flat side down and they should overlap at the center of each "X." In groups of four, arrange the rest of the pecan halves in the same way. Place the caramels in the top part of a double boiler or in a heavy saucepan; add the milk and butter. Cover and let the ingredients melt together over low heat; stir now and then until smooth. If necessary, let the mixture cool, just briefly, so that it is not runny. Spoon about 2 teaspoons of hot caramel over each "X" leaving the outer tips of the nuts showing. When done, let stand until the caramel is firm and set, about 45 minutes.

Melt the chocolate in the top part of a double boiler; remove the top pot from the bottom pot and stir the chocolate until smooth. Let the chocolate cool, just briefly, to a consistency that is not completely runny; spoon it over each tortoise to cover the caramel; try to leave the tips of the "X" uncoated. Let the tortoises stand until firm and set. Place the finished candies in a box or tin with wax paper between each layer. Cover and store in a cool place.

CARAMEL APPLES

Makes 5 or 6

5 or 6 crisp medium-size apples, unpeeled and well chilled
5 or 6 wooden ice-cream-bar sticks (sold at craft and hobby stores or used and cleaned)
½ cup coarsely chopped peanuts
A 14-ounce bag of caramels (about 50)
2 tablespoons water
Dash of salt

Wash and dry the apples; insert a stick into the blossom end of each; set aside. Also set aside a cookie sheet covered with a length of greased wax paper and a small shallow bowl filled with the peanuts. In the top of a double boiler or a heavy saucepan, combine the unwrapped caramels, water, and salt. Cover and let the ingredients melt together over low heat; stir now and then until the sauce is smooth.

Working quickly, dip an apple into the hot caramel sauce; turn it until it is evenly coated. Scrape the sauce off the bottom of the apple (it will get replaced by gravity) then roll the middle girth gently in the nuts. Place the coated apple on the lined cookie sheet and place the sheet in the refrigerator; repeat for the rest of the apples. If the caramel sauce gets too stiff to make a thin coating, gently reheat it adding a few drops of water if necessary. Chill the caramel apples until they are firm, then place them in paper cupcake-liners and wrap individually in sandwich bags. Store in a cool or refrigerated place.

POPCORN BALLS

Makes 1 dozen

3 quarts popped popcorn, without butter

1 cup light corn syrup
1 cup sugar
½ teaspoon salt
2 teaspoons vanilla extract
Food coloring, optional
Butter

Put the popcorn in a large roasting pan; place the pan in an oven set on "Low" or 170°. Combine the syrup, sugar, and salt in a heavy saucepan; heat over medium heat, stirring continuously until the mixture boils, then boil gently without stirring at all for 4 minutes. Remove the pan from the heat and stir in the vanilla and enough food coloring, if you wish, to color the balls. Slowly drizzle this syrup over the pan of popcorn; quickly mix to combine and coat evenly.

Butter your hands lightly. As soon as you can tolerate the popcorn's heat, quickly shape the mixture into 3-inch balls; work fast so that the syrup doesn't harden. Set the finished popcorn balls on a greased cookie sheet. When cooled slightly, wrap the balls individually in colored cellophane or sandwich bags, or foil or plastic wrap.

CARAMEL POPCORN BALLS

Set up the popcorn as described. Melt 42 unwrapped caramels (a 14-ounce bag contains about 50) along with 3 tablespoons of water, covered, in the top part of a double boiler; stir now and then until the sauce becomes smooth. Slowly drizzle the caramel sauce over the popcorn and shape into balls as described.

PEANUT BRITTLE

Makes 1 pound

Butter
1 cup sugar
1½ cups light corn syrup
Dash of salt
1½ cups skinless peanuts
¼ teaspoon baking soda
¼ teaspoon vanilla extract

Lightly butter a cookie sheet; set it aside. Put the

sugar in a heavy skillet; make a well in the center and pour in the syrup and salt. Put the skillet on a cold burner; turn the heat up to medium-high, then cook, stirring continuously, for 5 minutes. Reduce the heat to a slow simmer; stir in the peanuts and continue to cook, stirring frequently, for 20 more minutes.

Remove the skillet from the heat and immediately stir in the baking soda and vanilla; continue stirring. When the foaming subsides, pour the mixture onto the buttered cookie sheet spreading it out evenly. Let the peanut brittle cool and set before breaking it into pieces. Store in an airtight container.

PUERTO RICAN MILK CANDIES

Makes 1½ dozen

4 **cups whole milk**
1 **cup sugar**
¼ **teaspoon cinnamon**
¾ **cup shredded coconut**

Pour the milk into a heavy saucepan and bring to boiling over medium heat without stirring too much; keep an eye on it because, once boiling, it will rise quickly. Reduce the heat to low and allow it to simmer, stirring occasionally, for 20 minutes, then continue simmering for another 15 minutes stirring constantly.

After this simmering process, gradually drizzle in the sugar, stirring constantly as you do so, until it is dissolved. Stir in the cinnamon and continue to cook and stir over low heat until it simmers again. When the milk finally starts to thicken, start stirring quickly and continue to do so for about 5 minutes, or until the mixture becomes thick, richly cream-colored, and pulls away from the sides of the pan. Pour the mixture into a buttered 8-by-8-by-2-inch pan and allow it to cool to lukewarm.

While the candy cools, put the coconut in a measuring cup and use the tips of scissors to snip the shreds into smaller lengths; place the snipped shreds in a plate. When the candy has cooled

enough to handle, roll it into 1-inch balls, then roll each ball in the snipped coconut to embed and coat. Store, covered and refrigerated, for up to 1 week.

ALMOND LIQUEUR BALLS

Makes 2 dozen

⅓ **cup Amaretto or other almond-flavored liqueur (or substitute Grand Marnier)**
⅓ **cup light corn syrup**
3 **cups (a 12-ounce box) very finely crushed vanilla wafers**
About ½ cup blanched whole almonds

Stir together the liqueur and the corn syrup; drizzle this mixture over a mixing bowl containing the vanilla wafer crumbs; mix so that all the crumbs become well moistened into a rough dough. Cover and refrigerate until chilled.

In the meantime, place the almonds on a rimmed baking pan in a single layer. Place the pan 4 to 6 inches away from the oven's broiler and briefly roast on the broil setting until golden. Let the almonds cool, then finely chop them in a blender, being careful not to chop them so finely that they become ground.

When the crumb mixture is chilled, shape it into 1-inch balls; roll each ball in the chopped almonds. Store in the refrigerator, in a single, covered layer.

CHOCOLATE-ALMOND LIQUEUR BALLS

Replace the vanilla wafers with chocolate wafers.

VELVETY CHOCOLATE BALLS

Makes 1½ dozen

1 **small package (6 ounces) semisweet chocolate morsels**
3 **tablespoons heavy whipping cream**
3 **tablespoons sweetened powdered chocolate cold-drink mix**

Put the chocolate morsels in the top part of a double boiler; add the cream and stir continuously until the chocolate is melted and well blended with the cream. Remove the top boiler pan; cover the surface of the chocolate directly with plastic wrap and refrigerate for about 30 to 45 minutes, or until the chocolate is firm enough to hold its shape but not stiff.

Working quickly use either 2 teaspoons or your fingers to shape the chocolate mixture into 1¼-inch balls; roll each ball in the chocolate mix. Place the balls on a plate in a single layer, cover, and return to the refrigerator; they will keep for up to 2 weeks. Let the balls stand at room temperature for 5 to 10 minutes before serving them as an after-dinner, coffee accompaniment.

CRANBERRY DELIGHT

Makes 3 dozen

3 cups fresh cranberries
1¼ cups strained fresh orange juice
4½ envelopes (4½ tablespoons) unflavored
 gelatin
2¼ cups sugar
1½ cups chopped walnuts
About ½ cup confectioner's sugar

Combine cranberries and orange juice in a non-aluminum cooking pot. Gently simmer, covered, over medium heat for 10 or 15 minutes, or until all the cranberries pop. Let the cranberries cool to lukewarm, then whirl them, a little at a time, in a blender or processor until puréed. Strain the liquid into a clean non-aluminum cooking pot; discard the skins. Sprinkle the gelatin atop the cranberry mixture; stir to dissolve. Stir in the sugar, then cook over medium heat, stirring continuously, until the sugar is completely dissolved and the mixture becomes quite thick.

When the mixture is thick enough to heavily coat a spoon, remove the pot from the heat and stir in the walnuts. Spread the mixture into a generously buttered 8-by-8-by-2-inch pan and let it set, uncovered, at room temperature for 12 hours, or until firmly set.

Cut the candy into 1¼-inch squares; remove the pieces from the pan and place them in a single layer on a wire rack to dry for another 12 hours. Dredge each candy square in the confectioner's sugar. Store in a single layer or between layers of wax paper for up to 2 weeks.

DIET ORANGE JEWELS

Makes 5 dozen

1¼ cups cold water
4 envelopes (4 tablespoons) unflavored gelatin
4 one-gram packets Weight Watchers
 Sweetener or Sweet 'N Low or any other
 artificial sweetener to equal 2½ or 3
 tablespoons of sugar
½ cup undiluted frozen orange juice
 concentrate, thawed

Put the ¼ cup of cold water in a bowl; sprinkle the gelatin atop and let it stand. Bring the remaining cup of water to a boil, add it to the bowl containing the gelatin, and stir for 2 or 3 minutes until the gelatin dissolves completely. Stir the artificial sweetener into the mixture and allow it to cool to room temperature.

Stir the orange juice concentrate into the cooled gelatin mixture, then pour it into an 8-by-8-by-2-inch pan. Chill the candy until firm, then cut it into 1¼-inch squares. Store covered and refrigerated. Each square has less than 10 calories.

DIET APPLE JEWELS

Replace the orange juice concentrate with unsweetened apple juice concentrate, along with a dash of cinnamon.

FREEZER JAMS

These jams are simple to make and can be stored for up to three weeks in your refrigerator, or in your freezer for up to one year. You don't cook the fruit, so it retains its just-picked flavor. Follow the directions according to your chosen fruit.

Fresh fruit, see below
Fresh lemon juice, see requirements under each fruit
Sugar, see requirements under each fruit
¾ cup water
1 box (5 tablespoons) powdered pectin
Six or seven 8-ounce lidded plastic containers

Prepare the fruit of your choice according to specific directions; be sure to use fully ripe fruit with all blemishes cut out. When the instructions say to chop finely or grind, use any of these methods: (1) whirl half-cupfuls of fruit at a time at medium-low speed in a blender; (2) grate or chop several cups of fruit at a time in a food processor; (3) run the fruit through a food mill or a meat grinder; (4) chop the fruit very finely by hand and mash some, slightly, with a potato masher.

Measure the prepared fruit into a large mixing bowl, making sure that the amount you have is exact; if you are lacking some fruit, stir in enough water to meet the exact amount; do not add any more fruit that what is called for. If a fruit calls for lemon juice, mix it in now; always use strained fresh lemon juice.

Mix the amount of sugar called for into the bowl of prepared fruit so that it is blended well; let the mixture stand for 10 to 15 minutes. In the meantime, combine the water and the pectin in a saucepan; bring to boiling, then boil hard for 1 full minute, stirring constantly. Stir the pectin mixture into the bowl of fruit and continue stirring, nonstop, for about 3 minutes (only 2 minutes for raspberries and blackberries). Quickly ladle the jam into the containers, leaving ½-inch headspace; cover right away with lids. Let the filled containers stand at room temperature for 24 hours, or until set. Store 1 container in your refrigerator for immediate use and freeze the rest.

APRICOT FREEZER JAM

Halve and pit, but do not peel, about 1¾ pounds of apricots; chop and measure to get 2½ cups. Stir in 2 tablespoons lemon juice. Use 5½ cups sugar. Makes 6 cups.

PEACH FREEZER JAM

Peel, pit, and quarter 2 pounds of peaches; chop and measure to get 2⅓ cups. Stir in 2 tablespoons strained fresh lemon juice plus 1 teaspoon ascorbic acid crystals (such as Fruit Fresh) to prevent darkening; lacking the crystals, you can crush 3,000 milligrams worth of vitamin C tablets into a powder and dissolve them in the lemon juice; however, this will make the jam a bit cloudy. Use 5 cups of sugar. Makes about 6 cups.

STRAWBERRY FREEZER JAM

Wash and hull 1 quart berries; crush thoroughly, a cup at a time, with a potato masher; measure to get 2 cups. No lemon juice is required. Use 4 cups of sugar. Makes 5½ cups.

RASPBERRY FREEZER JAM (ALSO BLACKBERRY)

Wash and stem 1 quart berries; crush, 1 cup at a time, with a potato masher. Sieve half of the pulp to remove some of the seeds; measure to get 3 cups of pulp. No lemon juice is required. Use 5⅓ cups of sugar. Makes 6⅓ cups.

SWEET CHERRY FREEZER JAM

Stem and pit about 3 pounds of cherries; chop and measure to get 2 cups. Stir in 2 tablespoons strained fresh lemon juice. Use 4½ cups of sugar. Makes 5½ cups.

SOUR CHERRY FREEZER JAM

Same as Sweet Cherry Freezer Jam, above, but omit the lemon juice.

FREEZER ORANGE MARMALADE

Cut the tips off 2 medium oranges; score the skin into quarter-wedges and remove the peels along the scores; reserve the fruit pulp. Use a teaspoon to scrape the bitter white inner membrane off the peels. With scissors or a knife or a food processor, cut the peels into very thin strips or shreds; place them in a small saucepan along with ¾ cup water; simmer, covered, for 15 minutes. In a small bowl, crush the reserved fruit pulp sections, discarding membranes and pits. Stir the hot peel mixture and its liquid into the crushed fruit. Measure this combined mixture into a larger bowl to get 1⅔ cups; add water, if necessary, to meet the amount. Stir in ⅓ cup strained fresh lemon juice. Use 4¼ cups of sugar. Do not use powdered pectin boiled in ¾ cup water; instead, use half a bottle (⅓ cup) of liquid pectin and stir it into the bowl of fruit for 3 minutes. Makes 2 to 3 cups of marmalade.

FREEZER JELLIES

These simply made, no-cook jellies will keep their summer-fresh taste in your freezer for up to one year. They will keep in your refrigerator for up to three weeks.

Fresh fruit, see below
Sugar, see requirements under each fruit
¾ cup water
1 box (5 tablespoons) powdered pectin
Six or seven 8-ounce lidded plastic containers

Prepare the fruit of your choice according to specific directions; be sure you use fully ripe fruit with all blemishes cut out. When the instructions say to crush the fruit, crush it halfway through the cooking period, and again at the end of the cooking period; use a potato masher or the bottom of a sturdy glass tumbler.

Fruit juices for jellies should be filtered rather than strained. The traditional method is to let the juice and its pulp dribble through a hanging jelly bag. If you don't have a jelly bag, there are three other methods you can use:

(1) Use the cone-shaped part of a manual drip coffee set (do not use an automatic coffee system). Line the cone with the filter paper you would normally use for coffee and set it over a clean pitcher or coffeepot. Pour in the fruit pulp and let it drain; discard the filter paper when done.

(2) Set a large funnel into a large glass or beaker so that the juice has plenty of room to drain. Line the funnel with filter paper or damp, unbleached muslin or 4 layers of damp cheesecloth. Let drain.

(3) Line a wire mesh strainer with dampened muslin or 4 layers of cheesecloth. This method will take more time to drain than the others.

Do not squeeze the filtering juice; it makes for a cloudy jelly. Measure the juice into a mixing bowl, making sure that the amount you have is exact; if you are lacking some juice, stir in enough water to meet the exact amount; don't add any more juice than what is called for.

Blend the required amount of sugar into the bowl of filtered juice and let it stand at room temperature for 15 minutes. In the meantime, combine the ¾ cup of water with the pectin in a saucepan; bring to boiling, then boil hard for 1 minute, stirring constantly. Stir the pectin mixture into the bowl of juice and continue stirring, nonstop, for 3 minutes. Quickly ladle the liquid jelly into the plastic containers leaving ½-inch headspace; cover right away with lids. Let the filled containers stand undisturbed at room temperature for 24 hours, or until set. Store one container in your refrigerator but wait 1 full week before using it. Freeze the remaining containers.

STRAWBERRY FREEZER JELLY

Wash and hull 3 quarts of ripe strawberries; purée in a blender or food processor (or crush well); heat just slightly to release the juices and bring out the color. Filter to make 2½ cups of juice. Use 5 cups of sugar. Makes 5 cups.

RASPBERRY FREEZER JELLY

Prepare 3½ to 4 quarts of berries as for strawberry jelly. Filter to make 3 cups of juice. Use 6 cups of sugar. Makes 5½ cups.

BLACKBERRY FREEZER JELLY

Same as for Strawberry Freezer Jelly.

GRAPE FREEZER JELLY

Wash and crush 5 pounds of Concord grapes in a non-aluminum pot; heat slightly to release the juices, then filter to measure 3 cups of juice. Use 5¼ cups of sugar. Makes 5⅓ cups.

FREEZER PRESERVES

Freezer preserves are simply made, are lower in sugar content that most jams and jellies, and will keep well in your freezer for up to one year. They will keep in your refrigerator for up to three weeks. Follow the basic directions, below, using the specific instructions listed under each fruit.

Basic Directions: Combine the fruit with the sugar and either cook until tender or let stand overnight (refrigerated in hot weather). Strain the sugar-juice into a clean cooking pot. Pack the fruit just ⅔ of the way up into several sturdy 16-ounce lidded plastic containers. Let the fruit cool at room temperature until lukewarm, then refrigerate it, uncovered, while you go on to the next step.

Bring the juice to a boil; stir gently, maintaining a steady boil, until the syrup is somewhat thickened and able to coat a tablespoon with a thin glaze. Remove from the heat, skim off any surface scum, and let the syrup cool to room temperature; do not refrigerate any syrup in order to cool it as it may crystallize.

Pour the completely cooled syrup into the chilled, fruit-filled containers leaving ½-inch headspace. Cover the surface of the fruits directly with plastic wrap and attach the lids. Store 1 container in your refrigerator, but wait a full week before using it. Freeze the remaining containers.

APPLE PRESERVES

Peel, core, and quarter (or slice or chop) 4 pounds of firm ripe apples. In a pot, dissolve 8 cups of sugar in 5 cups of water; bring to a boil, then cool to lukewarm. Add the apples, return to the heat, and gently simmer until the apples are transparent, about 30 minutes. Strain the syrup into another pot. Pack the apples into containers; let cool, then refrigerate as directed. Add a few sticks of cinnamon and whole cloves to the syrup and boil as directed. Let the syrup cool to room temperature. Remove the spices and pour the syrup over the apples. Cover and freeze as directed. Makes about 6 cups.

PEAR PRESERVES

Peel, core and quarter (or chop or slice) 4 pounds of ripe pears. In a pot, dissolve 6 cups of sugar in 6 cups of water; add the pears and boil until the fruit is clear and tender. Let the pears plump for 6 to 12 hours at room temperature. Strain the syrup into another pot. Pack the pears into containers: let cool, then refrigerate as directed. Boil the syrup as directed, adding a stick of cinnamon and a few whole cloves, if you wish; let cool to room temperature. Remove the spices and pour the syrup over the pears; cover and freeze as directed. Makes 6 to 7 cups.

SPICY PEACH AND WINE PRESERVES

This makes a refreshing dessert. Combine 2 cups of dry red wine, 1⅓ cups sugar, 4 inches of broken cinnamon sticks, and 1 teaspoon of whole cloves in a saucepan. Boil until the syrup is reduced to 1½ cups; remove the spices. Peel, halve, and pit 3 pounds of peaches; add them to the hot syrup and boil gently for 2 minutes. Let the mixture stand, covered, for 6 to 12 hours at room temperature. Pack both the syrup and the peaches into containers leaving ½-inch headspace. Cover and freeze as directed. Pears may be substituted for peaches in this recipe. Makes 5 cups.

FOURTEEN EASY PUDDINGS

*Each flavor makes 6 half-cup servings
or fills one 9-inch pie shell*

These puddings are easily made in just a few minutes. They are much cheaper than their commercial counterparts yet far superior in flavor. Use Vanilla Pudding as a starting point, then follow the directions for 13 variations. Use as a pudding or as a pie filling.

VANILLA PUDDING

⅓ cup sugar
4 tablespoons cornstarch
⅛ teaspoon salt
2¾ cups milk
1 to 1½ teaspoons vanilla extract
2 tablespoons butter, optional

Pudding Directions: Mix sugar, cornstarch, and salt in a saucepan. Very gradually, stir in the milk until blended. Cook over very low heat, stirring constantly, until the mixture thickens and comes to a boil. Continue stirring and let the pudding simmer rapidly for 1 minute. Remove from heat and stir in vanilla. If you like your pudding extrarich, swirl in the butter until melted. Pour the pudding into 6 half-cup pudding glasses and let cool slightly. To prevent a skin from forming, cover each glass or the surface of the pudding itself with plastic wrap. Serve warm or chilled.

Pie Filling Directions: Prepare the pudding as directed above, but do not let it boil. Cool, stirring now and then, for 10 minutes. Pour the filling into a cooled baked 9-inch pie shell; chill until firm and serve topped with whipped cream.

FRENCH VANILLA

Cook pudding as directed, thickening, then simmering for 1 minute. Stir a little of the hot pudding into a bowl containing 2 lightly beaten egg yolks, then stir the bowl's contents back into the pudding. Stir constantly over the lowest possible heat for 2 minutes; if you are using a heavy, heat-holding pot, stir without heat for 1 minute before setting over heat for a second minute. Cool to lukewarm. Stir in 1½ teaspoons vanilla; pour into glasses and chill before serving.

FRENCH VANILLA FLUFF

Follow the above French Vanilla directions; cool to lukewarm, then stir in 1½ teaspoons vanilla extract. Fold in 2 stiffly beaten (but not dry) egg whites. Pour into glasses and chill. This method will make any flavor pudding more delicate.

BUTTERSCOTCH

Replace the white sugar with ½ cup plus 1 tablespoon firmly packed brown sugar. Cook as directed, swirling 3 tablespoons of butter, not optional (and not margarine), in with the vanilla extract.

CHOCOLATE

Increase the sugar to ⅔ cup. Blend 3 tablespoons unsweetened cocoa powder into the sugar, starch, and salt mixture before adding milk.

MOCHA

Prepare Chocolate, above, but blend in 1 rounded teaspoon instant coffee powder or freeze-dried bits along with the cocoa powder.

MEXICAN CHOCOLATE

Prepare Chocolate, above, but use only ½ teaspoon vanilla extract along with ½ teaspoon orange extract. Top with shaved chocolate.

COCONUT CREAM

Add ½ to ⅔ cup shredded coconut to the sugar, starch, and salt mixture. Prepare as directed, but use ½ teaspoon coconut extract instead of the vanilla. Makes 7 servings.

NUT PUDDING

Make any of the puddings from this recipe as directed; cool partially, stirring now and then. Just before pouring the pudding into glasses, gently fold in ½ to ⅔ cup slivered almonds or chopped walnuts or your choice of chopped nuts. With plain vanilla or chocolate puddings, reduce the vanilla extract to ¾ teaspoon and add ¼ teaspoon almond extract. Makes 7 servings.

BANANA CREAM

Increase the cornstarch to 5 tablespoons and the sugar to ½ cup. Prepare and thicken as directed, using only 2 cups of milk. Remove from heat and let cool partially, stirring now and then. Fold in 1 cup mashed, very ripe banana along with only ½ teaspoon vanilla extract. Pour into cups and chill.

LEMON

Replace vanilla extract with ½ teaspoon lemon extract and 1 or 2 drops of yellow food coloring.

PISTACHIO NUT

Replace vanilla with ¾ teaspoon pistachio or almond extract and enough drops of green food coloring to turn the pudding a lime color. Before pouring it into glasses, cool the pudding by stirring it, then fold in ½ to ¾ cup skinned, chopped, and smashed pistachio nuts. Makes 7 servings.

STRAWBERRY

Whirl enough strawberries in a blender or food processor to get 1 cup of purée or else mash them well; heat briefly to release color and juices, then set aside to cool. When the berry purée is lukewarm, make the pudding. Increase cornstarch to 6 tablespoons and sugar to ⅔ cup. Prepare and thicken as directed, using only 2 cups milk. Cool partially, then stir in the strawberry purée. Omit vanilla extract and butter. Pour into glasses and chill.

PEACH

Increase cornstarch to 5 tablespoons and sugar to ½ cup. Prepare and thicken as directed, using 1 cup of milk mixed with 1 cup canned apricot or peach nectar. Cool partially, then stir in 1 cup mashed or puréed peaches. Omit vanilla extract and butter. Pour the pudding into glasses and chill. Puréed or mashed peaches can be fresh, home-cooked, or canned in light syrup; decrease sugar if canned. Make Apricot Pudding the same way.

LOW CALORIE PEACH PUDDING

Makes 6 servings

This fluffy, wholesome pudding is sweetened almost entirely with fresh, summer peaches. Count only 50 calories per serving.

About 3 medium well-ripened peaches
1 teaspoon strained fresh lemon juice
2 tablespoons sugar (or the equivalent in artificial sweetener)
¼ teaspoon salt
1 envelope (1 tablespoon) unflavored gelatin
¼ cup cold water
¾ cup boiling water
A few drops red and yellow food coloring, optional
2 egg whites, at room temperature

Wash, peel, quarter, and pit the peaches; whirl the chunks in a blender to get 1 cup of purée; lacking a blender, mash them smooth with a potato masher. Pour the purée into a large mixing bowl, stir in the lemon juice, sugar, and salt; cover and set the bowl aside. In a small bowl, sprinkle the gelatin over the cold water, wait until it softens, then mix in the boiling water; stir continuously until the gelatin dissolves. Pour the dissolved gelatin mixture into the bowl of purée; stir to thoroughly blend the ingredients, then stir in enough food coloring to make an orange color. Cover and refrigerate for 2 to 3 hours, or until the mixture mounds slightly when dropped from a spoon.

In a medium-size bowl, use an electric mixer to beat the egg whites until stiff peaks form; set aside. Remove the slightly jelled peach purée from the refrigerator and beat it at medium speed for 3 or 4 minutes, or until it becomes fluffy and can hold its shape. Fold the egg whites gently but thoroughly into the peach mixture. Lightly pile the pudding equally among 6 half-cup pudding cups; cover and refrigerate until set.

OTHER FRUIT FLAVORS

Replace the fresh peach purée with 1 cup of purée made from your choice of peeled and pitted apricots, nectarines, plums, or pears; the fruits should be both sweet and well ripened.

CROSS REFERENCE

RICE PUDDING, 97

FROZEN YOGURT ON A STICK

Makes 8

Besides cherry flavor, you can choose yogurts and gelatin mixes in any flavor you like.

1 cup water
1 3-ounce package cherry-flavored gelatin mix
1 cup milk
1 cup cherry-flavored yogurt
8 5-ounce waxy paper cups
8 wooden ice-cream-bar sticks (sold cheaply at craft stores, or used and cleaned)

Bring the water to a boil in a saucepan; stir in the gelatin mix until it is dissolved. Remove the pan from the heat and stir in the milk. Pour the mixture into a mixing bowl and chill it in your refrigerator for about 2½ hours, or until it is partially set and mounds slightly when dropped from a spoon. Before removing the bowl from the refrigerator, stir the yogurt so that it is smooth and blended; set it aside. Use an electric mixer at medium speed to beat the gelatin mixture until it is fluffy. Stir in the yogurt by hand. Pour the mixture equally among the paper cups; insert the sticks and freeze until firm. To eat, peel off the paper cup.

ORANGE-VANILLA CREAMY POPS

Makes 12 to 14

For an adult version, pour the prepared mixture into a plastic freezer container, freeze, and serve as ice cream.

1¾ cups heavy whipping cream, well-chilled
1 can (14 ounces) sweetened condensed milk, well-chilled
1 large can (12 ounces) frozen, undiluted orange juice concentrate, thawed but chilled
1 teaspoon vanilla extract

12 to 14 waxy paper cups or plastic cups with a 5-ounce capacity
12 to 14 wooden ice cream bar sticks.

In a well-chilled bowl, use an electric mixer to beat the cream only until softly mounded; do not whip it. Stir in the sweetened condensed milk, orange juice concentrate, and vanilla; beat for no more than a minute, just until the mixture regains its softly mounded texture.

Pour the mixture into the cups, insert the sticks, and freeze overnight or until solid. To serve, peel off the paper cup or briefly submerge the plastic cup in hot water to loosen the pop.

QUICK CRANBERRY SHERBET

Makes 1 quart

1 can (16 ounces) jellied cranberry sauce
⅞ cup orange soda pop

In a mixing bowl, beat the cranberry sauce by hand until smooth. Slowly pour the soda pop down the side of the mixing bowl so that no carbonation is lost; very, very gently, mix to blend. Pour the mixture into an 8-by-8-by-2-inch baking pan and freeze until firm but not solid. Break the frozen mixture into chunks and place them in a chilled mixing bowl. Use an electric mixer to beat the mixture until fluffy. Pour it into a plastic container; cover and freeze until firm before serving.

QUICK ORANGE SHERBET

Replace the cranberry sauce with 1 cup of frozen, undiluted orange juice concentrate which has been halfway thawed. Use a full 4 cups of 7-Up or any lemon or lemon-lime or grapefruit soda pop. Mix as directed; pour the mixture into a 9-by-11-by-1½-inch baking pan; freeze and beat as directed.

FRESH FRUIT ICE POPS

Makes 6

About 2 well-ripened fresh pears, or peaches, or nectarines
1 cup orange juice
1 teaspoon strained fresh lemon juice
6 waxy paper cups or plastic cups with a 3-ounce capacity
6 wooden ice cream bar sticks

Peel, core, and quarter your choice of fruit. Whirl enough fruit chunks in a blender to measure 1 cup of purée; blend in the orange and lemon juice. Pour the purée into the cups and freeze for about 30 to 60 minutes, or until almost firm. Insert the sticks in the center and freeze overnight, or until solid. To serve, peel off the paper cup or briefly submerge the plastic cup in hot water to loosen the pop.

WINTERTIME POPS

When the listed fresh fruits are unavailable, replace them with canned and drained fruits to measure 1 cup; applesauce can also be used. Besides orange juice, you can use any flavor sweetened or unsweetened fruit juice.

FROZEN ICE POPS

Each recipe makes 11

Frozen ice pops can be made from a variety of ingredients; listed here are directions for two. If you like the fresh vitamin C provided by fruit juices, choose the recipe made with fruit juice concentrate; if you want to make frozen pops from what's on hand in your cupboard, choose the recipe made with gelatin dessert mix. Wooden ice cream bar sticks can be bought very cheaply in packages of 100 at craft and hobby shops or else you can clean and re-use the sticks from store-bought pops.

FROM FRUIT JUICE DRINK CONCENTRATES

2¼ cups cold water
1 teaspoon unflavored gelatin
1 container (12 ounces) frozen fruit juice drink concentrate, thawed
11 waxy paper cups or plastic cups with a 3-ounce capacity
11 wooden ice cream bar sticks

Combine the water and gelatin in a large sauce-pan. Heat and stir until the gelatin dissolves, but do not let the water boil; let cool to room temperature. Blend the juice concentrate into the gelatin-water, then pour the combined mixture into the paper cups; set the cups in the freezer. After about 2 or 3 hours, insert the sticks and freeze overnight. To serve, peel off the paper cup or briefly submerge the plastic cup in hot water to loosen the pop.

Some frozen fruit juice drink concentrate suggestions are: lemonade, limeade, tropical fruit punch, grape-lemon drink, cranberry cocktail, black cherry drink; do not use pineapple. Some frozen concentrates may call for more than 3 cans of water in their dilution directions; if this is the case, divide the number of cans of water called for by two and use that halved amount of water with the concentrate. Use a bit more gelatin and a few more cups and sticks.

FROM GELATIN DESSERT MIXES

1 small package (3 ounces) fruit-flavored gelatin mix
½ cup sugar
2 cups boiling water
2 cups cold soda pop or fruit juice
11 waxy paper cups or plastic cups with a 3-ounce capacity
11 wooden ice cream bar sticks

Combine the gelatin mix and the sugar in a bowl or pitcher. Pour in the boiling water, then stir until dissolved; let cool slightly. Pour in any flavor soda-pop or fruit juice that complements or matches the flavor of the gelatin mix; do not use pineapple. Mix to blend, then pour the combined mixture into the paper cups. Freeze for about 2 or 3 hours, then insert sticks and freeze overnight.

To serve, peel off the paper cup or briefly submerge the plastic cup in hot water to loosen the pop.

Some gelatin mix and soda pop or juice suggestions include: black cherry gelatin and cola soda pop; grape gelatin and lemonade or grape juice; mixed fruit gelatin; and either Hawaiian Punch or fruit-punch soda pop.

SODA POPS

Makes 14

The flavor of these creamy frozen pops depends on whatever soda pop you may choose. Root beer soda pop produces a frozen black cow; cream soda makes a vanilla pop. Other soda pop flavors that are particularly good in this recipe are: black cherry, cola, chocolate, fruit punch, orange, and grape.

If you have no sweetened condensed milk on hand, a recipe for it is provided below.

1 **can (15 ounces) sweetened condensed milk**
1 **bottle (28 ounces) your choice of soda pop (or use two 12-ounce cans)**
14 **waxy paper cups or plastic cups with a 3-ounce capacity**
14 **wooden ice cream bar sticks**

Pour the sweetened condensed milk into a large pitcher. Gently but thoroughly, stir in the soda-pop. Pour the liquid into the cups. Freeze for 2 or 3 hours; insert a stick in each cup's center, then freeze overnight or until solid. To serve, peel off the paper cup or briefly submerge the plastic cup in hot water to loosen the pop.

SWEETENED CONDENSED MILK

Use a wire whisk or an egg beater or a blender to thoroughly combine 1 cup of light corn syrup, ⅞ cup evaporated milk, and 3 tablespoons nonfat dry milk. Makes the equivalent of one 15-ounce can of sweetened condensed milk.

VITAMIN-PACKED CHOCOLATE POPS

Makes 12

1 **cup chocolate milk**
1 **or 2 eggs**
⅓ **cup (half a 6-ounce can) frozen orange juice concentrate, thawed**
4 **tablespoons confectioner's sugar**
2 **cups chocolate ice cream, softened**
12 **waxy paper cups or plastic cups with a 3-ounce capacity**
12 **wooden ice cream bar sticks**

Combine the milk, eggs, orange juice concentrate, and sugar in a blender container (don't use a food processor); whirl until smooth. Adding half of the ice cream at a time, whirl again until smooth and thick. Pour the mixture into the cups; freeze for about 2 to 6 hours, then insert the sticks and freeze overnight. To serve, peel off the paper cups or briefly submerge the plastic cup in hot water to loosen the pop.

NON-ALLERGENIC VANILLA ICE MILKS

Makes 5 to 6 cups

NON-DAIRY ICE MILK

Here's an ice cream substitute for people who are allergic to animal milk. You can buy soy milk in either powdered or liquid form in many supermarkets and most health food stores. If you are using a soy-based baby formula as your soy milk, reduce the oil in the recipe to 1 tablespoon.

3 **eggs, at room temperature**
¾ **cup sugar**
½ **cup light corn syrup**
3 **cups soy milk**
⅓ **cup salad oil**
1½ **tablespoons vanilla extract**
⅛ **teaspoon salt**

Use an electric mixer at low speed to beat the eggs until frothy; add the sugar and continue beating until the eggs become thick and light. By hand, stir in each remaining ingredient separately until the mixture is blended.

Pour the mixture into an 8- or 9-inch square pan; cover loosely and freeze. In roughly 2 hours, when only a 4-inch square in the center of the pan remains unfrozen, break the mixture into big chunks and place them in a large chilled mixing bowl. Use an electric mixer on low speed to beat the mixture; gradually increase the mixer's speed until the mixture becomes smooth and somewhat fluffy. Turn the mixture into a large, lidded plastic container; cover and freeze until solidly set.

DAIRY ICE MILK

Use any kind of fresh, non-skimmed animal milk here; regular cow's milk or, for people with allergies, goat or reindeer milk; do not use buttermilk.

3 eggs, at room temperature
¾ cup sugar
½ cup light corn syrup
4 cups any fresh, non-skim milk
1 tablespoon vanilla extract
1 teaspoon almond extract
⅛ teaspoon salt

Follow the same directions as for Non-Dairy Ice Milk in the previous recipe.

DIETER'S CHOCOLATE FREEZE

Makes 1 quart

Here are 87 calories per ½ cup as opposed to the 145 calories in the same amount of chocolate ice cream.

½ cup sugar
4 tablespoons unsweetened cocoa powder
1 envelope (1 tablespoon) unflavored gelatin
Dash of salt
2½ cups skim milk
1 teaspoon orange, brandy, or vanilla extract

Combine the sugar, cocoa, gelatin, and salt in a saucepan; use a wire whisk to gradually blend in the milk. Heat at a very low setting, stirring constantly, until both the sugar and gelatin dissolve; do not boil. Let cool slightly, then stir in the extract. Pour the mixture into an 8-by-8-by-2-inch baking pan and freeze for about 3 to 6 hours, or until the mixture is almost set but not hard (if it freezes solid, let it soften). Scrape the almost-set mixture into a mixing bowl; use an electric mixer to break up the chunks and to blend. When it is smooth, pour it into a plastic container; cover and freeze until firm.

Chapter 9:

PETFOODS, HEALTH AND BEAUTY AIDS, AND HOUSEHOLD HELPERS

Sections:

☐Petfoods and Supplies
☐Health and Beauty Aids
☐Household Helpers

BEEF HEART PETFOOD FOR DOGS AND CATS

Makes about 5 or 6 cups, or the equivalent of six or seven 6½-ounce cans of petfood

Use one beef heart for cats, two or more for dogs. You can also use lamb or veal hearts to equal 3 or 4 pounds. This petfood freezes well.

1 beef heart, about 3 or 4 pounds
Lard, or bacon fat, or suet, or butter
Assorted vegetables, optional
Rice, optional, for cats

Rinse the heart and remove any blood vessels and connective tissue. If the heart is split, stuff it with some lard; close it by wrapping string around it. Place the heart in an ovenproof casserole; add 1 inch of water. Cover the casserole and bake at 325° for 2½ to 3 hours, or until the beef heart is tender; replenish the water halfway through the cooking time. Let the cooked heart cool, then cut it into coarse chunks; reserve the cooking broth.

For Cats: During the last 30 minutes of baking, add—only if your cat likes them—chunked carrots or peas or ⅓ cup raw rice. When the heart is done, run it (and any vegetables and rice) through a meat grinder into a bowl; mix in enough cooking broth to moisten. The grinding can also be done in a food processor.

For Small Dogs: During the last 30 minutes of baking, add any of the vegetables your dog likes— carrots, celery, onions, potatoes—all in chunks. When done, run the beef heart pieces and the vegetables through a meat grinder into a bowl; mix in enough cooking broth to moisten. You can also do the grinding in a food processor.

For Big Dogs: During the last 30 minutes of baking, add vegetables as described, above. When the heart and vegetables are done and cooled, cut the heart into bite-size chunks and set aside. Use a potato masher to mash the vegetables coarsely in their cooking water. Let the water boil down, if necessary, then make a gravy out of it: in a jar, shake together some flour and cold water; add it to the pot of vegetables and cooking broth; heat to thicken; repeat as necessary. Stir in the heart chunks; cool and serve.

LIVER PETFOOD FOR DOGS AND CATS

Makes 5 to 6 cups, or the equivalent of six or seven 6½-ounce cans of petfood

Buy cheap, thick liver for this petfood. Many butchers and supermarkets will sell frozen 3- to 5-pound hunks of liver for considerably less than liver sold in smaller amounts. This petfood freezes well.

About 4 pounds beef, pork, or lamb liver
Any meat broth you may have on hand, or milk, or water
Oil, or lard, or bacon fat

Wash each liver and peel off any outside membrane. Bring a pot of water to a rolling boil. Drop all the liver into the boiling water, reduce the heat to a simmer and cook, uncovered, for several minutes until the liver is done. Cooking time will depend on size; do not overcook; the centers should be pinkish. Discard the cooking liquid.

For Cats: Put the cooked liver through a meat grinder; moisten with any available meat broth or milk or water plus some oil or melted lard or bacon fat. Lacking a meat grinder, use a blender or food processor: cut the liver into chunks and whirl, ½ cup at a time for the blender and 1 cup at a time for the processor, adding enough broth and oil to facilitate the whirling. Mixed with equal amounts of cooked rice, this liver is a cure for diarrhea in cats. Liver catfood can also be combined with commercial canned catfoods such as beef by-products, tuna, fish, and chicken in order to fool your cat into not getting bored with plain liver. After refrigerating cooked liver, moisten it with some water, milk, or broth.

For Small Dogs; By hand, cut the cooked liver into small pieces. Put 1 cup of the pieces in a blender or food processor container; whirl into a purée, adding some broth and oil until the purée is the consistency of gravy. Mix this gravy into the small pieces of liver.

For Big Dogs: Same as for little dogs, above, but cut the cooked liver into bigger pieces. Purée some of the liver into a gravy as directed. Mix the liver pieces and gravy with dry dog chow.

KIDNEY PETFOOD FOR DOGS AND CATS

Makes about 5 or 6 cups, or the equivalent of six or seven 6½-ounce cans of petfood

3 or 4 pounds beef or lamb kidneys
Any meat broth you may have on hand, or milk

Wash the kidneys; remove the outer membrane; place in a heavy pot with salted water to cover. Cover the pot, bring to a boil, then simmer slowly until tender, from 30 to 60 minutes depending on size; do not overcook; the center should be slightly pink. Remove the kidneys and let them cool; discard the cooking water. Cut the cooked kidneys into big chunks; remove any large tubules.

For Cats: Put the cooked kidney chunks through a meat grinder twice or chop well in a food processor; moisten the ground meat, if necessary, with broth or milk. For variety, you can combine this kidney catfood with commercial cans of tuna catfood.

For Small Dogs: Cook the kidneys along with any of the vegetables your dog likes—carrots, celery, etc. Put the cooked kidney chunks and the vegetables through a meat grinder once or chop them in a food processor.

For Big Dogs: Cook the kidneys along with vegetables as described above. By hand, cut the meat into bite-size pieces. Smash the vegetables with a potato masher and combine them with the meat.

CHICKEN PARTS PETFOOD FOR CATS AND SMALL DOGS

Every time you cut up a whole chicken, save and freeze the necks, backs, and giblets. When you've saved enough, make this petfood. Once cooked, it freezes well.

Chicken necks and backs
Chicken giblets (hearts, kidneys, livers)

Boil the necks and backs in water to cover for 50 minutes; add the giblets and continue boiling 3 more minutes. Remove the chicken necks, backs, and giblets and let them cool; reserve the broth. Use your hands to shred off all the chicken meat from the necks and backs; there's a lot of meat on the necks so dig in between the small vertebrae bones but be careful not to include any of these bones with the meat. Cut the skins into bite-size pieces. Chop the giblets into bite-size pieces; discard the white, tendon-like part of the kidneys. Mix together the shredded chicken meat and the chopped skins and giblets.

For Cats: Serve as is or combine with liver or tuna.

For Small Dogs: Combine equal amounts of dry dog chow and cooking broth; let stand until the chow has absorbed the broth. To serve, mix 2 parts chopped chicken pieces with 1 part softened chow.

MACKEREL FOR CATS

Makes 1¾ cups, or the equivalent of two 6½-ounce cans of catfood

For some reason the canned mackerel sold for human consumption is cheaper and purer than the mackerel sold in catfood cans. Compare the price of ⅞ cup mackerel for cats (that's a 6½-ounce can) and the same amount of mackerel for humans, and you will find a considerable difference. You also get more for your money with the mackerel intended for humans because there are no added cereal fillers and this mackerel has plenty of vitamin-rich fish oil to make your cat's coat shiny and to discourage fur balls. Mackerel for humans is sold in all supermarkets near other canned fish such as tuna and sardines; most brands come in bright red cans.

1 can (16 ounces) mackerel for humans

Drain the oil from the can; you may want to reserve it for mixing in with other homemade or commercial catfoods. Pour half the fish into a bowl and use a fork to break it up into small, mushy pieces. If there are bones, you can remove them or else mush them up well; they will be very soft and digestible for cats. If the mackerel is particularly soft, you can do this right in the can. Repeat for the other half of the can, then serve.

CAT REPELLENT

1 small can ground ginger

Most cats rear away at the smell of ground ginger. Sprinkle this spice liberally on the spots where you don't want cats to linger. Indoor use of ginger as a cat repellent is most effective, but outdoor use can be effective if you frequently repeat the sprinkling. Ground ginger will not stain rugs or upholstery and it vacuums up without a trace.

LITTER PAN LINERS

Cut off and discard the top two-thirds of a 15- to 24-inch wide plastic garbage bag; fit the bottom of the bag into and over the corners of a standard size cat litter pan and you now have a much less expensive litter pan liner that is exactly the same as the cat pan liners sold exclusively for that purpose. If your cat is a deep digger, use the cut-off top of the bag to doubly line the litter pan before adding the litter. To make a pan liner for large-size litter pans, use a 24- to 30-inch wide plastic garbage bag.

FRESH EGG SHAMPOO

Makes 1 application

This shampoo leaves hair protein-enriched and squeaky clean.

1 large egg, separated
3 tablespoons clear shampoo, such as castile or baby shampoo

In a small bowl, beat the egg white until foamy and soft but not stiff. Gently blend in the yolk followed by the shampoo. Transfer the mixture to a plastic cup.

Wet your hair with warm but not hot water; massage half the egg shampoo into your scalp; it will not suds much. Rinse well and repeat; this time it will suds a lot. Leave the second application on your hair for 1 minute, no more, before thoroughly rinsing.

FRESH EGG CONDITIONER

Makes 1 application

1 egg yolk
½ teaspoon olive oil
¾ cup lukewarm water

Use a rotary beater to vigorously beat the egg yolk until it is thick and light colored. Slowly drizzle in drops of the oil, beating well between additions. Slowly add and beat the water into the egg mixture. Transfer the mixture to a plastic container.

After shampooing, massage all the conditioner into your hair and leave it on for a few minutes before thoroughly rinsing.

DANDRUFF TREATMENT

Makes 1 application

10 aspirin tablets, 5 grains each
¾ cup warm water

Dissolve the aspirin in the water. After shampooing, massage this liquid into your scalp and leave it on for about 10 minutes, then rinse thoroughly.

LIQUID SOAP

Makes about 2 cups

Save all the end-of-the-bar soap slivers and turn them into newly scented liquid soap. You can also use those small, practically useless soaps collected from hotels and motels.

¾ cup dry soap scraps broken into 1-inch pieces
1 to 3 cups hot water
Food coloring
Scented oil or perfume
A pump bottle

Whirl the soap pieces to a coarse powder in a blender container; any pieces bigger than 1 inch should be smashed with a hammer before whirling. Put the powder in a non-aluminum pot, add 1½ cups of the hot water, and bring to a boil; stir and simmer, uncovered, for about 5 minutes. During this time, add drops of food coloring to suit your taste and enough water, in gradual doses, to make a soft, liquid soap. Remove from heat, continue stirring to help the mixture cool, adding more water if necessary to keep the soap liquid. When the soap is lukewarm, stir in your choice of scented oil or your favorite perfume to suit your taste. Pour the mixture into an empty pump bottle.

STYPTIC LOTION

Makes ½ cup

Ask your druggist for both alum and glycerin.

½ cup water
1 teaspoon powdered alum
¼ teaspoon glycerin

Combine the water and alum in a measuring cup. Stir in the glycerin until well mixed. Pour the mixture into a small bottle. To use, shake the bottle, moisten a cotton ball with the styptic lotion, and apply.

CLEANSING GRAINS

Makes 1 application

Facial soap
1 teaspoon cornmeal

Wet your face; work up a lather in your hands using your choice of facial soap; add the cornmeal to one upturned, soapy palm; rub the meal into the lather then wash your face with this gentle but effective scrub; avoid the eye area. For dry skin, substitute granulated sugar for the cornmeal.

RASPBERRY VINEGAR FACE SPLASH

Makes 1⅔ cups

This is the original, pH-balanced face splash for normal to oily skin. It is both invigorating and non-drying. Further, any commercial face splash or pH-restorer is only an inferior, synthetic version of what this or any vinegar can do. Vinegar splashed onto a wet, just-washed face forms what is called an acid mantle, which allows your skin to replenish the just-washed-away facial oils, but prevents the build-up of excess oils that clog pores. Any vinegar will accomplish the balance, but distilled vinegar or the following fruit-scented distilled vinegars are the most pleasant.

3 cups fresh raspberries
1 cup white distilled vinegar

Measure 1 cup of the raspberries into a non-aluminum bowl. Use a potato masher to just slightly mash the berries; pour 1 cup of vinegar atop. Place plastic wrap directly on the surface of the berry mixture. Let stand at room temperature for 18 to 24 hours.

Strain the vinegar into a clean, non-aluminum bowl; discard the raspberries. Measure a fresh cup of raspberries into the vinegar; mash slightly. Cover and let stand as directed above.

Follow the instructions in the preceding paragraph once more, using the last cup of raspberries. Strain the completed raspberry vinegar along with ⅔ cup of water into an attractive bottle; shake to combine and replace the bottle's cap or cork.

To Use: Wash and rinse your face as you usually do. Pour a teaspoon or two of the raspberry vinegar into a cupped hand and quickly splash it over your entire face. Let set a few seconds before blotting your face dry. Try not to get the vinegar in your eyes.

STRAWBERRY VINEGAR

Replace the raspberries with 3 cups washed hulled strawberries.

ORANGE VINEGAR

Add the peel of 1 orange to 1 cup of white vinegar; do not include the white, bitter part of the peel. Let the mixture steep in a non-aluminum, covered container for 1 week. Pour the vinegar plus ⅔ cup water (or, if you wish, orange-flower water) into a bottle and use as directed.

MINTY MOUTHWASH

Makes 1 quart

¾ teaspoon boric acid
1 packet Weight Watchers or Sweet 'N Low, or the saccharin equivalent of 2 teaspoons sugar
3 drops of oil of peppermint
4 cups water
Green food coloring

Combine in a clean quart-size bottle the boric acid, artificial sweetener, oil of peppermint, and 1 cup of the water. Close the bottle and shake well until the ingredients are dissolved and mixed. Add the remaining 3 cups of water and a drop of food coloring to turn the mouthwash light green. Shake the bottle to mix, then swish some mouthwash in your mouth and adjust the oil of peppermint if necessary. Store at room temperature. Do not swallow.

CINNAMON MOUTHWASH

Replace the oil of peppermint with oil of cinnamon and use red food coloring instead of green. For a spicy mouthwash, use 2 drops oil of cinnamon with 1 drop oil of cloves.

BABY OIL

Makes 1 pint

If you use baby oil for your baby or yourself, you can save some money. The variety sold exclusively for babies is nothing but perfumed mineral oil. Your baby won't notice the missing perfume and you can smell of your favorite scent instead of a baby's.

1 pint bottle of light mineral oil
Your favorite perfume (not cologne), optional

For babies, simply use the odorless mineral oil as is. For yourself, pour the mineral oil into a bowl; by drops, stir in the perfume until the oil is lightly scented. Pour the scented oil back into its bottle through a funnel. Use as you usually do. Besides perfume, you can use any essential oil, such as oil of lemon or oil of orange.

RICH COCOA BUTTER CREAM

Makes ⅓ cup

This excellent, chocolate-scented hand and body cream is far richer in skin-nourishing cocoa butter than any commercial product, yet it is far less expensive. Use it to relieve flaky winter skin, to

prevent summer suntans from turning your skin to leather, and to prevent stretch marks during pregnancy. Ask your druggist for the 1-ounce sticks of pure cocoa butter as they are not usually displayed.

2 ounces (2 sticks) cocoa butter
4 tablespoons petroleum jelly
4 teaspoons mineral oil

Break the cocoa butter into chunks. Place the chunks in the top of a double boiler along with the petroleum jelly. Heat and stir over a low flame until liquid. Remove the top pot from the double boiler so that it is no longer in contact with any heat, then use a wire whisk or a fork to beat the mixture until it starts to thicken and look like melting margarine on a hot day. Add the mineral oil and continue beating, vigorously now, until the cream is cool and an opaque yellow. Use a rubber spatula to scrape the cream into an attractive widemouth jar. Cover and store at room temperature. If you store the cream for over 3 months, little bits of the cocoa butter will start to re-solidify; they are very small and dissolve as soon as they come in contact with the warmth of your skin.

COCOA BUTTER AND COCONUT OIL CREAM

Replace the mineral oil with coconut oil; you can buy it at health food stores. After beating in the coconut oil, gradually beat in enough drops of coconut extract to scent the cream.

DEODORANTS

LIQUID DEODORANT

Dissolve 1 tablespoon of powdered alum in 1½ cups of water; stir in 1 tablespoon of rubbing alcohol. Pour the mixture into a clean, plastic spray bottle. Shake the bottle before each use. You can also scent this deodorant with your favorite cologne or toilet water.

CREAM DEODORANT

In the top of a double boiler, heat and constantly stir until smooth 1 tablespoon *each*: petroleum jelly, baking soda, and talcum powder. Scrape the mixture into a clean jar; allow it to cool, then cover. Apply with fingertips.

DEODORANT POWDER

Thoroughly combine ½ cup baking soda with ¼ cup Ammens Medicated Powder. Pour into an empty powder container or into a sugar shaker normally used in baking. Sprinkled liberally into each armpit, this powder will absorb underarm odor for about 6 hours.

PERFUME FROM FLOWERS AND HERBS

Here is a way to capture the fragrance of any fresh flower or herb into a perfumed oil. Choose a strong-smelling flower variety like lilies of the valley, roses, apple blossoms, clover, lavender, or whatever grows and smells nice in your garden. Leafy herbs can include mint, pennyroyal, sage, basil, and lemon verbena.

1 **quart-size (approximately) clear glass jar**
A **1- or 2-cup (approximately) clear glass jar**
A **clean, new, perfectly dry kitchen sponge, about 4½ by 3 inches**
Light mineral oil
Fresh flowers or herbs, all one variety
A **square of cheesecloth or clean nylon stocking, if necessary**
A **rubber band, if necessary**
Masking tape

The 2 jars will be used together and must have openings that are exactly or almost exactly the same size. Some suggestions are: a quart-sized spaghetti sauce jar with an applesauce or jelly jar; an 18-ounce peanut butter jar with a mayonnaise jar; or a large and a small canning jar. Try to choose jars with small openings to avoid having to use a cheesecloth barrier. Before beginning, check the weather report to make sure you will have three to five sunny and warm days in a row.

Completely saturate the sponge in the mineral oil. Place it in the smaller jar; do not cut it in half to do this. Using blossoms only (no leaves or stems), pack the larger jar full of flowers. If you are using herbs, use both leaves and stems, making sure to bruise all the leaves to release the fragrant oils. Set the large jar right-side-up in front of you. Look at the illustration opposite and hold the sponge-filled jar upside-down. If the sponge falls out of the inverted jar, you will have to set up a cheesecloth barrier. Place a square of single layer cheesecloth over the large jar's opening and place a rubber band around both the cloth and the jar's neck to hold the sponge in place.

Opening to opening, place the upside-down, sponge-filled jar directly atop the right-side-up, flower-filled jar. Make a tight seal between the jars with as much masking tape as is needed. Set this jar arrangement in direct sunlight all day long; bring the jars inside at night. The next day, replace the flowers or herbs with fresh ones and repeat the sunning. After three days of this, check the oil for fragrance. If you want a stronger scent, repeat with fresh cuttings for one to three more days. Using a funnel, carefully squeeze the scented oil from the sponge into a small bottle. Use as perfume. Makes a nice gift.

LEMON, ORANGE, OR LIME OILS

Use freshly grated peelings instead of flowers in the bottom jar. Do not include the white, bitter part of the peel.

INSECT REPELLENTS AND BITE RELIEVERS

REPELLENTS

• Oil of pennyroyal is an effective, non-chemical insect repellent safe for children and adults. Many health food stores carry oil of pennyroyal. Mix and bottle ⅓ cup 80-proof vodka with 1 to 2 teaspoons oil of pennyroyal. Apply sparingly. Don't be concerned that you will smell as if you've been drinking; the pennyroyal has a lemon-mint smell stronger than that of the vodka.

If you cannot find a store that sells oil of pennyroyal, you can easily grow that herb and make your own. Pennyroyal is a member of the mint family and can be grown in any home garden; to turn it into an oil, follow the directions in the preceding Perfume from Flowers and Herbs recipe.

• Mix and bottle ½ cup 80-proof vodka with 1 teaspoon of citronella oil. The oil is sold in most drugstores. Don't be concerned that you will smell as if you've been drinking; the citronella smell is stronger than the vodka's. Apply sparingly.

MAKING PERFUMES FROM FLOWERS AND HERBS

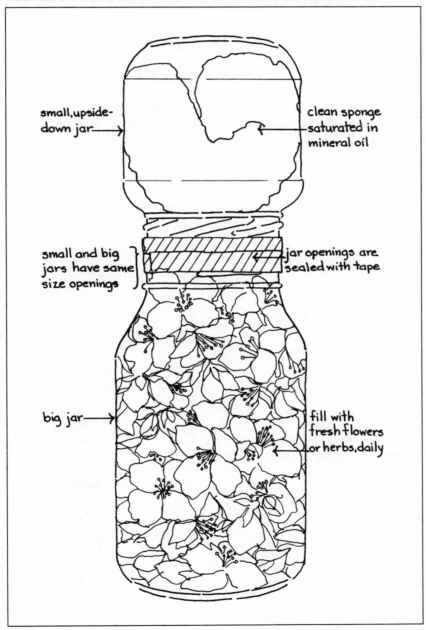

small, upside-down jar

clean sponge saturated in mineral oil

small and big jars have same size openings

jar openings are sealed with tape

big jar

fill with fresh flowers or herbs, daily

RELIEVERS

• This always works for mosquito bites: Lightly moisten the bite area by licking it, then liberally sprinkle on enough table salt to coat. Wait one full minute and the itching will have stopped entirely.

• Buy a small bottle of aromatic spirits of ammonia at the drugstore. Use a small cotton swab to apply a small amount to the bite. This reliever is exactly the same as the insect-bite sticks sold at a higher price.

• Lightly moisten the bite area, then sprinkle on some meat tenderizer.

• Make a spreadable paste out of baking soda and water. Apply liberally to the affected area. Also good for relieving poison ivy itching.

GRANDMA'S COUGH SYRUP

Makes 1 dose

2 teaspoons honey
1 teaspoon strained fresh lemon juice
¼ teaspoon glycerin

Thoroughly blend the ingredients, then swallow whenever needed.

ASPER-GARGLE

Makes 1 dose

This remedy may not be as pleasant as the preceding one, but it is quite effective in soothing a painfully sore throat.

¾ cup very warm water
2 aspirin tablets, 5 grains each
½ teaspoon salt

Measure the water into a drinking glass; it should be very warm but not so warm that it would further irritate your throat. Add the aspirins and salt and stir until dissolved. Gargle repeatedly with the mixture until it has all been used.

MOIST TOWELETTES

Makes about 4 dozen

These handy wash-up towels cost less than half the price of their commercial counterparts while they contain no harsh alcohols or bizarre preservatives and they stay fresh and moist just as long.

20 to 24 squares of white Bounty-brand paper towels
1 cup witch hazel
1 teaspoon glycerin, optional (available at drugstores)

Separate and stack each of the paper towel squares from the roll; cut each square in half. Place the rectangles in front of you vertically, fold each rectangle into thirds as if you were folding up a business letter; then fold the letter in half, as if you were closing a book. Place all but 4 of the folded towelettes on a single or double layer in a large shallow lasagne-type pan; set the pan aside.

In a shaker jar, combine the witch hazel and glycerin. (The glycerin is not essential; however it allows the towelettes to remain moist for long periods of time as well as being good for the skin.) Drizzle the liquid evenly over the pan of folded towelettes and allow them to absorb for several minutes. Press the towelettes to help them absorb any excess liquid; if any liquid remains, press in 1 or more of the reserved towelettes.

Stack the moistened towelettes in a lidded plastic 2-cup container; cover securely and use as needed when traveling with children, on picnics, in the car, etc. If the towelettes begin to dry out, simply pour in a little more witch hazel.

WINDSHIELD WIPERS

If you have used glycerin in your towelettes, they can be used as an effective automobile windshield-wiping cloth in even the coldest weather.

CARRY-ALONG TOWELETTES

Pack up to 10 moist towelettes in a Zip-Loc sandwich bag to carry in a purse, tote bag, or lunchbox.

WIPEY-DIPEY TOWELETTES

Replace the witch hazel and glycerin with 1 cup light mineral oil or 1 cup baby oil; saturate and package the folded towelettes as directed. Use as a half-price, alcohol-free diaper wipe for baby.

METAL POLISHES

SILVER POLISHES

• Heat 1 cup of water to boiling in a non-aluminum saucepan; remove from heat and stir in 4½ tablespoons soap flakes and 4 tablespoons whiting. You can buy whiting very cheaply at drugstores; ask your druggist for it as it isn't usually displayed. Vigorously stir the soap and whiting until dissolved, then let cool. When cool, stir in 1½ teaspoons either clear or sudsing ammonia. Pour the mixture into a clean bottle. Shake well before using.

• Rub silver with a baking soda and water paste. For all silverware except pieces with raised patterns and cemented handles, you can also make a soaking solution. First, line a glass or enamel pan with aluminum foil. Place the silverware in the lined pan. Bring 2 quarts of water to a boil; stir in and dissolve 2 tablespoons baking soda; remove from heat. Pour the solution over the silverware and let it stand for an hour or two until tarnish disappears. Rinse in water and dry.

COPPER AND BRASS POLISHES

• Combine ½ cup *each*: salt, flour, and vinegar. Brush this mixture liberally onto brass or copper and let stand 1 hour. Wipe off.

• For blackened copper-bottom pots, dissolve salt in vinegar to make a runny paste. Dip a cloth into the mixture and rub the copper with it until it shines.

• Use toothpaste (not the gel kind) on a soft cloth; rub until the brass or copper shines.

• Save lemon halves after using up the juice. Dip the cut side in table salt so it picks up a generous amount, then rub it on the brass or copper until it shines.

STAINLESS STEEL POLISH

• Use lighter fluid on a soft cloth.

• Combine 3 tablespoons baking soda with 4 cups of water; store in a jar or a bottle. To use, sponge the steel with the solution in the direction of the steel's grain; rinse.

LIQUID WAX FOR WOODEN FLOORS

Makes 1 quart

⅛ cup chopped paraffin (sold next to pectin and jelly-making supplies in the supermarket)
1 bottle (16 ounces) heavy mineral oil
1 bottle (16 ounces) light mineral oil
Several drops oil of lemon, optional (sold at drugstores)

Slowly melt the paraffin over very low heat in the top part of a double boiler; do not use anything other than a double boiler. Remove the top part of the double boiler from the bottom part, stir both of the mineral oils into the liquid paraffin, set both bottles aside. If you wish, also stir in a few drops of oil of lemon for a fresh scent. Allow the mixture to cool. Pour the floor wax back into the empty mineral oil bottles. Be very careful to remove the original labels from these bottles; securely tape on appropriate labels along with the following directions.

To Use: Apply liberally and in circular motions onto clean, dry, dust-free wooden floors; use several layers of cheesecloth to apply. Let the wax dry thoroughly, then buff lightly.

COOKING OIL "SPRAY"

Makes 1½ cups

Here is a non-spray version of anti-stick cooking

sprays. A little goes a long way. Whole wheat pastry flour is available at all health food stores.

½ **cup whole wheat pastry flour (no substitutions)**
1 **cup vegetable shortening**

Measure the flour into a medium-size mixing bowl; add heaping tablespoons of shortening to the flour, working it in well with your fingertips before adding more. When the ingredients are uniformly combined, scrape them into a lidded plastic container; cover and store at room temperature.

To use: With your fingertips, rub a thin film of the mixture over the bottom of the cooking pan. Do not use this mixture when a baking recipe calls for greasing and flouring a pan, but do use it when cookies require a lightly greased pan, and for frying eggs.

HOMEMADE PASTES

Each makes 1 cup of paste to be used on paper

CORNSTARCH PASTE

6 **tablespoons cornstarch**
1 **cup cold water**
4 **teaspoons light corn syrup**
½ **teaspoon white distilled or cider vinegar**
¼ **heaping teaspoon oil of wintergreen or 6 drops of oil of peppermint (ask your druggist for either of these)**

Put the cornstarch and water in a jar; cover and shake to dissolve. Pour half of the jar's liquid into a small saucepan. Stir in the syrup and vinegar; heat the mixture over medium-low heat; stir constantly and remove the pan from the heat when the mixture is fully thickened. Reshake the jar's remaining contents; gradually pour this liquid into the hot saucepan mixture. Stir gently until smooth, then add the oil. Pour the mixture into a widemouth jar; let cool; cover and let ripen for a few days before using.

QUICK FLOUR PASTE

1 **cup cool water**
4 **level tablespoons flour**
4 **teaspoons light corn syrup**

In the top part of a double boiler, blend the flour into the water; cook, stirring constantly, until thick. Remove the top part of the boiler from the bottom and stir the syrup into the mixture. Pour the paste into a widemouth jar; let it cool, then cover and let it ripen for a few days before using.

ALUM PASTE

1 **cup cool water**
¼ **cup flour**
2 **tablespoons sugar**
1½ **teaspoons alum**
A **few drops of oil of peppermint, or wintergreen, or peppermint extract, optional**

Combine the water, flour, and sugar in a saucepan; cook the mixture until it becomes clear. Remove the pan from the heat; stir in the alum and mint scent. Pour the paste into a widemouth jar; let it cool, then cover and let it ripen for a few days before using. The alum in this paste keeps it from drying out in the jar for long periods of time, but it should not be given to children who are apt to eat it.

CANNED HEAT

Use under fondue pots and chafing dishes, in power emergencies, as a camping stove, or to start a camp, fireplace, or barbecue fire. Gives hours of continuous heat.

Many **6½- or 7-ounce tuna fish or catfood cans, empty**
Lots of **cardboard, about three 8-by-11-inch pieces per can**
Paraffin, **about 4 ounces per can (sold next to pectin and jellymaking supplies in the supermarket)**

Clean and dry as many tuna or catfood cans as you'll need. Cut the cardboard into strips that are as wide as the height of the cans you're using; 1½ inches is about average; corrugated or slick non-porous cardboard won't work here. Place the cardboard strips flush against the walls of the can, and continue doing so, creating a continuous spiral of cardboard. End at the center of the can, making sure that the cardboard strips are fitted as snugly as possible.

Melt the paraffin in a double boiler; *never* melt it in a plain pot as it may ignite if its temperature gets too high. Slowly pour the liquid wax into the cans of cardboard so that the cardboard absorbs the wax. Leave the top ¼ inch of the cardboard in each can unsaturated for easy lighting. Let the cans cool and then store indefinitely. Light and use as you would any canned heat.

WINDSHIELD WASHER FLUID

Makes 2 quarts

3 **cups rubbing alcohol**
4 **cups water**
Several drops of blue food coloring
2 **teaspoons liquid dishwashing detergent**

Pour the alcohol, water, and blue food coloring into a gallon-size plastic jug; cover and shake well to combine. Add the dish detergent; cover and shake again. Remove whatever label is on the jug and securely tape on a new label; the label and the blue food coloring help ensure that the jug will not be mistaken by another family member for any other product.

ORGANIC INSECTICIDE

Makes about 1 cup

2 **medium onions**
8 **large garlic cloves**

Peel and coarsely chop the onions and garlic; pack them into a 2-cup glass jar; pour in enough

water to reach the top of the jar. Cover the jar tightly and let it steep in a dark place at room temperature for 1 week. Strain the liquid into a small spray bottle and mist liberally over any outdoor plants where there is an insect problem.

This insecticide uses the same principle as planting chives or scallions next to insect-prone plants. The spray works well on roses and is especially safe and effective on garden vegetables where chemicals are unwanted. For use on indoor plants, dilute it with equal amounts of water and use sparingly.

CHARCOAL LIGHTERS

Here are two fast, effective, inexpensive, chemical-free methods for lighting charcoal briquets in an outdoor barbecue grill.

• Use a rotary or electric can opener to remove the top and bottom rounds from a 3-pound coffee can. Use a pointed soda-pop can opener to puncture a series of triangles around the bottom rim of the can; space the triangles about an inch apart from each other.

Place the can in the bottom of an empty charcoal grill so that the triangle punctures are at the bottom. Fill the bottom third of the can with closely crumpled-up newspapers, then fill the rest of the can with charcoal briquets. Poke a lighted wooden match or paper drinking straw into one of the triangle punctures so that the newspaper within ignites. When the coals are burning well, use a pair of pliers to remove the can, leaving nicely glowing coals.

• Place a charcoal briquet in each slot of two papier-mâché, molded egg cartons; do not use plastic egg cartons. Close the cartons; place them, side by side, in an empty charcoal grill and set the paper on fire with several matches. By the time the paper cartons have burned away, the charcoal will be glowing.

Chapter 10:

STOCKING UP

Sections:

☐ Easy Home-Dried Foods
☐ What to Do with a Bumper Crop of Tomatoes
☐ What to Do with All that Zucchini
☐ What to Do with Extra Pumpkins

BEEF JERKY FROM YOUR OVEN

Makes about 6 ounces

Once dried, this high-protein, lightweight snack will keep indefinitely. Use the leanest beef possible to avoid spoilage. The secret to cutting the meat into thin uniform strips is to partially freeze it so it is firm when you slice it.

About 1¼ pounds flat boneless lean beef such
   as:
   flank steak, London broil, sirloin tip,
   partially frozen
2 tablespoons water
½ teaspoon Liquid Smoke
Salt
Pepper
2 shallow, rimmed baking pans, each about 9
   by 13 inches
Cake-type racks to fit the above pans

The beef should be partially frozen: it should be icy without being too solid to cut. Carefully trim and discard every bit of fat from the beef, then cut the beef into very thin ⅛-inch strips that are as long as possible. If you prefer a chewy jerky, cut with the grain of the beef; if you prefer crisper but more tender jerky, cut across the grain of the beef.

Set all the strips out flat and in a single layer on a long sheet of aluminum foil. Combine the water with the Liquid Smoke and liberally brush the top of every strip with the mixture. Follow this by liberally sprinkling the top of every strip with salt then sprinkle on pepper to taste. Turn all the strips over and repeat the brushing and sprinkling procedure. Place the strips, layer upon layer, in a large mixing bowl; place a plate directly atop the strips, then put a heavy weight such as a brick or several 1-pound cans atop the plate. Cover the bowl with plastic wrap and let it marinate in your refrigerator for 12 hours.

Remove the strips from the bowl and pat them dry between paper towels. Line the 2 baking pans with aluminum foil; set the racks inside the lined pans. Arrange the beef strips on the racks with their long edges close together but not overlapping. If you don't have enough room in your oven to accommodate both pans, or if you haven't enough racks, lay the strips directly across the oven's own rack; place this rack in the middle of the oven and cover the bottom oven rack with aluminum foil to catch the drippings.

Bake the beef strips at 175° for 6 to 10 hours, making sure to open the oven door every few hours to let moisture escape (if your oven is incapable of steadily maintaining this temperature, then bake at 200° for 5 to 7 hours), or until the meat has turned deep brown and feels dry throughout. Beef jerky should not be brittle, but it should be completely free of moisture and somewhere between crisp and chewy; a test piece should crack but it should not break in two when you bend it. Use paper towels to absorb any beads of oil on the strips, then let them cool completely. Store the finished jerky at room temperature in airtight containers. If the jerky is moist or extra-chewy, place it in plastic bags and freeze until ready to use; the lack of moisture allows for speedy thawing.

RANCH-STYLE JERKY

When sprinkling the just-cut beef strips with salt and pepper, also sprinkle them on both sides with equal amounts of onion powder and garlic powder to taste.

SPICY-HOT JERKY

Replace the Liquid Smoke mixture with 1 tablespoon Worcestershire sauce mixed with 1 tablespoon water. Sprinkle the just-cut strips with the salt and pepper as well as with a combined mixture of: 1 tablespoon chili powder, ½ teaspoon ground cumin, ½ teaspoon garlic powder, and ⅛ teaspoon cayenne pepper.

BEEF JERKY AU VIN

Replace the Liquid Smoke mixture with 2 tablespoons dry red wine mixed with 2 teaspoons strained fresh lemon juice. Sprinkle the just-cut strips with the salt and pepper as well as a combined mixture of ½ teaspoon garlic powder and ½ teaspoon finely ground oregano.

ORIENTAL BEEF JERKY

Replace the Liquid Smoke mixture with 1 tablespoon soy sauce mixed with 1 tablespoon water.

AIR-DRIED VEGETABLES

Most vegetables require lengthy preparation and the use of a food dehydrator to become successfully and safely dehydrated. The following vegetables and herbs are the exception. They require not much more than air drying in medium humidity in an ordinary kitchen.

Hang the vegetables in your kitchen in an overhead, shady spot where the air circulates well. The three most likely spots in every kitchen are: somewhere well above the oven, or near a radiator, or on the kitchen curtain rod. Drying time depends upon the humidity in your kitchen and the kind of vegetable. A test for dryness is included under every vegetable listed.

Most of the following vegetables will probably be added to your own existing recipes as a convenient flavor enhancer, but if you wish to rehydrate them and use them for their own sake, use the following formula: Pour 1½ cups of boiling water over each cup of dried vegetable. Let soak for 30 minutes to 2 hours, or until completely rehydrated. Cook as you would a fresh vegetable. Dried beans require overnight soaking; chopped vegetables usually require no more than 10 to 15 minutes rehydration time.

DRY BEANS (KIDNEY, NAVY, PINTO, AND SOY AS WELL AS OVERRIPE LIMA, GREEN, SNAP, AND WAX BEANS)

Dry the pods on the vine or else use a large needle and thin cord to string the tips of the bean pods into necklaces; hang them to dry. When the bean pods are light brown, shell the beans. The beans are dry when they shatter when hit with a hammer. If insects have been a problem in your garden, treat the beans by either freezing them for 3 days or heating them in a 150° oven for 40 minutes. Store the dried beans in airtight containers.

GREEN, SNAP, AND WAX BEANS

Wash and dry the beans. Use a large needle or a darning needle and thin cord or carpet thread to string the tips of the bean pods as you would beads. Leave about ½-inch airspace between each bean and hang to dry. They are dry when they turn dark green to brownish and are brittle.

CHILI PEPPERS

Do not touch your face or eyes when working with any chili pepper as the burning, hot oils are easily transferable. Thread the peppers into an attractive, hanging bunch using a darning needle and carpet thread. Hang to dry.

CORN

Carefully peel back the husks, leaving them attached at the base of the corn; remove the corn silks, then fold the husks back into their original position. Place the corn directly on the middle oven rack with space between each ear so that air can circulate. Bake at 325° for 1½ hours. Let the corn cool, then strip off the husks. Hang the corn so that the ears do not touch, until the kernels are dry and brittle. If you are dealing with home-grown corn, simply let it dry on the stalk until the husk dries out; remove the husk, and hang as described above until the kernels are dry.

Remove the dry kernels from the cobs and store in airtight containers. To cook dried corn, cover it with cold water and let soak overnight; the next day, simmer it for about 30 minutes, or until the kernels are tender. If you have access to a grain mill, this dried corn makes excellent, flavorful cornmeal.

HERBS

Gather garden herbs just when the plant begins to flower and just after the morning dew has evaporated. Cut the stems off the herbs, 5 or 6 inches from the tip. If the leaves are clean, don't wash them as some oils may rinse away, too, but if the leaves are dusty, quickly rinse in cold water; shake off the water and briefly leave the stems in the sunlight to evaporate the washing water.

Tie the herbs into small bunches and gather them with either rubber bands or wire twist-ties. Hang the bunches upside-down to dry for 1 to 3 weeks, or until the leaves crumble when rubbed between your hands.

MUSHROOMS

Use only commercially grown mushrooms. Use a damp cloth to wipe the mushroom caps clean; don't wash them; trim off the woody parts of the stems. Slice the mushrooms into ⅛- to ¼-inch slices. String them into a necklace using a thin sewing needle and ordinary sewing thread. Hang to dry until leathery to brittle.

If threading the mushrooms seems bothersome, set the slices on a non-stick cookie sheet (or a cookie sheet very lightly sprayed with spray-on vegetable oil, see page 146); set the cookie sheet in a 125° to 150° oven with the door propped ajar for 3 to 5 hours, or until the slices are leathery to brittle; turn the slices over every hour.

Store the dried slices in an airtight container. Drop the slices into any recipe that contains liquid, or else powder the dried slices by whirling them in a blender to use as a seasoning. Don't be alarmed if the dried mushrooms smell a lot like chocolate; the pure mushroom fragrance returns upon the addition of water.

ONION FLAKES

Peel and grate several onions and spread on very lightly greased cookie sheets. Bake at 125° to 150° with the oven door propped ajar for 4 to 7 hours, or until the flakes become brittle and light colored; turn the flakes once during the baking period.

PARSLEY FLAKES

Rinse bunches of parsley; shake off excess water; let drain on a dishrack. Line a shallow baking pan or cookie sheet with a single layer of paper toweling. One sprig at a time, pinch the parsley leaves off their stems and place the leaves in a single layer on the lined cookie sheet; you can pinch each triple set of leaves off all at once using thumb and forefinger. Let the parsley leaves dry on top of or in a cold oven for 2 to 4 days. To test for dryness: crumble a leaf between your fingers; it should be brittle and break up readily. Store in an airtight container.

POTATOES

See page 41.
[MAKE AHEAD CONVENIENCE MIXES/Side Dish Mixes/ Dehydrated Potatoes from Your Oven]

ORGANIC RAISINS

Commercially made raisins are dipped in lye solution and dried with sulfur fumes. Here's what they taste like naturally.

Several bunches fresh ripe Thompson seedless grapes

Bring a large pot of water to a brisk boil. Wash the grapes, attached to their stems, in cold water, then plunge them into the boiling water until their skins crack. Drain and cool. When cool enough to handle, remove all the grapes from the stems and spread them in 1 layer on a very lightly oiled, large, shallow, rimmed baking pan.

Set the pan in a 160° oven with the door propped slightly ajar. Bake for 2 to 6 hours, turning the grapes over every hour or so, until they have become pliable, wrinkled raisins. Let them cool, then store in an airtight container.

FRUIT LEATHERS

Choose the method you will use depending on the season and the humidity in your area. Should you choose the outdoor method and the weather won't allow for completion, you can always finish off the leathers in your oven. In any of these methods, begin making fruit leathers in the morning.

Several large cookie sheets or shallow baking pans, enough to fill 1 or 2 oven racks
High quality, clear plastic film, the thicker, the better, like Saran Wrap
Cellophane or masking tape
Choice of fruit, see below
Cheesecloth (if sun drying)

Prepare the Fruit Purée: Refer to the fruits listed below and plan on making enough fruit purée to fit the number of cookie sheets you will use. Approximately 1 to 1½ cups of purée will cover a 9-by-13-inch or similar size pan. Prepare and measure the fruit of your choice into a saucepan; add the specified amount of sugar; heat as directed. Several cups at a time, whirl the heated fruit in a blender or food processor until it becomes a purée; pour the purée into a bowl and let it cool to lukewarm.

Outdoor Drying Method: Plan to make the fruit leathers when you know you will have 3 sunny, warm, dry days in a row. If you can be certain of 3 days of these conditions, you can make the fruit leathers on a large scale, filling as many cookie sheets as you wish; you could even replace the cookie sheets with a folding card table or 1 or 2 large plywood squares measuring several feet across. But if there's a possibility that you will be granted only 1 or 2 dry sunny days, you should use only the cookie sheets or shallow baking pans because they will allow you to complete the recipe in your oven.

Tear off lengths of plastic film and stretch them across the cookie sheets and upside-down, shallow baking pans; the baking pans should be upside down so the rims will not interfere with even drying. (If you are working on a large scale, stretch the plastic film, overlapping, across the folding table or the boards.) Secure the plastic with tape.

Prepare the fruit purée according to the directions above. Ladle some of the lukewarm purée onto the plastic-filmed surface; use a rubber spatula to evenly spread the purée into a puddle ¼-inch thick; repeat to cover all the cookie sheets. Cover a level, outdoor table with a clean tablecloth, then place the cookie sheets on it. Devise a tent out of a single layer of cheesecloth to protect the purée from bugs and dirt.

Let the purée puddles dry in full sunlight shifting them out of shadows when necessary. At sunset, bring the purée indoors, then return it to the sunlight the next morning. Repeat this drying process to get 3 full, sun-drying days. On the third day, the purée should feel firm. Test for doneness by peeling one of the puddles off its plastic: if nothing sticks, it is done and you can package the leather according to the directions below. If the weather has been extra dry and windy, you might test for doneness on the second day of drying.

Oven Drying Method: Tear off lengths of plastic film and stretch them across enough cookie sheets and upside down baking pans to fill 1 or 2 racks of your oven; the baking pans work better when they are upside down because the rims won't interfere with even drying. Secure the plastic film with tape. Prepare the fruit purée according to the directions above. Ladle the lukewarm purée onto the cookie sheets; use a rubber spatula to evenly spread it into ¼-inch-thick puddles.

Place the cookie sheets or pans in a 140° to 150° oven or at the lowest temperature setting that your oven can steadily maintain. Set the pans 2 to 4 inches apart from each other to allow for some air circulation. Prop the oven door slightly ajar so that moisture can escape. Let the purée dry for 6 to 10 hours. Touch the oven racks and cookie sheets periodically; they should always feel mildly warm but never hot to the touch. Dry in this manner until the purée feels firm. Test for doneness by peeling one of the puddles off its plastic: If nothing sticks, it is done and you can package the leather according to the directions below.

Combination Outdoor/Indoor Drying Method: Follow the directions for drying the purée outdoors in the sun using only plastic-lined cookie sheets and baking pans as your surfaces. Dry for 1 or 2 days in the sun; then, if the weather turns

153

humid or cloudy, complete the drying in your oven according to the Oven Drying Method.

Packaging Directions: When the fruit leathers are done, cover each one with ample sheets of plastic film leaving a generous margin. Roll up the sheets of fruit leather, still on the plastic, into cylinders or cones. Wrap each roll individually in more plastic film. Store at room temperature for 2 months, refrigerated for 6 months, and frozen for 1 year.

APRICOTS

Peel, halve, pit, and cut away all blemishes. Measure the halves into a saucepan; stir in 1½ tablespoons sugar for every cup of apricots, then crush the mixture with a potato masher. Heat over low heat, stirring constantly and mashing further into a paste. Heat to just below the boiling point. Purée as directed.

PEACHES OR NECTARINES

Peel, pit, and cut away all blemishes. Cut the fruit into quarters, then measure the amount into a saucepan. Stir in 1½ tablespoons sugar per cup of fruit; crush, stir, and heat without boiling as for apricots, above. If the mixture looks too runny, heat it to boiling and simmer until it becomes syrupy. Purée as directed.

STRAWBERRIES

Wash, remove stems, and cut away all blemishes. Measure the berries, whole, into a saucepan; stir in 1 tablespoon sugar per cup of strawberries, then simultaneously crush and heat the berries. Bring the mixture to a full, rapid boil, then remove from heat. Purée as directed.

RASPBERRIES OR BLACKBERRIES

Wash, stem, and measure the berries into a sauce-pan; stir in 1 tablespoon of sugar for every cup of raspberries; or stir in 2½ tablespoons of sugar for every cup of blackberries. Crush and boil the berries until the liquid looks syrupy. Purée as directed, then strain to remove seeds.

PLUMS

Peel, pit, and cut away blemishes. Slice and measure the fruit into a saucepan; add 2 tablespoons of sugar per cup of plums. Crush and cook as for peaches or nectarines.

APPLESAUCE

For every cup of sweetened applesauce, stir in 3 tablespoons light corn syrup plus 1 teaspoon ground cinnamon. No need to heat or purée the mixture.

CRAN-GRAPE

For every 16-ounce can of either whole berry or jellied cranberry sauce, add ¼ cup grape jelly and ¼ cup light corn syrup. No need to heat the mixture, but purée it as directed.

FREEZER TOMATO PURÉE

Here's the answer to what to do with your bumper crop of homegrown garden tomatoes. This easy method produces a high quality tomato purée and takes only 45 minutes from start to finish. There's no constant stirring over a hot pot and the end product is a smooth and heavy purée that doesn't separate even when frozen.

Freezer Tomato Purée provides the base for the Tomato Sauce and Tomato Paste recipes that follow and for any tomato sauce that requires slow cooking. The amount of purée you will get from your tomatoes depends on juiciness, variety, and ripeness but, very roughly, 12 large tomatoes will yield 6 or 7 cups of purée.

Fully ripe tomatoes
A blender, or food processor, or food mill, or sieve
Plastic freezer containers or clean milk cartons

Wash and core a lot of tomatoes, trimming off any bruised spots; don't peel or slice them in any way; place them, hole side down, in a large pot. Pour in about ¼ inch of water or just enough to prevent the tomatoes from sticking to the pot before they begin to exude their own juices. Cover and boil on medium-low heat for about 30 minutes until all tomatoes—even the top ones—are very soft; do not stir or squish them while cooking; drain off any excess liquid if the tomatoes threaten to boil over or add more if they threaten to stick to the pot. Let the cooked tomatoes cool to lukewarm or speed cooling by placing the pot in a sinkful of cold water.

Drain off cooking liquid. Use a slotted spoon to transfer some of the tomatoes to a blender container filling it half full. If you can slip off and discard some of the tomato skins as you transfer the tomatoes, do so. Blend, first at medium, then at high speed, until the tomato purée is very smooth, about 30 seconds. Pour the purée into a sieve or strainer placed over a large mixing bowl; use a spoon to push every bit of the juicy pulp through, leaving only the skins and seeds. Repeat for the rest of the tomatoes. (If you don't have a blender, push the pulp through the sieve or strainer several times until it is free of lumps, skins, and seeds; or use a food mill. If you're using a food processor, you can whirl more than half a container at a time, but whirl only until the tomatoes are puréed. (If you whirl any longer you won't be able to strain out the seeds and skins.)

Pour the completed purée into 2- or 4-cup plastic containers or milk cartons leaving ½-inch headspace; label and freeze.

FREEZER TOMATO SAUCE

Tomato sauce is tomato purée which has been thickened through cooking. Follow the directions for Freezer Tomato Purée in the preceding recipe. After blending and straining the cooked tomatoes, return them to a clean, deep pot and cook, uncovered, over low heat until the consistency is to your liking; it should take about 30 minutes (less for Italian plum tomatoes); stir frequently and skim off any surface scum as it forms. As the sauce cooks, taste it now and then; if it is too acidic, add a pinch to a few teaspoons of sugar or a pinch of baking soda to neutralize; continue cooking, then check again to see if it needs further neutralizing. When the sauce is done and thickened to your liking, let it cool thoroughly to room temperature.

Pour the cooled tomato sauce into your choice of plastic freezer containers leaving ½-inch headspace. If you wish to have amounts equivalent to the small, 8-ounce or the larger, 15-ounce cans of tomato sauce available at the supermarket, use either 1- or 2-cup containers; some good containers of this kind include cleaned yogurt, sour cream, and cottage cheese containers as well as pint and half-pint milk cartons. Freeze for up to 1 year.

ONION and/or GREEN PEPPER-FLAVORED TOMATO SAUCE

When you make the tomato purée, add chunks of onions and/or green peppers to the whole cored tomatoes as they cook; blend and strain the chunks along with the puréed tomato pulp; continue with the above tomato sauce directions. If you like finely minced bits in your tomato sauce, add grated raw onions or peppers to the purée as it cooks into sauce. Freeze as directed.

GARLIC-FLAVORED TOMATO SAUCE

Add smashed garlic cloves to the purée as it cooks; remove after cooling. Do not freeze this sauce as the garlic flavor changes upon freezing.

BASIL, OREGANO, OR PARSLEY-FLAVORED TOMATO SAUCE

When you make the tomato purée, add fresh leaves or sprigs of basil or oregano or parsley to the whole tomatoes as they cook; blend and strain some of them along with the puréed tomato pulp, but don't add so many as to make the sauce turn brown. Continue with the Freezer Tomato Sauce directions on the previous page.

FREEZER TOMATO PASTE

Makes seven or eight 6-ounce "freezer cans"

If you have a lot of summer tomatoes and not too much freezer space, tomato paste is your best storage bet. You can use the product as a paste or you can combine one "freezer can" with ¾ cup boiling water to get 1¼ cups regular-strength tomato sauce. A "freezer can" contains the same amount of tomato paste as a 6-ounce commercial can and thaws in just a few hours.

4 quarts Freezer Tomato Purée from page 155 [this section]
7 or 8 waxy 5-ounce paper cups
Plastic wrap
7 or 8 rubber bands

Follow the directions for Freezer Tomato Purée;

after blending and straining the cooked tomatoes, return them to your very largest kettle or pot (even if the purée doesn't fill the pot halfway, the depth will prevent your stovetop from being spattered); lacking a large pot, use a splatter screen. Bring the purée to a bubbling simmer and cook, uncovered, until it is reduced to ⅓ of its original volume; skim off any scum that may surface. This will take 2 hours, more or less, depending on how large a batch you are making and whether you are using plum or regular tomatoes. Stir up from the bottom of the pot, first occasionally, and then more frequently as the tomatoes thicken; lower heat to prevent scorching.

Only when the tomatoes are very thick and mealy and they begin to stick to the pot's bottom despite stirring, transfer them to a double boiler; this will prevent the scorching that would surely occur in a regular pot as the tomato sauce turns to paste. Continue cooking in the double boiler for 1 hour, stirring frequently; replenish the bottom pot's boiling water as necessary. The paste is done when it can hold its shape in a rounded teaspoon turned upside down for 15 seconds without falling. Let cool thoroughly. Your finished tomato paste will have a homemade graininess that commercial pastes don't have. This graininess turns smooth as soon as water is added to the paste when it is used. If for some reason this graininess bothers you, press the finished, cooled paste through a strainer and you'll have a velvet-smooth product.

Put the cooled paste into the paper cups, filling them to the brim; cover each with a doubled square of plastic wrap; secure the wrap to each cup rim with a rubber band. Label and freeze for up to 1 year. If you wish to freeze for longer than 6 months, prevent freezer-burn by using doubled-up cups and 4 layers of plastic wrap as a cover for each. Each paper cup contains one 6-ounce commercial can's worth of tomato paste or ⅔ cup. Because there is so little water in them, the "freezer cans" defrost in a matter of hours; but if you need paste in a hurry, you can slice the frozen paste and add the slices to a small amount of boiling water.

CAN'T FAIL METHOD

No double boilers and no chance of scorching, but you've got to be home all day. In the morning, pour the 4 quarts of strained tomato purée into a kettle or pot that has about a 2-gallon capacity; bring purée to a low simmer over the lowest heat setting you can steadily maintain; forget about the pot except to stir it every few hours. When the tomatoes are much thicker than tomato sauce but not yet approaching the thickness of tomato paste, blend in roughly 2 tablespoons of olive oil for every 3 cups of sauce/paste in the pot; make sure all oil has been absorbed before adding more. Again, forget about the pot except to stir it every hour or so. The large pot, combined with the lowest possible heat, plus the addition of oil, will prevent the tomato paste from scorching and eliminate the need for a double boiler.

The paste is done when it can hold its shape in a rounded teaspoon turned upside-down for about 8 to 10 seconds without falling. This paste will never be as thick as the previous method's or commercial paste because of the addition of oil, but this will not make much difference because most recipes that call for tomato paste also call for some oil or butter, and the amount of oil you have added is hardly noticeable in relation to the amount of paste. Cool the paste, and package and freeze as above.

ITALIAN-STYLE TOMATO PASTE

The advantage to this tomato paste is that it stores well in your refrigerator and can be diluted in boiling water or stock for immediate use.

Make tomato paste as described in the previous recipe; do not make the Can't Fail Method or add any oil to it. Spread the paste ½ inch thick on a Teflon or lightly oiled cookie sheet. With a knife, score the paste into diamonds for easy drying; place the sheet of paste in your oven at its very lowest setting; prop the oven door slightly ajar. When the paste becomes dry to the touch but not too crusty, remove and let cool; cover the paste with cheesecloth and leave overnight at room temperature.

Remove and reserve the cheesecloth, then oil your hands very lightly and roll the dried paste into balls that are a little bigger than golf balls. Dip the balls in corn oil and place them in a clean widemouth jar; if you wish, separate each layer with a round of wax paper. When the jar is filled soak a piece of clean muslin or the reserved cheesecloth in corn oil and lay it loosely over the top layer of tomato paste balls. Close the lid; store in the refrigerator; use as any tomato paste.

STOCKING UP WITH TOMATO-BASED FOODS

The following foods use substantial amounts of the Freezer Tomato Purée and Tomato Sauce from the previous recipes. These foods can be made in quantity, without the trouble of canning, and stored for later use. The recipes for these foods can be found in the first volume of *Make Your Own Groceries:*

Tomato Catsup, page 76
Chili Sauce, page 76
Barbecue Sauce, page 77
Italian Tomato Sauces, page 89
Tomato Juice and Tomato Juice Cocktails, page 167
Easy Green Tomato Pickles, page 101

FRESH TOMATO BREAD

Makes 2 loaves

3 large ripe tomatoes
½ cup lukewarm, 110° water
2 packages active dry yeast
4 tablespoons sugar
1 teaspoon salt
¼ cup corn oil
5½ to 6 cups flour

Wash and core the tomatoes; don't peel or slice them; place them, hole side down, in a saucepan with a scant ¼ inch of water. Cover and simmer for 30 minutes, then let the tomatoes cool to lukewarm. Drain off and discard the cooking liquid, slip off and discard the skins. Plop the tomatoes into a blender; whirl them into a purée, then strain the purée into a bowl; push all the pulp through, leaving only the seeds to be discarded. Measure exactly 1½ cups of this tomato purée into a large mixing bowl and set it aside.

Measure the ½ cup lukewarm, 110° water into a cup; sprinkle the yeast atop; wait a minute, then stir to dissolve along with 1 teaspoon of the sugar; set the cup aside for 5 minutes until it is bubbly.

Stir the remaining sugar into the tomato purée followed by the salt, oil, and 1 cup of the flour. Stir in the yeast mixture, then gradually add enough of the remaining flour to form a moderately stiff dough.

Knead the dough for about 10 minutes on a well-floured surface adding more flour if necessary. When it is smooth and blistered, place the dough in a lightly oiled bowl, turn it once, then cover and let it rise in a warm place for 40 minutes, or until doubled in bulk. Punch the dough down; knead it a few turns, then shape it into 2 loaves. Set the loaves in 2 greased 9-by-5-by-3-inch loaf pans; cover and let them rise for about 30 minutes, or until doubled.

Bake the risen loaves at 350° for 40 to 50 minutes until lightly browned and hollow sounding when thunked with your finger. Remove the loaves to racks and let them cool. Serve warm with lots of butter or cheese. This bread freezes well.

HOW TO FORCE-RIPEN GREEN TOMATOES

Here are several ways to rescue green tomatoes before the first frost ruins them. The force-ripened tomatoes cannot compare to the vine-ripened kind, but they will be no worse than the hot-house supermarket variety.

• Pull up entire tomato-plant vines including roots and hang them upside down in your basement or any cool, dark place until ripe.

• Wrap each green tomato in 1 double-page sheet of newspaper. Place the wrapped tomatoes in a single layer in a basket or tray; set the basket in a shady basement spot or in a somewhat cool closet. Check for ripeness in 3 or 4 weeks.

• Set the green tomatoes in a single layer (not touching each other), in a loosely-woven basket or in a tray-like container that allows air to circulate freely from the bottom. Place the basket or tray, uncovered, in a cool, shady, dry basement spot. Turn the tomatoes over occasionally.

FROZEN ZUCCHINI PIZZA PIE

Makes 1 pie, serves 6

Make as many of these pizzas as you wish, then freeze them for future meals.

2 eggs
½ pound whole milk mozzarella cheese, shredded
About 4 or 5 medium zucchini
2 cups any spaghetti sauce, cooled

Lightly beat the eggs in a large mixing bowl; mix in 1 cup of the shredded mozzarella; set the bowl aside. Cut the tips off the zucchini, then shred enough to measure 4 well-packed cups. Squeeze out any excess moisture, then mix the shreds, by the cupful, into the egg-cheese mixture until all the zucchini is coated. Press the mixture into a well-greased 10-by-15-inch or similar shallow, rimmed baking pan. Bake this zucchini pizza crust for 10 minutes, then remove it from the oven and let it cool completely.

Pour the spaghetti sauce over the cooled zucchini crust. Sprinkle the remaining mozzarella over the sauce; gently press the cheese into the sauce with a metal spatula. Place the pan, uncovered and level, in the freezer until the pizza is solid. Cover with foil and label with this page number or the following cooking directions.

Cooking Directions: Defrost the frozen pizza. Bake in a 400° oven for 25 to 35 minutes, or until the cheese is bubbly. Let the pizza set for 5 minutes before cutting and serving.

ZUCCHINI PANCAKES

Makes about 14

Serve these zucchini pancakes as a dinnertime side dish, much as you would potato pancakes. You can serve some for tonight's dinner and freeze the rest as a freezer-to-oven vegetable.

2 cups packed shredded zucchini
½ cup flour
½ teaspoon salt
Pepper to taste
2 eggs, at room temperature
Oil for frying

Combine zucchini, flour, salt, and pepper in a large mixing bowl. Separate the eggs; put the whites in a clean medium-size bowl; mix the yolks into the zucchini mixture. Beat the egg whites until soft; do not allow stiff peaks to form; gently but throughly fold the whites into the zucchini mixture.

Heat ¼-inch of oil in a skillet until hot but not smoking. Drop heaping tablespoonfuls of the zucchini batter into the oil and brown pancakes on both sides. Drain the pancakes on paper towels; sprinkle with additional salt, if you wish. Serve immediately along with ketchup, or freeze for later use.

To freeze, place the cooked, drained pancakes in 1 layer on a cookie sheet; set the sheet, uncovered, in your freezer. When the pancakes are solidly frozen, put them in a plastic freezer bag along with this page number or the following cooking directions.

Cooking Directions: Preheat oven to 400°. Place the frozen pancakes in a single layer on an ungreased baking sheet. Bake for 10 to 15 minutes, or until the largest pancake is heated through.

ZUCCHINI REFRIGERATOR PICKLES

Makes 3 or 4 pints

2½ pounds young 5-inch zucchini
2 medium onions
2 cups white distilled vinegar
1 cup sugar
2 tablespoons salt

1 teaspoon celery seeds
¼ teaspoon turmeric
¼ teaspoon dry mustard, dissolved in 1
    teaspoon water

Read "Things to Know Before Making Pickles"
on page 77.

Cut the tips off each zucchini; do not peel; cut
into ¼-inch slices; set aside. Peel the onions, cut
them into thin slices, and separate into rings; set
aside. Combine the vinegar, sugar, salt, celery
seed, turmeric, and mustard in a large, non-aluminum cooking pot; bring to a boil; remove the
pot from the heat; stir in the zucchini slices and
onion rings. Marinate for 1½ hours; stir now and
then.

Return the cooking pot to high heat; bring the
mixture to a boil and simmer, uncovered, for 4
minutes. Heat 3 or 4 pint-size jars by running
very hot tap water into them; don't heat if you are
using plastic containers. When they are well
heated, use a slotted spoon to pack the zucchini
and onion slices into the jars. Slowly pour the
pickling solution over the vegetables and fill right
up to the jar's brim so that no vegetables are
exposed. Cover, let cool to room temperature,
then refrigerate.

ZUCCHINI COOKIES

Makes 5 dozen

1 cup flour
1 teaspoon baking soda
1 teaspoon salt
2 teaspoons cinnamon
½ teaspoon nutmeg
¼ teaspoon ground cloves
1 egg
⅔ cup corn oil
1½ cups packed brown sugar
1½ teaspoons vanilla extract
2½ cups packed shredded zucchini
2½ cups any granola cereal
1 cup chopped walnuts
½ cup raisins

Combine flour, baking soda, salt, cinnamon, nutmeg, and cloves in a large mixing bowl. Combine
in a blender container, in this order, the egg, oil,
sugar and vanilla; whirl until smooth. Pour the
liquid mixture into the dry ingredients; beat by
hand until well blended. One by one, incorporate
the remaining ingredients into the cookie batter.

Drop heaping spoonfuls of the cookie batter,
about 2 inches apart, onto greased cookie sheets.
Bake at 375° for 10 to 15 minutes, or until
browned at the edges. Transfer the hot cookies to
cool on racks. These cookies freeze well.

COCONUT ZUCCHINI BARS

Makes about 2 dozen

1¾ cups flour
1½ teaspoons baking powder
½ teaspoon salt
2 eggs
⅔ cup corn oil
½ cup packed brown sugar
½ cup granulated sugar
½ teaspoon orange extract
2 cups packed shredded zucchini
1½ cups (4 ounces) shredded coconut
Confectioner's sugar for sprinkling

Combine flour, baking powder, and salt in a large
mixing bowl. Combine in a blender container, in
this order, the eggs, oil, both sugars, and orange
extract; whirl until smooth. Pour the blender mixture into the flour; beat by hand until well
blended. Stir in the zucchini, then the coconut.

Spread the mixture equally into 2 greased 8-by-8-
by-2-inch pans (or into one 9-by-13-by-2-inch pan).
Bake at 350° for 30 to 40 minutes, or until a sharp
knife inserted at the center comes out clean. Let
the pan(s) cool on a well-dampened kitchen towel.
Cool thoroughly before sieving confectioner's
sugar atop and cutting into bars. These bars
freeze well.

ZUCCHINI LUNCHBOX CAKES

Makes 1 dozen

2 cups flour
2 cups sugar
2 teaspoons baking soda
1 teaspoon baking powder
1 teaspoon salt
2 teaspoons cinnamon
3 eggs
1 cup corn oil
½ teaspoon almond extract
2 cups packed shredded zucchini
1¾ cups coarsely chopped walnuts
1 cup raisins
12 plastic sandwich bags, optional

Combine the flour, sugar, baking soda, baking powder, salt, and cinnamon in a large mixing bowl; use an electric mixer to beat in the eggs, oil, and almond extract. When the mixture is well combined, stir in, by hand, the zucchini, 1 cup of the walnuts, and the raisins. Pour the batter into a greased 9-by-13-by-2-inch baking pan and sprinkle the top with the remaining nuts. Bake at 350° for 45 to 55 minutes, or until a sharp knife inserted in the center comes out clean. Cool the cake in the pan placed on a well-dampened kitchen towel. When the cake is cool, cut it into 12 equal portions. You can either eat the portions right away or freeze them as lunchbox cakes.

To freeze, slip each portion into a plastic sandwich bag and place, level and in 1 layer, in your freezer. Put the frozen bag in a lunchbox in the morning and it will have thawed by lunchtime.

MOIST ZUCCHINI BREAD

Makes 2 loaves

2½ cups flour
2 teaspoons baking soda
1 teaspoon salt
½ teaspoon baking powder
1 tablespoon cinnamon
3 eggs
1 cup corn oil
1¾ cups sugar

2 teaspoons vanilla extract
2 teaspoons freshly grated lemon peel
2 cups packed, shredded zucchini
1 cup chopped walnuts
1 cup raisins, optional

Combine and sift together in a medium bowl, the flour, baking soda, salt, baking powder, and cinnamon; set the bowl aside. Use an egg beater or a wire whisk to lightly beat the eggs in a large mixing bowl; add the oil, sugar, and vanilla and continue beating the mixture until it is thick and foamy. Stir in the lemon peel and the zucchini; add the flour mixture, blending thoroughly; stir in the walnuts and raisins.

Spoon the batter into 2 well-greased and flour-dusted 8-by-5-by-3-inch loaf pans. Bake at 350° for 50 to 60 minutes, or until a sharp knife inserted at the center comes out clean. Briefly cool the loaves in their pans by placing them on a well-dampened kitchen towel; then remove the loaves from the pans and cool thoroughly on wire racks. These loaves freeze well.

PINEAPPLE ZUCCHINI BREAD

Increase flour to 3 cups and sugar to 2 cups; add 1 well-drained 8¼-ounce can of pineapple to the liquid ingredients along with the zucchini.

ZUCCHINI FRUITCAKE

Increase the flour to 3 cups and add along with the cinnamon: 2 teaspoons allspice, 1 teaspoon nutmeg, and ½ teaspoon ground cloves. Replace the sugar with 2 cups packed brown sugar. Increase walnuts and raisins to 2 cups each. Stir 2½ cups mixed chopped candied fruit into the finished batter.

Bake the 2 loaves at 325° for about 1 hour and 15 minutes. Before removing the warm loaves from their pans, drizzle ½ to 1 cup brandy or dark rum over them; let the loaves cool completely in their pans. Wrap each loaf well and either freeze for up to a year or let ripen in your refrigerator for 2 weeks before serving.

161

CHOCOLATE ZUCCHINI BUNDT CAKE

Makes 1

2¼ cups flour
2 tablespoons cornstarch
½ cup unsweetened cocoa powder
½ cup ground almonds
1 tablespoon baking powder
1 teaspoon baking soda
1 teaspoon salt
1 teaspoon cinnamon
¾ cup vegetable shortening
2 cups sugar
3 eggs
2 teaspoons vanilla extract
¼ teaspoon almond extract
2 cups packed shredded zucchini
½ cup milk
2 cups confectioner's sugar
3 tablespoons milk
1 teaspoon vanilla extract

Combine in a medium-size bowl: the flour, corn-starch, cocoa, almonds, baking powder, baking soda, salt, and cinnamon; set the bowl aside. Combine the shortening and sugar in a large mixing bowl; use an electric mixer to beat them together until creamy. Add the eggs, one at a time, beating well after each addition; beat in the two extracts. By hand, stir in the zucchini. Alternately, stir the dry ingredients and the milk into the zucchini mixture.

Turn the batter into a well-greased and flour-dusted 10-inch Bundt pan. Bake at 350° for about 60 minutes, or until a sharp knife inserted in the center comes out clean. Cool the pan on top of a dampened kitchen towel for 20 minutes; then carefully invert it on a wire rack; remove the pan and let the cake cool completely.

Make a glaze by vigorously beating the confectioner's sugar, milk, and vanilla until very smooth. Drizzle the glaze over the cake; let it set, then serve. If you intend to freeze the cake for future use, do not glaze it until thawed and ready to serve.

PUMPKIN CHIPS

One pound of pumpkin makes 4 cups of chips

Fresh pumpkin
Oil for frying
Vegetable shortening for frying
Salt to taste

Peel and seed the pumpkin; cut it into paper-thin slices of uniform size. To cut slices paper thin, use your choice of a vegetable peeler, a very sharp knife, a food processor, the slicing slot of a hand grater, or a cabbage-shredder. Rinse the slices under cold water, then let them soak in ice water for 1 hour.

Drain the slices; pat them dry between paper towels. Pour equal amounts of oil and shortening into a large heavy saucepan to a depth of 3 inches; heat to 360° on a deep-frying thermometer, or until very hot but not smoking. Fry the pumpkin slices, a handful at a time, for a few minutes or until amber-crisp; stir the slices after the spattering subsides to prevent sticking. Drain the chips on paper toweling; sprinkle with salt to taste, and repeat with the remaining slices. Cool and store in airtight containers.

SPICED PUMPKIN CHIPS

Sprinkle every 2 cups of hot fried chips with a mixture of 2 teaspoons curry powder, 1 teaspoon onion powder, and ½ to 1 teaspoon salt.

PUMPKIN TEMPURA

Makes about 4 cups

Serve these crisp, batter-fried pumpkin slices with tonight's dinner or freeze them to have on hand as a freezer-to-oven side dish.

3 cups peeled fresh pumpkin cut into 3-by-1-inch strips, ⅛ inch thick
Flour for dredging
Oil for frying
1 cup flour
½ teaspoon sugar
½ teaspoon salt
1 egg, lightly beaten
2 tablespoons oil
1 cup ice water

Dredge the pumpkin strips by shaking them, cup by cup, in a small bag containing flour; shake off excess flour; set the strips aside. Pour oil into a frying pan to a depth of 1 inch; heat slowly while you go on to make the batter. Combine the remaining ingredients; beat until just moistened; some lumps should remain. Increase the frying pan's heat to high so that the oil becomes hot but not smoking.

Working fast so that the batter remains cool, dip the pumpkin slices in the batter, then fry them in the hot oil for 3 or 4 minutes, or until golden. Drain on paper towels. Serve hot or freeze for later use.

To freeze, place the cooled tempura in a single layer on ungreased cookie sheets; freeze uncovered until solid, then transfer to plastic freezer bags. Seal and label with this page number or the following cooking directions.

Cooking Directions: Preheat oven to 400°. Place the frozen tempura in a single layer on an ungreased baking sheet. Bake for 10 to 12 minutes, or until the largest piece is heated through.

HOMEMADE PUMPKIN PURÉE

Cut a 9- or 10-pound pumpkin in half through the stem portion; you'll need a very sharp knife for this. Scoop out and discard all the strings and reserve the seeds; see the following recipe for directions for toasted pumpkin seeds. Grease a large shallow baking pan with vegetable shortening, then arrange the pumpkin halves, cut side down, in the pan; prick the skin with a sharp knife tip to let excess moisture escape. Bake, uncovered, at a preheated 350° for 1 hour to 1 hour and 15 minutes, or until the flesh is very tender when pierced and the skin yields easily to light pressure. Let the pumpkin cool.

Scoop out pulp and either whirl to a purée, 1 or 2 cups at a time, in a blender or food processor, or mash thoroughly with a potato masher, or run through a food mill or a meat grinder. When nice and smooth, set the purée in a wire strainer and allow the excess water to drain off. Let it drain for 30 minutes, or until the pumpkin looks like thick mashed potatoes; drain well so the purée will not be watery.

Cover and refrigerate the pumpkin purée for up to 2 days or freeze it (in amounts for favorite recipes) in plastic containers, leaving ½-inch headspace; freeze for up to 1 year. You can count on 2 cups of cooked pumpkin purée to equal a 1-pound can of the canned variety; use exactly as you would the canned purée in your own or any of the following recipes.

TOASTED PUMPKIN SEEDS

Fresh pumpkin seeds
Salt
Vegetable shortening

Clean fiber off the seeds and rinse well. Place the seeds in a bowl of lukewarm water to cover; stir in a generous amount of salt, about 2 teaspoons per cup of seeds; stir to dissolve the salt. Let the seeds soak about 4 to 6 hours at room temperature.

To toast, grease a rimmed baking sheet very generously with shortening; use enough to make a thick white film over the sheet as opposed to a transparent film. Drain the seeds in a strainer, then spread them in a single layer over the greased sheet; sprinkle lightly with salt if you

wish. Bake at 300° until golden, crispy-brown, and somewhat puffed. Serve warm.

PUMPKIN BUTTER

Makes 3 cups

2½ cups pumpkin purée
¾ cup sugar
¼ cup apple cider or strained orange juice
½ teaspoon cinnamon
¼ teaspoon allspice
¼ teaspoon nutmeg
⅛ teaspoon ground cloves

Combine all the ingredients in a heavy saucepan. Bring to a boil, then reduce heat to low and simmer slowly for 10 minutes, or until the mixture is thickened to your liking. Let the butter cool; it may thicken further upon cooling so you might want to stir in a few more tablespoons of cider or juice before packing it into containers. Freezes well and tastes especially nice on muffins.

PUMPKIN BREAD

Makes 2 loaves

3½ cups flour
2½ cups sugar
2 teaspoons baking soda
1 teaspoon salt
1 teaspoon cinnamon
1 teaspoon nutmeg
¼ teaspoon cloves
2 cups pumpkin purée
1 cup corn oil
4 eggs

Combine the first 7 dry ingredients in a large mixing bowl; set aside. In another large bowl, use a rotary egg beater to blend the pumpkin and oil; add the eggs, 1 at a time, beating well after each addition. Use a rubber spatula to stir the dry ingredients into the pumpkin mixture; stir to no more than just moisten the mixture; do not over-stir into a smooth batter.

Turn the mixture into 2 well-greased and flour-dusted 9-by-5-by-3-inch loaf pans. Bake at 350° for 1 hour, or until a sharp knife inserted in the center comes out clean. Cool the pans for 15 minutes by placing them on a well-dampened kitchen towel. Remove the loaves from their pans and finish cooling on racks. These loaves freeze well.

FROZEN PUMPKIN TOASTER SLICES

When the loaves are cool, use your sharpest knife to cut them into ¾-inch thick slices. Stack with a small sheet of wax paper between each slice; wrap the stack of slices in a plastic bag; label and freeze.

To serve, put the frozen slices in a toaster and toast once or twice; or heat briefly on both sides under a broiler or in a toaster-oven. Like toast, these slices are good buttered.

PUMPKIN NUT BREAD

Stir 1 cup of coarsely chopped walnuts into the pumpkin mixture along with the dry ingredients.

PUMPKIN-ORANGE BREAD

Reduce the corn oil to ⅔ cup and add to it ⅓ cup frozen-and-thawed orange juice concentrate.

WHOLE WHEAT PUMPKIN BREAD

Use 2 cups all-purpose flour combined with 1½ cups whole wheat flour. For extra nutrition, you can add to the dry ingredients: ¼ cup nonfat dry milk, 2 tablespoons soy flour, and 1 tablespoon wheat germ.

CHEWY PUMPKIN LUNCHBOX BARS

Makes 1 dozen

2 cups flour
2 teaspoons baking powder
1 teaspoon baking soda

½ teaspoon salt
2 teaspoons cinnamon
1 teaspoon nutmeg
½ teaspoon ground cloves
4 eggs
2 cups pumpkin purée
2 cups sugar
¾ cup corn oil

Combine the first 7 dry ingredients in a medium-size bowl and set aside. In a large mixing bowl, use an electric mixer to beat the eggs slightly, then beat in the remaining ingredients. Stir the dry ingredients into the egg-and-pumpkin mixture then beat until well blended.

Pour the mixture into 2 greased and floured 8-by-8-by-2-inch pans. Bake at 350° for 30 to 35 minutes, or until the edges begin to pull away from the sides and the center springs back when lightly touched. Let the cakes cool in their pan, then cut each pan into 6 large bars. Serve the bars right away or freeze them as lunchbox bars.

To freeze, slip each bar into a plastic sandwich bag and place, level and in 1 layer, in your freezer. Put the frozen bag in a lunchbox in the morning and it will have thawed by lunchtime.

FROZEN PUMPKIN MUFFIN BATTER

Makes 1 dozen muffins

1½ cups flour
½ cup sugar
1 tablespoon baking powder
¾ teaspoon salt
½ teaspoon cinnamon
½ teaspoon nutmeg
1 egg
⅓ cup corn oil
½ cup pumpkin purée
½ cup milk

Combine the first 6 dry ingredients in a large bowl; set aside. Use a rotary egg beater to lightly beat the egg in a medium-size bowl; beat in the remaining ingredients until smooth. Quickly add the pumpkin mixture to the bowl of dry ingredients; stir only briefly by hand to get a lumpy batter; do not over-stir the batter. Pour the batter into a quart-size plastic container or a clean milk carton. Seal, label, and freeze.

Cooking Directions: Let the batter thaw in your refrigerator for about 12 hours or overnight. Fill greased muffin tins ⅔ full with the batter; sprinkle the tops with sugar and bake at 400° for 20 minutes.

LEMON PUMPKIN-NUT COOKIES

Makes 2 dozen

2½ cups flour
1 tablespoon baking powder
1 teaspoon salt
½ teaspoon cinnamon
½ teaspoon nutmeg
¼ teaspoon ginger
10 tablespoons butter
1½ cups packed brown sugar
2 eggs
1 cup pumpkin purée
¾ teaspoon lemon extract
1 cup coarsely chopped walnuts

Combine the first 6 dry ingredients in a medium-size mixing bowl; set aside. Use an electric mixer to cream together the butter and sugar until light and fluffy. One at a time, add the eggs; beat well after each addition. Blend in the pumpkin and lemon extract. By hand, stir the dry ingredients into the creamy pumpkin mixture; stir in the walnuts.

Drop the dough by the tablespoonful, 2 inches apart, onto lightly greased cookie sheets. Bake at 375° for 10 to 15 minutes, or until slightly browned around the edges. Remove the hot cookies to racks to cool. Once cooled, these cookies freeze well in plastic bags.

Chapter 11:

GROW YOUR OWN GROCERIES

Sections:

☐Home Garden Groceries
☐Indoor-Grown Groceries

POPCORN

You will probably have to order your popcorn seeds through a mail order catalog since the seeds are not often sold on racks. The yellow hybrid varieties produce larger ears with bigger popped-corn than the short, strawberry-ear varieties. Don't plant popcorn near regular sweet corn lest they cross-pollinate and ruin your sweet corn. Grow popcorn just as you would sweet corn. Water the plants regularly and any time they show signs of wilt, especially when the tassels begin to appear as this is also the time when the ears are just forming.

Once the ears are mature, stop watering and let the stalks turn brown and completely dry out. Pick the ears; pull the husks back to expose the kernels, then use lengths of cord to tie back the husks. Use the cord to string the ears together into a long, hanging garland. Hang the garland to dry in a cool, dry place for about one month. The corn kernels are dry enough to harvest when they can easily be pushed off the cob with your thumbnail; if they don't come off easily, let them dry for another month.

Collect the dry, harvested popcorn kernels in a shallow dishpan or tray; spread them into a single layer and, working outdoors, use a hair drier to blow off all the chaff and hulls. Store the popcorn in airtight containers. Freezing popcorn kernels right up to the time of popping ensures that they will all pop, so you might want to store the containers in your freezer.

NUTTY CORN SNACKS

The nutty corn kernels sold in bags are made from extra-large, hybrid corn but you can make your own, smaller version from any home-garden sweet corn. Once the ears of one or more stalks of corn are mature, stop watering and let the stalks turn brown and completely dry out. Follow the directions in the previous Popcorn recipe

for picking, hanging, drying, and collecting the kernels.

Pour oil into a frying pan to a depth of 1 inch; heat it to very hot but not smoking. Drop a handful or 2 of dried corn kernels into the oil; put a cover on top just in case some decide to really pop high; remove with a slotted spoon when the kernels are slightly puffed. Drain on paper towels and sprinkle liberally with salt. This method also works with hulled sunflower seeds.

SUNFLOWER SEEDS

Sunflower seeds are almost ripe when the back of the flower head has turned dry and brown with no traces of green left. To prevent the birds from eating all the seeds, wrap a single layer of cheesecloth around each head and allow the entire plant to dry out. If the seeds are already large enough, cut off the flower head leaving 1 or 2 feet of stem attached; invert the flower head onto a tray or hang it upside down in a cool, dry place so that the seeds can completely dry out.

The seeds are ready to harvest when they separate easily from the head as you run your thumb over the surface. Remove the seeds by hand or with a stiff, wire brush; if the center seeds are still moist, remove them anyway and spread them out to dry further.

To hull the seeds, let them soak overnight in cold water, then remove the softened husks and collect the inside sunflower seed kernels. This is a time-consuming chore, but the rewards are seeds that contain 55% protein by weight plus calcium and every B vitamin; in fact, sunflower seeds are the only vegetable to contain the entire range of B vitamins. Another hulling method is to crack each unsoaked husk lengthwise with pliers. Let the sunflower seeds dry on paper towels, then store in airtight containers. Because of their high oil content, it is best to freeze the seeds; they can be frozen for up to a year.

To roast sunflower seeds for a snack, sauté them in a thin layer of oil, drain on paper towels, and salt to taste. The seeds can also be puffed according to the previous, Nutty Corn Snacks recipe.

PUMPKIN SEEDS

You can roast seeds from any variety of pumpkin with good results according to the directions on page 164, but for abundant, really superior, roasted pumpkin seeds, you might consider growing or buying a variety called Lady Godiva Pumpkin, named for its naked seeds. The flesh of this pumpkin is stringy and not very good for cooking, but the many seeds within are completely shell-free so that you don't have to hull them or soak them in brine. These pumpkins seeds are available in the major seed catalogs.

Cut a Lady Godiva pumpkin in half; remove the seeds and rinse them free of strings. Allow the seeds to dry, then sauté them in a ⅛-inch film of oil; drain on paper towels and salt to taste.

PEANUTS

Peanut seeds are available through all major seed catalogs. The compact bush varieties are Spanish, which are the little peanuts used in candies; Virginia, which are known as cocktail peanuts; and Valencia, the jumbo, circus-type peanuts; avoid the vine or runner varieties because they require a lot of growing room. Plant as directed.

When the dark green leaves of the mature plant turn to a pale, yellowish green color, it is time to test for ripeness; this may take until mid-October in some northern areas. Burrow your fingers under the soil and pull off one peanut pod; if the pod snaps off easily continue the test; if it does not, let the plant ripen further. Open the peanut pod; the nuts inside should show a deep pink color on the seed coat, and the inside of the pod should be dark with tiny veins showing. If the nuts are watery and white-to-pink in color, wait

about 2 weeks before re-testing. Be sure the pods are ripe because immature peanuts are bitter tasting. If you live in the north half of the country, you can't expect the more distant pods to be ripe even when the center ones are.

To harvest the peanut plants, loosen the soil around the main stem, then gently pull up the entire plant along with its roots. Set the roots on newspapers; shake off extra dirt, then pick off the pods. Rinse the pods to remove their dirt. Prepare, using any of the following methods.

PEANUTS ROASTED IN THE SHELL

Place the clean peanut pods in 1 or 2 layers in a deep shallow baking pan. Bake at 350° for about 25 to 30 minutes. Stir the pods from time to time as they bake. Open up a few of the peanut shells just before completion to make sure they are roasted to your liking.

OIL ROASTED PEANUTS

Remove the raw peanuts from their pods; if they are small, you can leave the skins on; if not, blanch them by putting them in boiling water for 3 minutes, then drain, slide the skins off with your fingers, and dry well between paper towels.

Heat peanut or vegetable oil to a depth of 1 or 2 inches in a heavy skillet; the oil must be deep enough to cover the nuts. When the oil is about 300°, fry and stir the nuts until they just begin to brown. Use a slotted spoon to place the nuts on paper towels where they will continue to brown and sizzle. Sprinkle the nuts immediately with salt that you have made fine by whirling in a blender container.

DRY ROASTED PEANUTS

Remove the raw peanuts from their pods. Blanch the nuts by putting them in boiling water for 3 minutes, then drain, slide the skins off with your fingers, and let the nuts dry on paper towels. Spread the blanched peanuts, 1 layer deep, in a large shallow baking pan. Roast in a 350° oven for 15 to 20 minutes, or until golden brown. Be

169

sure to stir the peanuts from time to time as they roast. Remove from the oven and sprinkle the hot nuts immediately with salt that you have made fine by whirling in a blender container.

Another, slightly oilier dry-roasting method is to place raw, unblanched peanuts in a large roasting pan as described above. Bake at 350° for 35 minutes, or until golden when a skin is removed. Cool the nuts, then slip off the skins. Sprinkle with fine salt as described above.

GARLIC

Plant single cloves of ordinary grocery-store garlic, point-side up and 1 inch deep in loose garden soil. Space the cloves 4 inches apart from each other and plant in the fall just as you would plant any other bulb. Water generously when springtime arrives, then stop watering when the brown at the leaf-tips begins to move down the leaves and the leaves begin to droop and break. When this happens, let the plant mature without watering it until most of the leaves turn brown.

To harvest, loosen the soil around each bulb and remove the whole plant; shake off excess dirt. Spread out or hang the plants to dry in partial shade for a week or until the leaves and skins are papery. Trim off most of the leaves and roots but keep some of each to prevent spoilage. Braid or tie the stems to get hanging garlands of garlic bulbs. Hang in a cool, dry spot for up to a year.

HOT PEPPER FLAKES

Hang and dry hot chili peppers according to the directions on page 151. To make hot pepper flakes, coarsely shred just the outer, dry chili, and not the seeds; use a mortar and pestle or a blender; be very careful to let the whirled chili powder settle completely before removing the blender container cover. To each teaspoon of hot pepper flakes, add ½ to 1 teaspoon of the very hot seeds. Store in an airtight container. Use sparingly.

HORSERADISH

You can buy horseradish roots through most seed catalogs as well as from fresh vegetable markets in autumn and during the Passover season in spring. Purchase no more than two or three of the 4-inch roots as horseradish has spreading, weed-like qualities and thrives in even the worst conditions. Plant the roots horizontally, 12 inches apart and 2 or 3 inches deep in either spring or autumn and let the plants mature over the summer; they will look a lot like mustard or collard greens. The roots will grow their best during late autumn and should only be unearthed just before the first frost is predicted.

To harvest, loosen the soil around the entire plant and pull the plant up by its roots. If some of the outer roots snap off, you can count on them becoming next year's plants. Remove the roots and replant several 3-inch lengths for next year. Bring the roots inside, wash them well, and prepare according to the following directions. The root doesn't store well unless it's prepared, so either make some for your neighbors or wrap and store the extra, unpeeled roots in your freezer for winter use. The strength of your homegrown, home-prepared horseradish will be a real eye-opener compared to the supermarket variety.

To Make 1 Cup of Prepared Horseradish: Set aside a small bowl filled with cold water. Mix ½ cup white distilled vinegar and ¼ teaspoon salt in either a blender container or a mixing bowl; use only white vinegar as cider vinegar will turn the horseradish brown. Wash and scrub 2 medium-sized horseradish roots; use a potato peeler to scrape off all brown skin and rough spots. Drop the cleaned root into cold water before continuing to the next.

Blender Method: Cut the roots into small cubes—enough to fill 1 heaping cup. Place a handful of the cubes in the blender containing the salted vinegar; whirl at medium speed until fully grated. With the blender still running, add another handful of horseradish; when grated, continue adding the remaining horseradish in this manner.

Food Processor Method: Cut roots into 1-inch

chunks. Finely grate the chunks in a food processor; add the salted vinegar and turn the machine on and off very quickly to combine the ingredients.

Grater Method: Grate roots on a cheese-grater to make 1 cup. Pour into the bowl of salted vinegar and stir to blend.

Pack the prepared horseradish into a small jar, seal tightly, and store in refrigerator. If the horseradish is too fiery for you, you can tame it by grating some long white radish into it or let it mellow, untouched and refrigerated, for a month or so.

RED HORSERADISH

After packing horseradish into a jar, pour in some beet juice.

HORSERADISH WITH BEETS

Grate 1 or 2 cooked beets along with the horseradish roots and use red wine vinegar. Optional: 1 teaspoon sugar. Makes 1⅓ cups.

GRAPE LEAVES

Many Middle Eastern recipes require brined grape leaves as a wrapper for the stuffing. Not only are jars of grape leaves expensive and hard to find, but they usually contain about 25% unusable leaves. If you have access to a grapevine (absolutely any variety will do as long as it hasn't been sprayed with an insecticide), you can freeze the leaves for free.

Pick the grape leaves sometime in the spring or early summer when they are fairly light green and just as soon as they reach full size; dark green leaves picked in late summer will be leathery and have stringy veins. The best time to pick the grape leaves is in the morning or at least before 11:00 a.m. Plan to process the leaves as soon as you've finished picking them so they won't get wilted or soggy upon freezing.

Gather as many leaves as you wish; try to make

them all close in size and avoid any that are as big or bigger than your hand. Trim off the stems. Do not wash the leaves; any dirt or dust on them will be boiled away during processing. Pile the leaves, one directly on top of the next, into stacks of 20; slip the stacks into sturdy plastic freezer bags and freeze on a level surface.

When ready to use the frozen leaves, all you need to do is scald them. Fill your largest cooking pot with water, adding about a tablespoon of salt per quart of water; bring to a steady boil and plunge the unwrapped stack of frozen leaves into the water. Wait for the water to return to a boil, then continue boiling the leaves for about a minute or until they become limp; you may have to push the leaves down into the water with a wooden spoon to accomplish this. When the leaves are just limp, transfer them to a colander; rinse them under cold water to prevent further cooking, then use as directed in whatever recipe you're using. Repeat the scalding for as many leaves as you need.

ROSE HIP TEA

Most common garden roses produce either bland or bitter tasting hips, so if you are considering purchasing any rose bushes, you would do well with any non-hybrid Rugosa rose variety. Not only do Rugosa roses offer an abundance of fragrant flowers that produce the largest and sweetest tasting hips but they are probably the heartiest of all rose varieties and are resistant to diseases, insects, weather extremes, and neglect. About three Rugosa rose hips contain more vitamin C than an average orange.

Allow the roses to bloom, wither, and go to seed on the bush or vine without cutting them off so that hips will form. It is very important that you use no insect sprays on these roses unless they are safe enough for vegetables; insecticides intended for flowers rather than vegetables are poison.

FRESH ROSE HIP EXTRACT

Pick the rose hips as they individually ripen; they should still be hard and at their most vibrant in color. Remove all stems, leaves, and blossom ends; wash well and measure into a non-aluminum pot. For every cup of rose hips in the pot, add 1½ cups of cold water. Bring to a boil, reduce the heat, then cover and simmer for 20 to 30 minutes, or until tender. Remove from heat; mash the hips with a potato masher and let the mixture stand, covered and at room temperature, for 24 hours.

Strain the liquid extract into a bowl with a spout. Make a test cup of tea keeping track of the amount of extract you use; measure this amount of extract into clean ice cube tray compartments and freeze solid; transfer the cubes to a plastic bag. Add one cube per cup of boiling water as needed for a tea that is high in vitamin C.

DRIED ROSE HIPS

Pick the shriveling hips in late autumn after the first frost; the frost will kill off the chance of any burrowing insects. Wash the hips, then cut off both end tips so that some flesh is exposed. Spread the hips in a single layer in a shallow baking pan and bake at 140° to 160° for 3 to 10 hours; prop the oven door slightly ajar to let moisture escape during this time. The hips are dry when they are hard and brittle enough to shatter when hit with a hammer. Store in an airtight container.

To make tea, boil 1 heaping tablespoon of hips to each cup of water; simmer, covered, until the tea reaches the strength you desire. Strain into a teacup and sweeten to taste. For a more potent cup of tea, crush or grind the hips before boiling.

HERBAL TEAS

CHAMOMILE

The seeds can be bought from any seed catalog, but do not get the bitter, perennial, ground-cover varieties. Choose the annual, 3-foot, bushy variety (either Matricaria chamomilla or Matricaria recutita) for its sweetness and profuse flowers; these plants are short-lived but, like dill, they will self-sow to offer at least two harvests each summer.

To harvest, pinch off the flower heads when the yellow centers are well developed but firm; the flower petals should be standing out horizontally rather than folding back toward the stem. Dry the flower heads in a single layer on a large tray or shallow pan in a shady, dry place with good air circulation. When the heads are dry to the point of being powdery, store in airtight containers.

To make tea, use 1 heaping teaspoon per cup; pour boiling water atop and steep until a deep yellow.

MINT

Plant peppermint or spearmint in partial shade and plant sparingly as mint plants spread like weeds. Either make a tea out of fresh, bruised leaves or else dry the mint plants according to the herb drying directions on page 152. Brew dried, crushed mint leaves in boiling water; serve hot or iced.

LEMON VERBENA AND LEMON BALM

Both are fragrant with a strong lemon flavor. Grow, harvest, dry, and use exactly like mint tea, above. Lemon verbena or lemon balm leaves are good mixed with commercial teas, too.

LOOFA SPONGES

Seeds for homegrown loofa (or luffa) squash sponges are sold in the "just-for-fun" or the children's section of many seed catalogs. The purplish squash vine is easy to grow and will provide you with many invigorating sponges for baths and showers.

Let the squashes completely ripen on the vine, then stop watering the plant. When the squashes have turned spiny and completely brown, pick them and hang them to dry in a cool, dry, well-ventilated place. When the squashes are brittle, lightly crush the outer skin and place them in a roasting pan. Pour boiling water atop the squashes so that they are submerged and let them soak until you can easily peel off all the outer skin. Cut the peeled sponges into whatever sizes you want.

BEAN SPROUTS

Bean sprouts like mung bean, lentil, wheat, and rye are briefly cooked and eaten or else used within a recipe before the leaves develop. The sprouts are high in non-starchy protein and measure from 1 to 3 inches in length. You can grow your own sprouts in any kitchen using untreated, sprouting beans available at many supermarkets, most health food stores, and through all major seed catalogs.

Choose one of the following two sprouting arrangements: Arrange a non-metallic, shallow-bottomed colander over a plate or basin; cover the sprouts loosely with a damp towel to hold in moisture and warmth between rinsings. Another sprouting arrangement is one or two widemouth canning jars with the flat, round center disc removed. Replace the disc with a double layer of cheesecloth that just slightly sticks out of the outer jar ring; you could also choose to replace the disc with a matching-size piece of fiberglass or plastic window screen; don't use metallic screen.

Pick the beans over and discard any broken ones. Rinse the beans, place them in a non-metallic bowl, and cover with about 4 times their volume of cool-to-tepid water; let them soak at room temperature for about 12 hours or overnight. The next morning, drain off all the unabsorbed water and place the beans in the sprouting arrangement of your choice. Place the sprouting arrangement in a dark, warmish, 70° spot such as a cupboard or a breadbox or a rarely used drawer, or under a large, upturned cooking pot.

Rinse the seeds at least 3 times (4 times is better) a day by completely filling up the sprouting container with cool-to-tepid water, then allowing the water to completely drain off. Refer to the list below to complete the various bean sprouts. When complete, rinse off the loose seed hulls, discard any unsprouted seeds, and drain on paper toweling. Store, refrigerated, in a rigid plastic container for 4 to 7 days.

MUNG BEANS

Bean sprouts should be about 1 inch long in 3 to 5 days; you can let mung bean sprouts grow to commercial size, about 2 to 3 inches, by sprouting for 5 to 7 days but you run the chance of their developing an unpleasant odor.

A ¼-cup of mung beans will yield from 1 to 3 cups of sprouts, depending on how long you let the sprouts grow. Use mung bean sprouts, stir-fried, in Oriental recipes.

LENTILS

Lentil sprouts will be from 1 to 1½ inches in 2 to 4 days. Use ½ cup of lentils to get 3 cups of sprouts. Use as you would mung bean sprouts in Oriental dishes and in vegetable combinations.

WHEAT AND RYE

Wheat and rye berries will sprout to ¼ inch in about 2 days. Use ¼ cup of either berry to get 1 cup of sprouts. Use wheat or rye sprouts in pilafs for a high-protein combination or add them to bread recipes. If you have just-baked loaves of sprouted wheat or rye bread, wrap them in a plastic bag for 45 minutes before serving in order to soften the sprouts near the outer crust; wrapping and freezing the loaves will also soften the sprouts.

SALAD SPROUTS

Small, thin, salad sprouts like alfalfa, curly cress, radish, and mustard are eaten raw in salads or as a garnish after the first two leaves of the sprout are fully opened. The sprouts have a crisp, strong flavor and measure about 1½ inches long. You can grow your own salad sprouts in any kitchen using sprouting seeds available at health food stores and in all major seed catalogs.

Line the bottom of a glass or non-metallic, 1- or 2-inch deep, baking dish with either ½ inch of vermiculite or 4 layers of cheesecloth. Rinse the seeds; sprinkle them in an even, solid layer atop the vermiculite or cheesecloth and cover with cool-to-tepid water. Soak the beans for 4 hours, no more than that, then drain off all the unabsorbed water. Cover the pan loosely with plastic wrap. Place the pan in a warmish, 70° to 72° spot that is out of direct sunlight. Spray the seeds daily with cool-to-tepid water to keep the vermiculite or cheesecloth wet; there is no need to completely rinse the sprouts. As soon as the seeds pop open, remove the plastic wrap, set the sprout pan in indirect and then, later, direct sunlight to make the leaves green. Refer to the list below to complete the various salad sprouts. When the leaves open, uproot the sprouts, drain, and store, refrigerated, in a plastic bag for up to a week.

Another, more direct method is to sprinkle the soaked seeds over a 1-inch layer of potting soil; cover with plastic wrap and keep the soil damp. When the seeds pop open, remove the plastic wrap and place the pan in indirect then, later, direct sunlight. Pull up the sprouts as you need them.

ALFALFA SPROUTS

The sprouts should be leafy in 3 to 5 days. One teaspoon of seeds yields 1¼ cups of sprouts. Use the sprouts generously in salads or in ham sandwiches. You can also sprout alfalfa in a sprouter jar described in the previous Bean Sprouts recipe.

CURLY CRESS OR GARDEN CRESS (PEPPERGRASS)

The little green seedlings will be leafy in 3 to 6 days. One teaspoon of seeds will yield ¾ cup of peppery, potent sprouts. Sprinkle the sprouts over salads or cottage cheese or snip them and mix them into cream cheese for a snappy spread for crackers.

RADISH

The 2-inch sprouts should be ready in 2 to 5 days. One teaspoon of seeds will yield ¾ cup of radish-flavored sprouts. The flavor gets hotter as the sprouts get older or dehydrated. Sprinkle over salads.

MUSTARD

The sprouts are ready in 5 or 6 days. One teaspoon of seed yields ¾ cup of sprouts. Use as a salad garnish.

SPROUT MIX

Combine ¼ teaspoon *each*: alfalfa, curly cress, and radish seeds for a tasty, complementary mix. The sprouts will be ready in 3 to 5 days and will yield 1 cup. Use in salads or over cottage cheese.

Chapter 12:

FOR THE AMBITIOUS

Sections:

☐Cheesemaking
☐Meatcutting Tricks

RIPENED STARTER-MILK

The milk you use for starting cheese has got to be ripened so that a small amount of lactic acid develops. Lactic acid prevents other kinds of bacteria from growing in and thus ruining any cheese you make. Ripening the milk takes several steps because you want an all-encompassing but weak strain of lactic acid in the milk; more acid will develop as the cheese is made to give it a tart taste.

2 cups fresh milk
1½ teaspoon fresh cultured store-bought buttermilk

Pour 1 cup of the milk into a clean, scalded, heavy-gauge glass jar; add the buttermilk; cover and shake the jar to mix the contents. Allow the jar to stand, undisturbed, for 16 to 24 hours at a room temperature of between 70° and 75°.

When the milk is curdled like buttermilk, scald a second clean glass jar and pour the remaining 1 cup of fresh milk into it. Scald and cool a ½-teaspoon measure, then use it to transfer ½ teaspoon of curdled milk from the first jar into the second jar. Cover and shake well. Allow the second jar to stand, undisturbed, at between 70° and 75° for 12 to 18 hours, or until slightly curdled. The second jar of milk is the ripened starter-milk you will use in cheesemaking recipes; refrigerate it until ready to use. The first jar of curdled milk is fresh buttermilk and can be used in any recipe calling for buttermilk.

SMALL CURD COTTAGE CHEESE

Makes about ¾ pound

1 quart whole milk
1 quart skim milk
An oral fever thermometer
3 tablespoons Ripened Starter-Milk from preceding recipe

A candy thermometer
Fine mesh cheesecloth

Before beginning, please remember to use absolutely clean, non-aluminum utensils and milk with the most recent date you can find.

Warm the Milk: Use either a large double boiler or make your own arrangement by placing a large non-aluminum cooking pot within a slightly larger water-filled pot. Pour the milk into the top, smaller pot and slowly heat the water so that the milk reaches about 72°; check the temperature of the milk with an oral fever thermometer. Stir in the Ripened Starter-Milk.

Curdle the Milk: Cover the pot of milk loosely with aluminum foil or a clean towel. Let the milk stand, completely undisturbed, at a 70° to 75° room temperature for about 16 to 24 hours, more or less. Do not be tempted to stir the milk during this time. If the weather is chilly, you may have to reheat the water in the outer cooking pot to maintain the milk's 72° temperature.

A firm, jelly-like curd will form after the 16 to 24 hours and a watery whey will float on the surface. Test to see if the curd is ready to cut by inserting the flat of a dinner knife or metal spatula between the side of the cooking pot and the curd; gently pull the curd away from the side of the pot; if the curd first holds together then breaks precisely and quickly, it is ready to be cut; if the knife glides through the curd without separating it, let the milk stand for a few more hours before testing it again.

Cut the Curd: Use a long-blade knife to cut the curd, in its container, into ¼-inch cubes. See Illustrations A, B, C, and D, opposite.

First, cut vertical lines spaced ¼-inch apart completely through the curd. Second, cut horizontal lines spaced ¼-inch apart completely through the curd. Third, return to the vertical-line cuts and repeat, but this time, hold the knife at an angle so as to under-cut the curd pieces, making each slice

SMALL CURD COTTAGE CHEESE

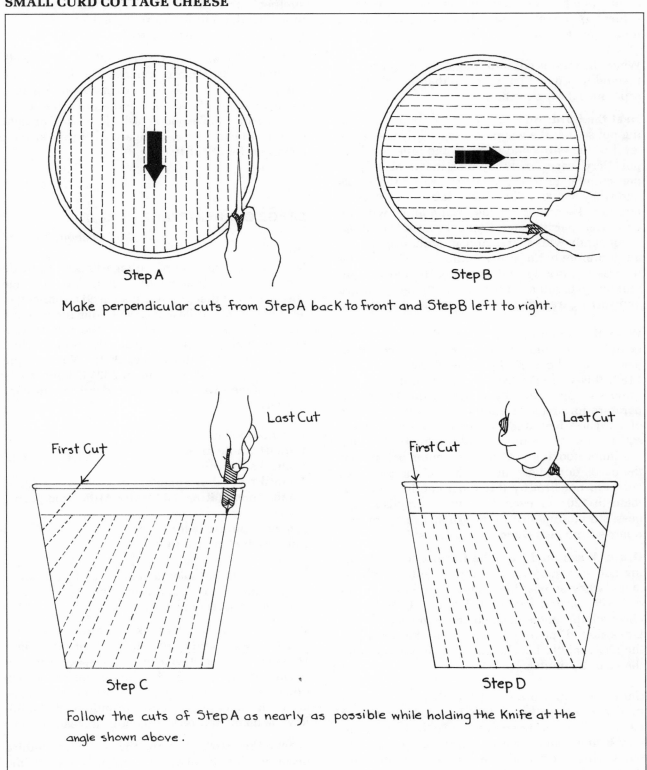

Step A

Step B

Make perpendicular cuts from Step A back to front and Step B left to right.

First Cut

Last Cut

Step C

First Cut

Last Cut

Step D

Follow the cuts of Step A as nearly as possible while holding the knife at the angle shown above.

about ¼-inch lower than the one before. Fourth, return to the horizontal line cuts and, again, under-cut at an angle.

When the curd is cut into rough, ¼-inch pieces, let it stand for 10 to 15 minutes so that the whey can separate out even further.

Heat the Curd: Add 72° water to the outer cooking pot so that the water comes slightly above the level of the curds and whey in the inner cooking pot. Very, very slowly, by increments of only 1° per minute, raise the temperature of the curds and whey to 100°. This should take about 30 to 40 minutes; keep tabs on the temperature with an oral fever thermometer. While the curd is heating, stir it gently with a large non-aluminum spoon for a full minute out of every 5 minutes. The stirring insures uniformity and prevents the curds from clumping together. Increase both temperature and stirring frequency at about 95°.

When the temperature of the curds reaches 100°, switch to a candy thermometer and continue heating by about 1° increments per minute to 115°; this will take from 10 to 15 minutes; continue stirring. Carefully maintain the 115° temperature for about 25 minutes, or until the pieces of curd are firm and do not break easily when squeezed between thumb and forefinger. Remove the inner cooking pot from the outer pot so that the curds don't heat any further. If the pieces of curd are not firm by this time, continue to heat them to 120° or even 125° to accomplish firmness; stir continuously at this higher temperature; remove from heat when the curds test firm.

Drain, Wash, and Cool the Curd: Use a measuring cup or a soup ladle to dip off and discard as much whey as possible. Generously line a colander with several layers of dampened, fine-mesh cheesecloth; set the lined colander in a clean sink. Use a slotted spoon to lightly spoon the curds into the cheesecloth. Let the curds drain for no more than 2 or 3 minutes.

Gather all four corners of the cheesecloth, then immerse this gathered bag into a large pot of clean, cool water. Lower and raise the bag repeatedly in the water for 4 or 5 minutes so that any whey rinses off and the curds become cool. Replace the water with ice water and rinse for

another 4 or 5 minutes. Place the cheesecloth bag in a colander and let it drain; shake the colander now and then to hasten draining.

Salt and Cream the Cheese: When only well-drained curds remain, remove the cheesecloth and transfer the curds to a mixing bowl. Stir in ½ teaspoon of salt; taste, then add more salt to taste. Stir in 3 or 4 tablespoons of half-and-half or light cream to taste. Store, refrigerated, in an airtight container for about 10 days.

LARGE CURD COTTAGE CHEESE

Makes about ¾ pound

Mild-tasting, large curd cottage cheese is made very much like the tangier, small curd cottage cheese except that you will also need a rennet tablet. Look in the Yellow Pages of your phone book under "Dairy Laboratories" for the rennet supplier nearest you or else order the rennet from: Chas. Hansen Laboratory, 9015 West Maple Street, Milwaukee, Wisconsin 53214. Rennet tablets, wrapped well, will keep indefinitely in your freezer.

1 **rennet tablet**
1 **quart whole milk**
1 **quart skim milk**
An oral fever thermometer
3 **tablespoons Ripened Starter-Milk from page 178**
A candy thermometer
Fine mesh cheesecloth

Before beginning, please remember to use absolutely clean, non-aluminum utensils and milk with the most recent date you can find.

Prepare the Rennet: Break 1 rennet tablet into quarters; wrap and freeze all but ¼ for future use. Dissolve ¼ rennet tablet in 2 tablespoons of cool water; set it aside. If the manufacturer's directions that come with your rennet differ from the above, ¼ tablet per 2 gallons of milk formula, follow the manufacturer's directions instead.

Warm the Milk: Follow the same procedure described for Small Curd Cottage Cheese in the previous recipe. When the milk reaches 72°, stir in the Ripened Starter-Milk and just 1½ teaspoons of the dissolved rennet solution.

Curdle the Milk: Follow the same directions as described for Small Curd Cottage Cheese. Because of the rennet, the milk should curdle in a shorter time, about 12 to 18 hours, more or less. Test to see if the curd is ready to cut.

Cut the Curd: Cut the curd into ½-inch to ⅝-inch pieces as described and illustrated in the previous recipe. When the curd is cut, stir it slowly with a non-aluminum spoon or, better yet, your hand for a full minute every 5 minutes; do this for about 15 minutes so that the whey can separate out even further.

Heat the Curd: Heat the curd as described for Small Curd Cottage Cheese very, very slowly in about 1° increments to 110°. This should take about 40 to 50 minutes; increase both temperature and stirring frequency at about 100° to 105°. Carefully maintain the 110° temperature for 10 to 20 minutes, or until the pieces of curd are firm when tested; remove from heat. If the pieces of curd are not firm by this time, or if they seem to be firming up too slowly, continue to stir and heat them to 115° to 120° until the curds test firm.

Drain, Wash, and Cool the Curd and Salt and Cream the Cheese: Follow the same directions described in Small Curd Cottage Cheese.

THREE MEALS FROM A LEG OF LAMB

Each cut will serve 2 to 3

CHOPS

Select a full-cut, about 7-pound, leg of lamb, then ask the supermarket meatcutter or your butcher to cut off 3 or 4 slices of sirloin chops from ¾- to 1-inch thick; tell the meatcutter to cut the slices up to a point about an inch in front of the rump bone. The chops, sometimes called lamb steaks, can be broiled, pan-broiled, or braised.

KEBAB OR STEW MEAT

At home, cut off the rump portion, B, as shown in the illustration, including the rump bone as your border line. The rump portion, B, should be boned, then cut into 1½-inch cubes for either shish kebab or stew meat; trim off any fat.

For kebabs, marinate the cubes for 5 hours in a mixture of ¼ cup melted butter, ¼ cup olive oil, ½ cup fresh-squeezed lemon juice, 1 tablespoon crushed oregano, and ¼ teaspoon pepper; don't use any salt at all in the marinade. Skewer the meat along with your choice of vegetables, and barbecue, basting with extra marinade, until the meat is slightly pink at the center. Serve over pilaf. This is a good marinade for the chops, too.

For stew, brown the cubes in a tablespoon of butter, add 1 medium, chopped onion and sauté until just limp. Pour enough water over the cubes to

THREE MEALS FROM A LEG OF LAMB

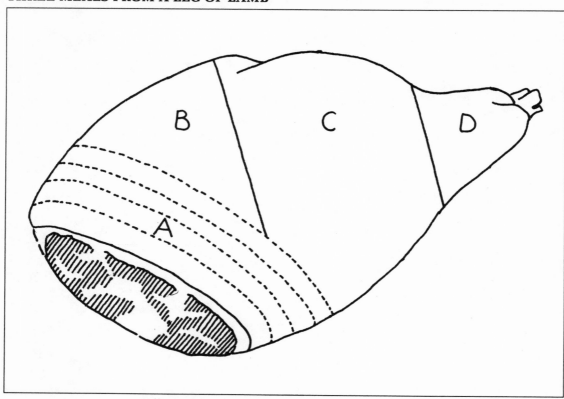

barely cover them, then cover and simmer for 1 hour. Refrigerate the stew overnight, then skim off all the congealed fat before continuing with your choice of the following recipes. For Irish stew, add 2 or 3 peeled and quartered potatoes and simmer for 30 more minutes; thicken the broth before serving with a flour-and-water paste. For Scotch stew, add ½ cup pearl barley and simmer 30 minutes, then add 1 or 2 cups of diced, raw carrots and simmer 20 or 30 more minutes. For Greek lamb stew, add 1 or 2 smashed and minced cloves of garlic along with the onion; to the skimmed stew, add several tablespoons of tomato paste to taste and ½ to 1 cup of rice or orzo macaroni, then simmer for 20 to 30 more minutes; season with pepper.

LAMB ROAST

Once the chops and rump section "B" are removed, section "C" will remain as a very meaty center roast. Trim off most, but not all, of the fat. Roll the meat up and use sturdy cotton cord to tie it into an oven roast. Place the roast, fat side up, in a roasting pan and bake in a 325° oven for 35 minutes per pound of meat; this is for medium-rare meat; adjust the cooking time according to your own preference.

EXTRAS

You'll be left with 1 perfectly good lamb shank which you can bone and use as a bit of stew meat. Or else, freeze the shank until you can get another to go along with it and make a hearty stew for two according to any of the stew directions, above.

Simmer the rump bone and any meat scraps in water to cover to get a hearty broth that gels when refrigerated. Skim off any fat and use the broth to make pilaf or Scotch broth.

HOME-BONED TURKEY ROASTS

BONELESS WHITE MEAT ROAST
Makes 7 to 12 servings

1 whole turkey breast, from 4 to 7 pounds
3 to 4 tablespoons butter
Cotton cord

Buy a whole turkey breast and either have the supermarket meatcutter split it in half for you or else cut down the center length of breastbone yourself, breaking the wishbone and cutting the breast into halves. Place each breast half, skin side down, on your work surface; find the splintered wishbone, slip a sharp knife under it, and cut it out. One of the breast halves will still have the sinewy breastbone attached to it; remove it by running the knife blade down the length of the breastbone.

Cut close to the bones of the rib cage, freeing them; scrape or slice away the smaller rib cage bones. Find the wing socket and remove it, then use your fingertips to feel the meat to be sure no small bones are still embedded; leave the skin attached. Pat the boned breast back into shape. Repeat the process with the remaining breast half.

Assemble the roast by placing 1 boned breast half, skin-side down, on your work surface; arrange dots of the butter over the exposed meat. Top the buttered breast with the other breast, skin-side up, and arrange it snugly so that the meatiest portions of each breast are at opposite ends. Tie the roast at 1-inch intervals with separate lengths of cord and stretch the skin over any exposed meat as you tie. Finish by tying the roast with 1 or 2 lengthwise cords. If the turkey breast has never been frozen, you can freeze the roast for future use; if the breast was frozen and thawed, cook the roast within the next 24 hours.

Place the roast in a shallow pan and bake at 325° for 20 to 25 minutes per pound of meat; baste frequently with butter. Let the roast set for 10 minutes before removing the cords and slicing.

BONELESS DARK MEAT ROAST

Makes 4 to 6 servings

3 or 4   turkey thighs, all the same size
Cotton cord

Place each thigh, skin-side down, on your work surface. Cut out the thigh bone with a sharp knife. Set aside 2 thighs with their skins attached; remove the skins from the remaining 1 or 2 thighs.

Assemble the roast by placing 1 unskinned thigh, skin-side down on your work surface; snugly roll up the other skinless thigh(s) singly or together; place the roll atop the thigh on the work surface, cover the arrangement with the remaining thigh, skin-side up. Tie the roast with separate lengths of cord at 1-inch intervals and tuck the skin over any extra flaps as you tie. Finish by tying the roast with a lengthwise cord. If the turkey thighs have never been frozen, you can freeze the roast for future use; if the thighs were frozen and thawed, cook the roast within the next 24 hours. Bake exactly as for Boneless White Meat Roast, on page 183.

BE YOUR OWN BUTCHER

MOCK VEAL SCALOPPINE

Remove the skins, then bone chicken thighs and breasts; there are boning directions in the previous recipe. Figure on either 2 thighs or 2 breast halves per serving. Place each boned cutlet in its own 10-by-10-inch plastic food storage bag or between layers of sturdy plastic wrap; give the meat plenty of room to expand. One at a time, place a wrapped cutlet on a very sturdy work surface or on your kitchen floor and hammer it repeatedly with the bottom of a very heavy skillet. It's easy to get carried away with the hammering

so try to hammer each cutlet to a uniform thickness of ⅛ inch without breaking or shredding the meat.

Use the pounded chicken scaloppine just as you would veal in any scaloppine recipe, such as Scaloppine Marsala, Piccante, or Parmigiana. Once pounded, the scaloppine should be used immediately as it doesn't even store well in your freezer.

TURKEY CUTLETS

Bone a whole or a half turkey breast according to the directions in the previous, Boneless White Meat Turkey Roast recipe; also remove all skin. Figure that about 1½ or 2 pounds of turkey breast will yield about 10 cutlets to serve 4 or 5. When slicing the cutlets from the breast, slice on the bias and try to make uniformly sized cutlets of the same thickness. Place several cutlets at a time in a single layer in a plastic food storage bag or between layers of sturdy plastic wrap. Place the wrapped cutlets on a sturdy work surface or on your kitchen floor and hammer repeatedly with the bottom of a very heavy skillet to a uniform thickness of ¼ to ⅛ inch; do not break the flesh.

Use the pounded cutlets just as you would use veal or chicken in any cutlet or even scaloppine recipe; the breaded recipes work best because turkey has very little fat of its own and it tends to dry out when sautéed without a coating. Unpounded turkey cutlets store well in your freezer; pounded cutlets should be used immediately.

PORK LOIN CHOPS

Buy a whole loin of pork and use a sharp knife to cut between each bone so that you get extra-thick pork chops. The price per chop will be cheaper than if the butcher sliced it.

INDEX

Make your home special

Since 1922, millions of men and women have turned to *Better Homes and Gardens* magazine for help in making their homes more enjoyable places to be. You, too, can trust *Better Homes and Gardens* to provide you with the best in ideas, inspiration and information for better family living.

In every issue you'll find ideas on food and recipes, decorating and furnishings, crafts and hobbies, remodeling and building, gardening and outdoor living plus family money management, health, education, pets, car maintenance and more.

For information on how you can have *Better Homes and Gardens* delivered to your door, write to: Mr. Robert Austin, P.O. Box 4536, Des Moines, IA 50336.

Better Homes and Gardens®

*The Idea Magazine
for Better Homes
and Families*